The International Student's to UK Education

Are you thinking of studying at university in Britain? Do you feel confused about which course is best for you, which university to choose, and how to apply? Are you wondering about what kinds of challenges you will be faced with, how best to approach them and how to overcome them? If so, this guidebook is for you.

Honest and accurate, this book acts as an international student introduction and cultural guide to UK Higher Education. It informs and guides students in their preparation for all aspects of UK HE, from university selection and application through to participation, and provides a clear understanding of how British universities function. Helping international students make the most of the many opportunities that university offers, this text will expand your knowledge of UK Higher Education with regards to:

- Application procedures;
- Finances;
- Self-awareness, cultural understanding and adaptation (social and academic);
- University administrative procedures, facilities and support;
- Work and career information and advice.

The International Student's Guide to UK Education is a comprehensive guide that will help students to develop critical and reflective ability in order to become independent, well-informed and empowered decision makers.

Martin Hyde is an experienced international office manager and Principal Lecturer in English and Language Studies at Canterbury Christ Church University, UK.

The International Student's Guide to UK Education

Unlocking University Life and Cult...

Martin

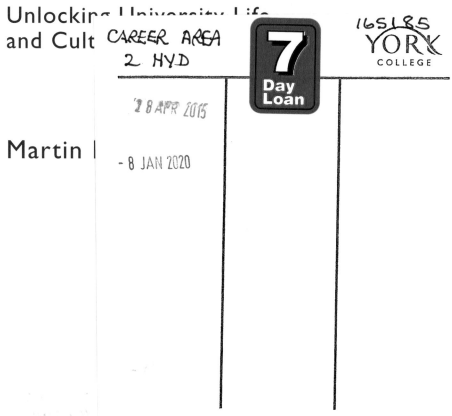

Routledge
Taylor & Francis Gr...
LONDON AND NEW YORK

First published 2012
by Routledge
2 Park Square, Milton Park, Abingdon, Oxon OX14 4RN

Simultaneously published in the USA and Canada
by Routledge
711 Third Avenue, New York, NY 10017

Routledge is an imprint of the Taylor & Francis Group, an informa business

British Library Cataloguing in Publication Data
A catalogue record for this book is available from the British Library

Library of Congress Cataloging-in-Publication Data
Hyde, Martin, 1960–
The international student's guide to UK education : unlocking university
life and culture / Martin Hyde.
p. cm.
Includes index.
1. Foreign study–Great Britain–Guidebooks. 2. Education, Higher–Great
Britain–Guidebooks. 3. Great Britain–Guidebooks. I. Title.
LB2376.6.G7H93 2012
378.41–dc23
2011036814

ISBN: 978-0-415-61806-9 (hbk)
ISBN: 978-0-415-61807-6 (pbk)
ISBN: 978-0-203-81828-2 (ebk)

Typeset in Galliard
by Keystroke, Station Road, Codsall, Wolverhampton

MIX
Paper from
responsible sources
FSC
www.fsc.org   FSC® C004839

Printed and bound in Great Britain by
CPI Antony Rowe, Chippenham, Wiltshire

In memory of my father – a teacher to the end

Contents

Acknowledgements

I would like to thank the editing team at Routledge and especially Maggie Lindsey-Jones, Rose James, and Geraldine Lyons, whose comments have been of invaluable help for shaping the final text. I would also like to thank all the international students who have shared information with me over the years about their experiences of studying at university in the UK, with special thanks going to Huang Shu-er for her openness and for her generosity with her time.

Chapter 1

Introduction to the guide

Dear international student (or future international student!), well done for buying this guide! Whether you are already at a UK university or are thinking of applying to study in one, this guide will help you understand the UK university system of study and how to get the best from your time studying in a university in the UK. The guide is designed both to help you prepare for study and to help you understand the various issues that arise as you are studying and living in the UK as an international student and how to best deal and cope with these issues.

The guide is organised from start to finish: from application to arrival, stay and return to your own country and culture. It realises that a lot of things will be different and perhaps strange for you and that the experience will be both challenging and exciting. It realises that study at a UK university is a life-changing experience for you both professionally and culturally as a person. The guide will continually ensure you take account of your own development and cultural adaptation and change and help you with this process – a process that at times can be confusing and difficult. The guide helps you as a 'whole person', taking account of your emotional, cultural and academic needs. Above all the guide makes you realise you are not alone in this experience!

Instead of simply telling you facts about UK university study and the UK study experience, the guide is designed to engage you in your own learning. To do this you are required, from time to time, to undertake self-development exercises. This is done to encourage 'active reading' and 'reflective learning': learning that will equip you to deal with the challenges and excitement of your new life in the UK as an international student. Above all, the guide is designed to help you – to help you avoid some of the problems and traps that being an international student can involve and to make you aware of how you can take best advantage of and enjoy the experience.

It would, after all, be unusual to buy a beautiful new car and yet not have an instruction manual of how drive the car and enjoy all its features, wouldn't it? Yet many students do just that – they buy an international education without having such a guide! This book is designed to act as such a guide for you. I hope you enjoy it and find it useful and that it helps you better understand and enjoy the experience.

The guide is organised and structured in the following way. You are the centre of the circle: an international student with your own culture, outlook and under- standings – around you are the different layers of academic culture and the classroom, university academic structure, university administrative support. Beyond the classroom is UK student culture and outside the university is the British life and culture. All of these will influence your experience and the guide will explain these different influences and help you to better understand them. You, as a cultural being, are always central to the experiences that these different layers of experience offer. Developing your understanding of how you understand yourself and understand your reactions to these various layers of experience is the key aim of this guide.

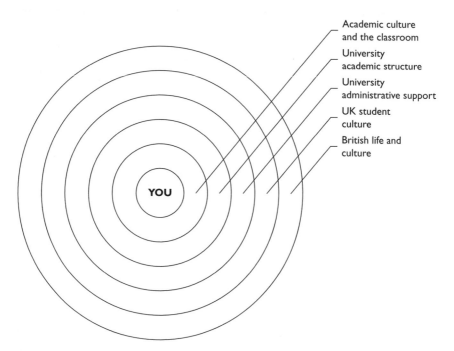

Academic culture
and the classroom

University
academic structure

University
administrative support

UK student
culture

British life and
culture

YOU

Figure 1.1 You and the influences upon you as an international student in the UK.

Chapter 2

Before you go

Understanding yourself and your needs

Introduction

One of the most difficult and most important choices you may make in your life is the choice of education to prepare you for the life ahead.

The world is rapidly globalising. Internet technologies and the media combined with the spread of multinational business means that everyone in the world is increasingly in contact with each other and that opportunities for work are now found abroad as well as at home. This interconnection provides a wealth of opportunities to explore – opportunities that in the past were not available. The spread of global financial services, and the liberalisation of countries both politically and economically, mean the world is an exciting place for those who choose to prepare themselves for it by developing the skills needed to operate in it. One of the main ways of doing this is to opt for an international education. In this section you will undertake a series of exercises designed to allow you to reflect on the world around you and to analyse your own wants and needs so that you are better able to make the right choices about your study programme in the UK and increase its value to you.

Question: What do you feel are the advantages of an international education?

Exercise

Consider the following ideas and decide if you agree with them:

Opportunity offered	Tick if you agree ✓
The development of international language skills – especially in English as it is the main world language of communication today	

The development of intercultural awareness and the ability to relate to and work with people from many different international backgrounds	
The opportunity for self-development and to become more self-aware through managing to adapt to a new cultural environment	
The development of the necessary self-confidence to become a global traveller and citizen	
The acquisition of the most up-to-date knowledge in the field I have chosen to specialise in	
The opportunity to meet new people and make friends with people from places and backgrounds I would not otherwise meet	
Other . . .	

Note: You are advised to try these exercises out: it is best to use the space of a notebook to write down your responses to the various sections where indicated in the chart.

The choice of country, university and programme of study will have life-changing consequences for you, so it is very important that you spend time reflecting upon the choice before you make it. This section of the guide will help you with this process. There is no doubt that it is very difficult, especially if you are just finishing high school, to know what career you may want to follow. Perhaps it is not a good thing to be too sure of what you want too young anyway! In fact you may have ideas about what you think you want, or your parents may have influenced you in your choice of future career, but in fact, once you begin your studies, you may find that the choice was not the right one for you. It is expensive to make a mistake in your choice, both in terms of time and money, so the more you know yourself and what you really want to study and perhaps do later in life, the better – even if this simply means you find out what you *do not* want to do or study!

Reflective exercise: Imagine the future in five years' time. Think of your ideal scenario. What are you doing as a job? What is your typical work day like? Now imagine the negative scenario. What are you doing as a job? What is your typical work day like?

It is wise to have a goal and to see what may help lead you to the goal and what may in fact lead you away from it!

Question: What skills and experiences will you need to develop to be good in your ideal job?

The fact that you have bought this guide suggests you have already decided to study in the UK. There are a wide variety of countries in which to choose to study these days. Nearly all countries with developed economies and even countries with developing economies offer opportunities for international education in their universities now. Even in countries where the spoken language is not English, you may find that the programmes of study are in fact taught in English. Of the English-speaking countries, the main choice is usually between North America (Canada and the USA), Australasia (Australia and New Zealand) and the UK.

Exercise

It is worth checking your thoughts about the relative advantages of each destination. Use the checklist in Table 2.1 to understand your reasons for choosing the UK compared to the other destinations.

Table 2.1 Why choose the UK?

Area of consideration	Advantage/disadvantage of the UK	Tick ✓ if important for you, cross ✗ if not
Reputation	UK has a very good worldwide reputation for the quality of its universities and education	
Cost	UK tuition fees are comparatively reasonable and the cost of living is not too high	
Simplicity of application	UK universities have an easy-to-use application system (UCAS) and visa system	
Variety of programmes	There are over 100 universities in the UK all offering an interesting range of programmes to choose from	

Table 2.1 continued

Area of consideration	Advantage/disadvantage of the UK	Tick ✓ if important for you, cross ✗ if not
Teaching style	The UK educational style is practical and gets students involved in their subject in an interactive way	
Political culture	The UK is the oldest democracy in the world and offers freedom of thought for me to develop my ideas	
Popular culture	The UK leads the world in many areas of popular culture, e.g. football, music, youth fashion	
Permission to work and study	The UK automatically allows students the right to work during their studies	
Multicultural society	The UK, and especially its big cities, are a melting pot for the world's people	
Location	The UK is in the EU. I am then able to visit most EU countries at low cost (budget airlines, Eurotunnel etc.)	
Food	The UK has some of the most exciting international cuisine in the world these days*	
Natural beauty	Although the UK is a small country it has lots of beautiful countryside†	
Respect for the environment	The people of the UK like to protect animals and nature and fight to restrict pollution	
Sport	The UK is the home of nearly all the major sports in the world (football, rugby, hockey, cricket, golf)	
History	The UK has a deep respect for tradition and history. This makes it very interesting for visits	
Safety	In the UK it is difficult for people to buy guns and it is unusual for UK police to be dangerous	
Transport	The UK has a well-developed transportation system. It is cheap and easy to travel within the UK‡	
The National Health System	The UK has a huge public health system that international student can use for free§	
The weather	The UK has a temperate climate: not too hot in summer and not too cold in winter¶	
Other		

*You probably did not think that the UK was good for food, but this reputation for bad food comes from a past period in UK history. In fact UK food is going through a revolution at present. You will find a variety of restaurants and food in any medium-sized city in the UK very hard to find anywhere else.

†You may not have associated the UK with beautiful and outstanding nature. In fact the UK has many stunning landscapes to explore (the Peak District, the Pennines, Snowdonia, Dartmoor, the Lake District, the Norfolk Broads, Ben Nevis, the Scottish Lochs and Highlands, the Yorkshire Moors and Dales, the Pembrokeshire coastline and the Cornish coastline).

‡The UK transportation system is complex to understand and usually very expensive. The trains and metro tend to be overcrowded and dirty. The system has suffered from being made private and a consequent lack of radical investment.

§The NHS is a comprehensive and effective part of UK life. Although it did suffer in the past from certain mismanagement and underinvestment, today it is in better shape and offers a high-quality service. International students do not have to buy private medical insurance if they study in the UK for over six months (in Scotland the six months rule does not apply). Use the website listed below to check the latest information.

¶The British themselves complain a lot about the climate, especially in winter, which can be long and depressing (see Chapter 8). However, the UK is lucky to have sufficient rainfall to avoid real problems of drought or wild fires or dangerously hot summers. It can however suffer from floods.

Useful website: http://www.educationuk.org/Life-in-the-UK/creating-your-life-in-the-uk/Health-advice-for-UK-international-students. If you do a web search under 'NHS and international student' you will find many other useful websites with lots of information and advice.

Question: Did you think of any other reason? Were there some reasons you hadn't thought of?

Advice: EU/EEA students. If you are an EU/EEA student you should apply within your country for your European Health Insurance Card (EHIC) before going to the UK. Note that dental charges are not usually covered for free on the NHS.

Overseas students should make sure that they take out health insurance if they are coming to the UK on a course of less than six months' duration or if they wish to cover dental treatment. It may be sensible for all international students to think about cover for repatriation in the event of death or severe injury.

Reflection: hopes and fears

Often before we go abroad to another country we have an image in our minds of what that country will be like and how we will live there. In reality, this does not always turn out to be true. Things we thought would be good turn out not to be true and things we thought could be bad may also turn out not to be.

Exercise

1 List the three things you think you know about and will like about being a
student in the UK.
2 Look at these again and think where the ideas and the images came from.
Can you trust these ideas and images?

Comment: It is best to be realistic and prepared for reality. There is a famous story of a boy called Dick Whittington who set off from the English countryside to escape rural poverty. He had been told that the streets of London were paved with gold. When he got there he found it full of rats and people trying to cheat him. This is an extreme warning! But the fact is that everywhere in the world there are similar problems. We often carry false ideas about things around in our heads – these are usually given to us by comments from other people (parents, teachers) or the media. It is best to approach the UK with an open but critical mind: you will find that the streets of London are not paved with gold, but you also may find that the English are not as cold and reserved as you had expected!

Motivation for studying in the UK

To be successful at studying abroad it is important to have the right motivation to overcome the inevitable difficulties that being out of your own culture brings.

The next exercise focuses on your motivation for studying in the UK. Generally there are two possible motivations for studying abroad – these are called 'push' or 'pull' reasons. Push reasons are generally negative and pull reasons are positive. If you are motivated by push reasons you may therefore have some motivation problems when studying in the UK. Push reasons do not come from within you – this is why they may be difficult reasons to continue to believe in, especially when met with difficulty.

Exercise

Look at the reasons in Table 2.2 and tick the ones that apply to you.

Table 2.2 Push and pull reasons

Reason for choosing to study abroad	✓
Push reason	
A To get away from difficulties at home or in my home country	
B Because I am bored at home/in my country	
C I can't get in to a 'good' (prestigious) university in my country	
D My parents have told me I must study in the UK	
E Study abroad will give me a holiday break to have fun after the hard work of school and before beginning a job	
F Lack of employment opportunities in my country	
G To start a new and better life abroad: it is the easiest way of getting into the country	
Pull reasons	
H The UK offers the kind of education and the programme of study I am interested in	
I I feel that a UK university education will help me in my career	
J I want to be surrounded by English in everyday life to become completely fluent	
K I have relatives/friends living in the UK who will support me	
L The UK is a relatively calm and stable society where I will be able to study without interruption by strikes or political violence	
M I am interested in the lifestyle of the UK and want to experience it and develop myself as a person	
N The programmes are quite compact – in England, three years for most undergraduate and one year for most postgraduate programmes: it won't take so long to get qualified	

WARNING!

If you have more Push reasons than Pull reasons, you need to ask yourself if studying abroad in the UK is a sensible idea!

Anecdote: Sunday was the eldest son of a lower-middle class Nigerian family from a village. He had done quite well at school in the local town. His father decided he should go to the UK to get a degree in business studies and then work in the UK as this would help the family. The money for the tuition fees was gathered from many members of the extended family and village friends. His father told him he would need to work to support himself once in the UK. Sunday was not really interested in business studies, he had always wanted to be a musician – but he was excited by the idea of going to the UK and so took the opportunity to go. However, once in the UK at university he was bored by the programme and failed the first year. He also found that part-time working in the Post Office (sorting letters early in the morning) tired him out. When he failed his first year he couldn't face telling his father so he pretended he had done well. The situation began to make him feel very depressed and desperate.

Question: What problems do you think Sunday will have with his future studies in the UK? What problems do you think await him if he has to return to Nigeria? How could this problem have been avoided?

Making the choice about what to study

WARNING!

Don't forget that it is *you* who is going to study abroad and not your parents! You must study something that *you* are interested in. Sometimes this may mean reaching a compromise with your parents, especially as they are the people who are probably sponsoring your education. Many universities offer combined honour programmes – also known in the USA as 'double-majors' (you can study two half-programmes at the same time for the same cost, e.g. business studies and music). This may represent a *head and heart* combination. Look at Table 2.3 and decide which are 'head' (rational) reasons, and which are 'heart' (emotional) reasons.

Table 2.3 Reasons for studying a particular subject

Reason for studying a subject	Head ✓	Heart ✓
This programme is one that has a higher chance of leading to a job		
This programme is one my parents want me to study		
This programme is in a growing area for employment in the future		
I love this subject area – I find it fascinating		
I have always been interested in this area of life and want to learn more		
I feel motivated to read and talk with people about this subject		

Advice: Both points of view are useful to consider. There are some subjects that may not necessarily lead to an obvious career or job at the end of it for you. Arts subjects like painting or music performance are not subjects that have obvious careers unlike, say, engineering or medicine, and of course parents worry about what their children will do in life – if they will have enough money to live well. On the other hand, it is very difficult to study well a subject that you have no passion or curiosity for. Ideally you need to find something to study that satisfies both 'head and heart'. If you have to make a choice, my view is that it is certainly better at undergraduate level to follow the heart, because you are more likely to be successful this way. You can always focus on the world of work as your motivation for study at masters level and undertake professional training later, once you know what jobs you are preparing for.

Self-analysis for choosing to study a subject abroad

Exercise

The flow chart in Figure 2.1 is designed to help you analyse your reasons for studying abroad. It is useful to have thought this through and to know *why* you are making this important and expensive choice. To do this properly you may need to do some research on your own country's educational possibilities as well as what UK universities offer.

PESTLE and personal SWOT analyses

Another two kinds of analyses you can do before you go to study abroad to help you with your choice of study are PESTLE and SWOT analyses. PESTLE – political, economic, social, technological, legal and environmental – analysis looks at the external environment you are in and what openings or opportunities there are for jobs and careers (see Table 2.4). A personal SWOT – strengths, weaknesses, opportunities and threats – analysis looks at your strengths and weaknesses. This is done as a form of self-analysis – to see in which areas you need to develop new skills to take advantage of the opportunities offered in the external environment.

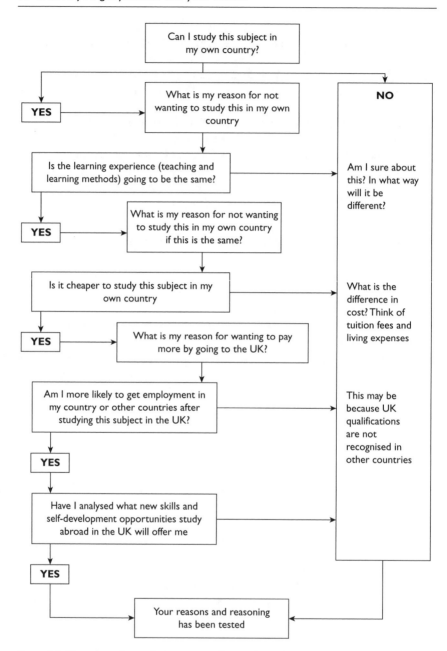

Figure 2.1 Flow chart for analysing reasons for studying abroad.

Exercise

Table 2.4 PESTLE analysis

	Situation for analysis	Questions to ask	Your notes
P	Political	Is the country liberalising? What opportunities are there in the private sector? Is the country increasingly under state control? Is the country likely to experience political turmoil?	
E	Economic	How is the economy doing (unemployment, gross domestic product [GDP] gross national product [GNP], inflation)? How fast is the country growing economically? At what stage in its development is the country and what professions are in demand?	
S	Social	Is there a developing middle class? Are fashions and tastes changing? What is the population age distribution? What opportunities does this provide? Which service sectors are in demand?	
T	Technology	How fast is technology spreading (mobile phones, Internet)? What opportunities does this provide for businesses and training?	
L	Legal	Is the country a safe environment to work, live or run a business in? What legal protection is there? What kinds of working contracts are available? How easy and profitable is it to set up and run a business?	
E	Environmental	What opportunities are there for green technology and renewable energy development? How does carbon emissions legislation influence the opportunity for new industries?	

WARNING!

Supply and demand

It is a good idea to check if there is an oversupply of professionals in certain areas of study in you own country or any other country you want to work in. In some countries too many doctors or engineers have been trained or there may be too many students with business degrees, for example. If many of these people cannot find work because there are not enough jobs in these sectors it may be unwise to join them! On the other hand, you may want to think if there are shortage areas (e.g. not enough dentists) or not enough people with MBAs! For example, it may be that there are too many people with undergraduate qualifications, e.g. engineers with a lot of technical knowledge, but who lack management and English language skills, which are also needed for the jobs on offer: in this case a postgraduate degree in management may well be a good idea.

Advice: Do the exercise above to assess the employment situation to help you make a sensible choice.

Anecdote: Several years ago Misako decided that she would study early childhood development with business studies with an option in entrepreneurship. This was a combined honours programme she found on offer at a UK university. Her reasoning was as follows: by doing a PESTLE analysis of the external environment in Tokyo she noticed that women are increasingly joining the workplace in Japan. This meant that if they had children and wished or needed to continue working, they needed a service where they could leave their children to be looked after during the day (child nursery provision). The Japanese as consumers are very concerned about quality of provision and so developing the latest knowledge of how to best look after children from the UK seemed ideal. From a personal SWOT analysis (see below) she also realised she was good at working with young children and liked it. An area of weakness was business start-up so she decided she needed to know how to go about setting up and operating a business. The above programme seemed like an ideal preparation for setting up her own quality nursery as a business in the city.

Personal SWOT analysis

As well as looking at the opportunities available and the areas in which it is sensible to prepare your career, you also need to take account of your own personality, likes and dislikes and areas of strength and weakness. The exercise in Figure 2.2 is designed to help you with this.

Advice: Once you have done this exercise you can design a study plan that will help you by both 'playing to your strengths' – to the ones that the modern world of work will reward you for – and by tackling and improving your weaknesses (the ones that will hold you back in your career unless improved).

Working after your studies

Suggestion: If you have an idea of where you may want to work after your studies, it is a good idea to check the working visa requirements of the country or countries you are interested in working in before beginning your studies.

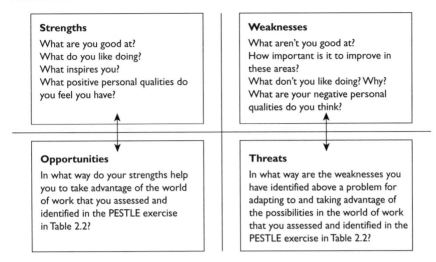

Figure 2.2 A personal SWOT analysis.

If your plan is to stay in the UK check to see if this is possible and, if so, what the requirements are.

Useful websites:

- For the UK http://www.ukba.homeoffice.gov.uk/workingintheuk
- For the USA http://www.usa.gov/visitors/work.shtml
- For Australia http://www.immi.gov.au
- For Canada http://www.cic.gc.ca/english/index.asp

Now that you have undertaken the above exercises, complete the following exercise which you should use for selecting your university programme of study.

Exercise

Do the self-analysis exercise in Figure 2.3 and then think of what programmes you could study that would fit in the 'Motivation Zone'.

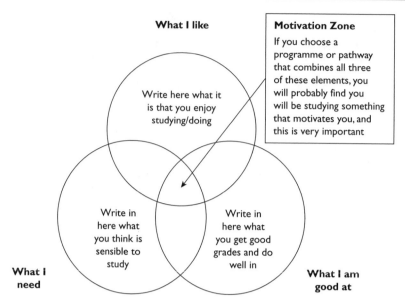

What I like

Motivation Zone

If you choose a programme or pathway that combines all three of these elements, you will probably find you will be studying something that motivates you, and this is very important

Write here what it is that you enjoy studying/doing

Write in here what you think is sensible to study

Write in here what you get good grades and do well in

What I need

What I am good at

Figure 2.3 Finding your Motivation Zone for your university study programme selection.

Recognition of qualifications

Question: Will the UK qualification I study be recognised in my own country and abroad?

WARNING!

It is very important that before you start your studies in the UK you find out if the UK qualification you receive will be recognised in your country or in any other country you wish to move on to after studying. You may find it useful to check if the university you will study at in the UK is on your national Ministry of Education list of approved institutions and if the qualification you will study will also be recognised in your own country or any other country for state jobs or by national universities if you wish to work or continue your studies in your country. If you are undertaking a professional qualification (e.g. law, medicine, nursing etc.) it is also likely that you will need to retrain or undertake certain adaptation examinations for example, in order to be able to practice in your own or another country. Again the UK qualification you will receive should be checked with the professional body governing the profession in the country you are aiming to practice in.

Note: UK qualifications are considered prestigious and are normally unproblematic for working in the private sector throughout the world.

Useful website: http://www.ukcisa.org.uk/student/ukstudent/recognition.php

You may find that the ENIC (European Network of Information Centres)/ NARIC (National Recognition Information Centre) is useful for this information if it covers your country: otherwise, if in doubt, you should contact your own country's Ministry of Education to check this out.

Useful website: http://www.enic-naric.net

Question: Will my own national school and university qualifications be acceptable for applying to UK universities?

Note: NARIC: to check if your own national qualifications are recognised by the UK education system you can visit NARIC to obtain a statement of comparability (check the fees for this at the website).

Advice: However, many universities in the UK subscribe to NARIC themselves and will check your qualifications themselves for comparability. Find out if you need to use NARIC yourself with the university if you are in doubt. The university international admissions office will normally have posted the qualifications it recognises on its website, or will answer an e-mail query. This could save you the comparability certificate fee!

Question: Do you need to get the certificate validated in any way? Some countries may occasionally require an apostille certificate/stamp to legalise the UK qualification you obtain. This involves paying for a notary to legalise the document and then getting this stamped by your national embassy in the UK

Useful website: http://www.apostillelegalisation.co.uk

Mind your English language!

One of the main areas of misunderstanding and problems with international study is the issue of the English language. Universities will ask for certain requirements to be met in order for you to be able to study in their universities.

Sometimes you may fail to reach the necessary entry score for the programme you wish to study or you may have a low score in one of the four language skills that have been tested (reading, speaking, listening and writing). In these cases universities may offer a Foundation Year (a full year of study that is designed to prepare you with your English level, your study skills and your knowledge of specific subjects) or pre-sessional programmes (a period of intensive English study and academic adaptation) as a way of preparing for the programme of study you wish to follow. Many students find that they need to do these programmes in order to make any progress in their English as it may not be possible to make fast enough progress with English language study in their own countries. For universities to be able to assess the best pathway (route of study) for you, they need to know your current English score. They can then recommend the right kind and the right length of English study you probably need. This is important because it will determine the length of time and the types of visas you need to be issued with.

Recommendation: Take an international English exam, such as the Secure English Language Test (SELT), before you apply and have the scores ready!

Advice: You should estimate that for each 0.5 International English Language Testing System (IELTS) band you need to improve you will need to do up to 10–12 weeks of intensive English study.

Comment: Understanding English language learning and study: many students do not understand the complexity of learning a foreign language such as English. It is very important to be realistic about this.

Exercise

Look at the statements in Table 2.5 and see if they match your views or not

Table 2.5 Beliefs about English language learning

Belief about English language learning	Agree ✓ Disagree ✗
English is an easy language to learn	
It takes about one year to learn a language well	
It won't take me long to learn English once I am in the UK	
I don't really need to study English because I will pick it up naturally once I am in the UK and using it daily	

Answer: You should have disagreed with all of these! English may be an easy language to start to speak, but it has a complex spelling system and a difficult pronunciation system for many people. It usually takes about five years of regular study to know a language well. The average person can expect to increase only 1.5–2.0 IELTS points after a full year of intensive English language study! Speaking and using English in a workplace is not the same as learning the language for academic study. The average daily use of social English is limited and will not help much for writing essays!

Preparing to be self-sufficient

Look at the list of day-to-day chores in Table 2.6. If you are able to do these simple tasks before you go to study abroad this will help you enormously.

Table 2.6 Daily chores in student life

Chore	Need to learn	Need to improve	Can do
Cooking basic meals			
Washing up the dishes			
Using a washing machine/launderette/spin dryer			
Ironing			
Basic shopping for food			
Hoovering and cleaning a room			

Advice: If you are not able to do any of these life chores, it is a good idea to learn them before you depart. This will make you more self-confident.

What to take/pack

When you pack to bring things to the UK you should consider the fact that many of the items you need for everyday life are available at very reasonable prices in the UK. Out of town stores such as Matalan or the big supermarket chains are good for clothing, especially coats and other items needed for the cold – which they sell at cheap prices. You will also find that general utility stores are plentiful in all cities and offer cheap packs for bedding and cooking utensils.

Recommendation: Use your airline weight limit to bring personal things that you cannot find in the UK, but perhaps buy the rest once you are here.

Further useful websites to visit before departing

You will find the downloadable booklets at the British Council website very useful to read before departure.

http://www.britishcouncil.org/eumd-immigration

Also visit the following website for information on cultural adaptation:

http://www.ukcisa.org.uk/about/material_media/pubs_crosscultural.php

Chapter 3

Choosing your programme, choosing a university and applying

In this chapter we will look at all the relevant information that you need to consider for choosing what and where to study in the UK. You will undertake information-searching exercises to develop your understanding of UK universities and programmes on offer and in doing so develop an understanding of what is best for you. The chapter also then explains what you need to consider in order to apply.

You can study at three levels in UK universities: undergraduate (UG), postgraduate (PG) and doctoral level.

Exercise

Match the following terms to their explanations

A	Undergraduate (UG) level	1	This is the level of study you usually do after you have graduated from your first degree. It is also called Masters level and is typically an MSc or MA.
B	Postgraduate (PG) level	2	This is the level of study you may go on to, usually after a Masters degree. It is also referred to as PGR (postgraduate research), although PGR may begin at Masters level
C	Doctoral level	3	This is the study you do after leaving your high school. It is also called a Bachelors degree. There are two main types: a BA (Bachelor of Arts) or BSc (Bachelor of Science). There are many others, e.g. BEng (Bachelor of Engineering)

Answers: A, 3; B, 1; C, 2

Language confusion note: In the USA 'graduate' is used where in the UK the term postgraduate would be used. A graduate programme in the USA is called a *post*graduate programme in the UK. In the UK an undergraduate degree can also be called a Bachelors (e.g. BA/BSc) or first degree, and a postgraduate degree (e.g. MA, MSc) is often referred to as a Masters.

Understanding 'levels of study'

In the UK there are two national qualifications frameworks which explain at what level programmes are taught. It is important to understand these levels, and Table 3.1 should help you with this.

The *National Qualifications Framework* (NQF) is developed for use in England, Northern Ireland and Wales. It consists of nine levels from secondary school through to university education. Scotland and the *Scottish Qualifications Authority* (SQA) has its own system called the Scottish Credit and Qualifications Framework (SCQF) based on 12 levels!

Table 3.1 The three levels of higher education

England, Northern Ireland and Wales NQF Level	Education level example	
8	Doctoral degree	
7	Postgraduate Masters degree	
6	Year 3 undergraduate degree (360)	University
5	Year 2 undergraduate degree (240)	
4	Year I undergraduate degree (120)	
3	Up to A2 level (foundation year) AS level	
2	GCSE grade C + (16 years)	School
I	Pre-grade C GCSE	
Entry	Basic knowledge and skills	
Scotland SCQF Level	Education level example	
12	Doctoral degree	
11	Postgraduate Masters degree	
10	Honours degree	University
9	Ordinary degree	
8	Higher National Diploma	
7	Advanced Higher (school) and Higher National Certificate (year I university)	
6	Highers (school)	
5	Intermediate 2	School
4	Intermediate I	
I–3	Access I–3	

Once you know what level of programme your own national qualifications allow you to apply to study at, the next step is to decide what programme you want to study.

Question: What is different about undergraduate study in Scotland from England?

Answer: In Scotland you study for four years and in the UK for three.

Choosing your university programme

Step 1: deciding if you want to follow a professional pathway or general pathway

This is one of the first choices you need to make when thinking of university study for the first time. The question is, 'Do you want to start professional job training to become a medical doctor, dentist, veterinary surgeon, engineer, or a service sector employee such as a nurse or a teacher, or are you less sure and would prefer to study something less specific – that keeps your options for future work more open?'

Note: For some professions, e.g. law or architecture, you can do a one-year 'Conversion Masters'. This means that after the first degree you may be able to then do training for a career in these professions even if you did not choose a specific undergraduate degree in these subjects. Note that you may need to have studied a related first degree – so it is best to check this before beginning your study pathway.

Pathways: A pathway is the full set of studies that you decide to follow – it can include English preparation, a foundation year or pre-sessional summer school preparation, undergraduate degree and postgraduate degree. It is good to think of pathways and research what possibilities there are open to you.

WARNING!

Professional recognition between countries: If you choose to study a professional pathway degree and return to work in your own country or another country, then you need to research if this professional degree is (a) recognised by the relevant professional body, and (b) if not, what further training programmes or exams you will need to take to be able to practice professionally.

Studying medicine/dentistry

Medicine is usually undertaken by direct entry onto a five-year programme (UCAS Code A100). UCAS is the Universities and Colleges Admissions Service. To apply for a medicine or dentistry degree, international students will usually have to sit the UK Clinical Aptitude exam (UKCAT, or sometimes the Biomedical Admissions Test – BMAT). You should check which exam you need to take for the universities you are interested in and when you need to take it.

Places for direct entry to medicine are limited; an alternative pathway some students may choose to follow is to study a degree in biomedical science (three years). After this they apply for 'Medicine Graduate Entry' (UCAS Code A101). This requires a further four years of study.

Studying law (to become a lawyer [barrister] or solicitor)

The quickest route into these professions is to get at least a 2.1 qualifying university law degree and then undertake the necessary further training and qualifications.

Further training depends on whether you want to become a barrister (lawyer) or a solicitor:

To become a barrister (lawyer)	A one-year Bar Professional Training Course (BPTC) followed by at least 12 months 'pupillage in chambers' (professional experience)
To become a solicitor	A one-year Legal Practice Course (LPC) followed by a two-year training contract (with a firm of solicitors, or the legal section of a government department or commercial firm)

WARNING!

This means that you need to study or train for at least an extra two or three years before being able to practice! Choosing a professional career means a long financial and academic commitment.

Note: Graduates in a non-law degree subject can still qualify as solicitors or barristers by taking a Postgraduate Diploma in Law (PDL) before then taking the LPC/BPTC. This means the expense of an extra year's study. The PDL prepares non-law graduates for a legal career as it covers the foundations of law in one year!

Note: Professional recognition: Undergraduate degree programmes such as architecture or civil engineering may be professionally recognised, e.g. the Royal Institute of British Architects (RIBA) recognition for a BA Architecture, or Institute of Civil Engineers (ICE) recognition for a BEng. Check to see if this is the case with the university programmes you are interested in.

Healthcare and education training programmes

Unfortunately it is not possible currently for overseas students to apply to train as a nurse or midwife by applying to enter directly into a university degree programme in the UK. This is because of the restrictions that apply to funded places which are only for home and European Union (EU) students.

A few universities do offer a 'top-up' (year 3 entry) BSc in Nursing which registered overseas nurses can apply for. The programme includes an Overseas Nursing Programme. When passed this allows nurses to become registered with the Nursing and Midwifery Council (NMC), which means they can work as a nurse in the UK National Health System. Places are limited as you will need to have an Overseas Nursing Programme (ONP) decision letter issued by the NMC that assesses you as eligible for entry to the programme.

Useful website: http://www.nmc-uk.org/Registration/Joining-the-register/Trained-outside-the-EU—EEA

Note: Finances for EU students on nursing and midwifery programmes: EU students on BSc nursing and midwifery programmes are funded by NHS bursaries and therefore do not have to pay fees. They must apply for this exemption from the NHS. EU students who have been ordinarily resident in the UK for three years can also apply for maintenance grants.

Useful website: The NHS bursary website http://www.nhsbsa.nhs.uk/Students/3261.aspx

Training to be a teacher

There are several routes to becoming a trained teacher in the UK. The most usual is through undertaking a PGCE (Postgraduate Certificate in Education) after having obtained a first degree (Bachelors). It is a one-year programme, much of it being very practical and school-based. Another route is through doing a Bachelor of Education (BEd) which can be three or four years long. This enables you to study for your degree and complete your initial teacher training at the same time. It is often a popular choice for those interested in teaching primary school children.

All trainee teachers must meet a set of professional standards determined by the government before they can be awarded Qualified Teacher Status (QTS). This is done by undertaking a period of initial teacher training (ITT) such as a PGCE, followed by an induction year in employment as a teacher in a school.

WARNING!

International students should be aware that a teaching qualification gained in the UK may not qualify them to teach in their home country: it is professional training for the UK education system. You should check first in your own country to see whether UK qualifications are acceptable. They are, however, often acceptable and even desirable in many international private schools.

Note: You will generally only be eligible for government-funded bursaries for teacher training if you have been in the UK for three years or more and have a residency visa.

Step 2: deciding on what type of degree programme

You will need to understand various words and concepts to be able to make your choice properly. Do the matching exercise in Table 3.2 to help you with this. Once you have done this think about the advantages for you of each type of study.

Think of the advantages and use these to help with your decision making.

You may also find other types of courses available – they represent shorter programmes that often form part of a traditional degree – so it is good to know what they mean. Match the English term to the explanation on Table 3.3 to help you understand.

Table 3.2 Degree types and their advantages

	Degree type	Description	Advantages
A	Honours degree	1	A four-year undergraduate course in which students undertake a placement year in industry (usually paid). In the USA this is called an 'internship'.
B	Top-up degree	2	A programme delivered by two institutions from different countries which both award their own national degrees upon successful completion.
C	Double degree	3	A flexible degree system by which a degree is obtained through a process of 'credit accumulation'. Students choose to study from a wide range of subject modules.
D	Modular degree	4	A degree that involves studying from two different subject areas. In the USA these are called 'Double' or 'Dual Majors'.
E	Sandwich degree programme	5	Studying only the final year of a degree to be awarded the full degree. This involves transferring credits in from another (often international) university.
F	Combined/joint honours degree	6	A degree that is of a higher academic value than an 'Ordinary' or 'Pass Degree'.

Answer: A, 6; B, 5; C, 2; D, 3; E, 1; F, 4

Table 3.3 Course names and their explanations

	English term		Explanation
1	Foundation degree	A	A programme (often one year long) that prepares students for entry to the first year of an undergraduate degree programme
2	Pre-sessional programme	B	Qualifications, taught mostly in FE colleges, that are equivalent to the first and second years of university study
3	PG Cert., PG Dip.	C	A preparation programme of short duration usually focusing on English language skills and academic writing
4	HNC (Higher National Certificate) and HND (Higher National Diploma)	D	A two-year degree (the first two years of university study). It usually has a work-based element
5	University Foundation Programme	E	The first part and second part of a Masters programme

Answer: 1, D; 2 ,C; 3, E; 4, B; 5, A

Masters specialisation: Big universities may offer specialist Masters programmes, smaller universities may offer Masters that begin with a general first phase of study (perhaps offering a PG Certificate) and then allow students to specialise in more specific areas in the next phase. Check what specialisms (often called options or electives) are running before beginning the programme.

WARNING!

Some universities may not run options if there are not enough students opting for the option. A phrase to look out for here is 'subject to student numbers'.

Step 3: deciding if you need a preparation course

Another common pathway for international students who have not obtained the equivalent of A Levels (or UCAS points) necessary to enter a UG programme directly, is to either take A levels in the UK at an A-level college (these can be expensive programmes, and usually take two years of study) or to do a university entry International Foundation Year/International Foundation Programme (IFY or IFP). A similar preparation – called a 'Pre-Masters' – may be necessary to enter a Masters programme if your degree is not of a sufficient level for direct entry or if your academic English level is not sufficient.

Note: Integrated or non-integrated IFP/IFY: These programmes are designed both to improve your IELTS score level and offer content teaching of modules to A level standard. You may need either or both – in which case this may be a good pathway for you. Some universities may add an HE Level 0 (NQF Level 3) year to a full UG degree programme. This kind of IFY is called an 'Integrated Foundation Programme'. For an overseas student this type of preparation year may have the advantage of meaning that you only require one visa. If you are an EU home student, it may mean you are eligible to apply for Student Loans Company (SLC) loans for the preparation year as well as for the rest of the programme. If the Foundation year is not integrated then it is called 'stand-alone' and if you are an overseas visa national student you will need one visa for the IFY and one for the remaining UG programme. If you are an EU student, you will not be able to apply for a Student Loan Company (SLC) loan to cover the cost of the IFY.

There are many private colleges offering international foundation programmes in the UK and universities may also have arrangements to recognise a foundation year taught in your own country, accepting students onto their programmes who successfully pass these.

Useful website: http://www.collegesinbritain.co.uk

WARNING!

Before you decide to undertake an IFP/IFY, integrated or not, instead of A levels, check which universities the IFP/IFY you study will allow you entry into. Generally the top-level universities (Russell Group) in the UK require A levels!

Question: What do you need to think about when applying to study on a course in the UK?

Advice: Make sure you have undertaken the exercises in Chapter 2 so you have a good idea of what you want to study!

Understanding tuition fees

Of course, as well as choosing a programme from the above self-analysis, the reality of money and the cost of a programme are often a crucial deciding factor.

Currently in UK universities there are two fees for studying on a programme and they are set broadly according to nationality and legal place of residence. There are two categories of fee status: *home* and *overseas*. UK universities charge fees at a higher rate to overseas students. These are students from outside the European Union (EU). They charge a lower rate (or nothing in Scotland) to those classified as home students – as these are subsidised by UK government funding.

Note: Home fees also apply to students from overseas British and EU territories, e.g. Bermuda (UK) or Greenland and the Faroe Islands (Denmark) and to European Economic Area (EEA) students who are resident working in the UK.

In 2011, the fees were often three times more expensive for overseas students than home students. In 2012, home students' fees are between £6,000 and £9,000 per year for UG programmes, narrowing the difference.

Question: Which fees status are you? Overseas or home? If you are not sure, visiting the following website may help: http://www.ukcisa.org.uk/student/fees_student_support.php

Fees within the UK for home students

Note: Fees in Scotland, Wales, Northern Ireland and England for home (EU) students vary. England and Northern Ireland are more expensive than Wales. Currently, policy in Scotland is that no tuition fees are charged for most EU students. It is a good idea to check the most recent situation as policies change.

Part-time courses and fees

If you are an overseas student you are not able to study in the UK on part-time programmes. EU students are able to do so. There are no fee loans available for part-time programmes.

Loans and payment for EU students

The Scottish Government pays all tuition fees through the Student Awards Agency for Scotland (SAAS) and EU students need to apply to SAAS for the payment of their tuition fees.

In England and Wales, if you're classed as an EU student and you're doing a full-time course in England, Northern Ireland or Wales, you can apply for a student loan to cover your tuition fees from the Student Loan Company. The SLC operate a unit dedicated to helping EU students with applying for loans and bursaries: Student Finance Services European Team, PO Box 89, Darlington DL1 9AZ, UK; Helpline +44 (0) 141 2433570; e-mail address EU_ Team@slc.co.uk.

WARNING!

Many students find that it is difficult to get through on the telephone. It is best to do as much as you can online!

Useful websites: http://www.student-support-saas.gov.uk
http://www.slc.co.uk
http://www.direct.gov.uk (put 'EU tuition fees loans' in search facility)

WARNING!

Many of the rules about fee status and eligibility for tuition fee loans or grants and for maintenance grants are complex. Universities usually have a fee status expert in their admission or student support team who can help with enquiries. If you are not sure, contact the university you are applying to and complete their fee status form.

Applying for a student loan as an EU student

EU students can apply for UK student loans to cover their tuition fees but generally EU students do not have access to loans to cover living costs (unless they have been resident in the UK for three years before starting to study).

Exercise

Before you take out a loan with the SLC it is best to make sure you have understood the terms and conditions of the loan. You can find all of this information by visiting the websites listed earlier. Complete Table 3.4

Table 3.4 What do you know about student loans?

Question to answer	Tick ✓ when you have answer
Are you eligible for a student loan?	
Are you eligible for a tuition fee grant or maintenance loan or grant?	
Do you know which form to complete for the grant and what is the latest date you can apply?	
Does the university you are applying to offer a bursary* for EU students?	
Do you know how to apply for the bursary?	
Do you understand the interest rate payment for the loan and the terms of repayment for this interest rate?	
Do you fully understand the repayment terms and what the income threshold is? For example, in 2011 it is set at 9% of salary earned above the £21,000 threshold	
Do you understand what the RPI is and how this is used to calculate loan repayment	
Are you aware of the international thresholds for repayment and how they vary? For example, in Poland in 2011 this is set at £9,000 equivalent	

Table 3.4 continued

Question to answer	Tick ✓ when you have answer
Are you aware of the 'default payment sum' for each country and what this means?	

*Bursaries. EU/EEA students may be eligible for bursaries from the university. A bursary is an award of money that does not have to be paid back. If you are an EU student check with your university or college how you apply for any bursary. Most universities and colleges let Student Finance England manage the bursaries on their behalf. If this is the case, you won't need to make a separate application for a bursary to your university. Instead, Student Finance England will assess you for the bursary. This is often awarded on a means-tested basis (this means that you have to send in information on your family income to the EU Team. If you have applied for a tuition fees loan they will automatically send a form to request this information from you).

Advice: The system may seem complex at first, but this is no reason not to understand your loan and its terms. If you get the answers to the above set of questions you will have a good understanding of the major features of the loan. It is very sensible to do this before taking out a tuition fees loan!

Advice: If you are an EU /EEA student who is paying the tuition fees and not applying for a UK student loan from the SLC, you should still complete certain sections of the loan application form to be able to obtain the bursary. Bursary payments are usually paid in two instalments later in the academic year.

WARNING!

Make sure you update the SLC on your current student address otherwise the bursary form may be sent to the address in your home country!

Note: If you already hold an EU university degree (an equivalent or higher qualification), you are not entitled to receive loans or grants from the government. Universities vary on their fees policy for this, so again check this with them.

Note: scholarships: Universities may offer scholarships. Most often these are mainly for overseas students at PG level only and are only partial scholarships (i.e. a fee reduction of say 30 per cent off the usual fee). Make sure that if the scholarship is for a UG programme the reduced fee is for the full length of the programme and not only for the first year!

If you are interested in a scholarship find out from the university the application procedure and the criteria that they use to award scholarships. Criteria may not only be based on your academic performance, but on what you can bring to the university. Thinking of it like this may help when you write your scholarship application letter: what is it that you have, rather than anyone else, that the university wants to pay you for?

WARNING!

Some universities use scholarships purely as a marketing device, giving all students a scholarship of perhaps £1,000. You may well find that even after the scholarship you are paying the same fee as another university offering the same programme that does not offer a scholarship!

Choosing your university

In many ways choosing a university is about finding the right one for you. This involves many factors.

Exercise

Look at the following list and tick the aspects that are important for you:

Aspect	Questions for consideration	Importance (high ✓✓ medium ✓ low 0)
Geography	England – North or South? Wales or Scotland?	
Urban or rural	London or a big city or a smaller provincial town? City centre or out-of-town campus?	
Cost of living	London and the South East is more expensive to live in than the North of England	
University reputation	National student survey results? League table position?	
Facilities	Sports, library, accommodation facilities?	
Student life	Social life, night life, cultural activities?	
Security and safety	Quiet location or crime-ridden location?	
Other?		

Understanding the university experience and what is right for you

Level of the university: traditional versus modern universities

The UK has several groupings of university and you may hear of these. Read the descriptions in Table 3.5 to better understand them.

Basically the first two groups represent more traditional universities that have a research focus. They tend to be at the top of league tables, while the other groups represent newer universities that tend to offer practical and work-focused curricula.

Table 3.5 University groups in the UK

Grouping	Description
Russell Group	The big and most famous research-led universities that lead the league tables. In the USA the equivalent are called the 'Ivy League'
1994	A group of 19 smaller research led-universities
Million Plus	Mainstream universities many of which used to be polytechnics and became universities in 1992
University Alliance	A group of 23 universities which focus mainly on business engagement

Note: league tables: Various league tables exist. They are designed by newspapers and are not government approved. Many students use them to help them decide which university to go to. Typical tables used can be found at the following websites.

Useful websites: http://extras.timesonline.co.uk/stug/universityguide.php
http://www.thecompleteuniversityguide.co.uk/league-tables
http://www.guardian.co.uk/education/universityguide

WARNING!

It is not always true that the higher in the league tables the happier the students! A National Student Survey is carried out each year and you can check the results.

Useful websites: For helping select universities http://unistats.direct.gov.uk
http://www.push.co.uk/uni-chooser
One of the key skills in selecting which university you want to apply to is having a realistic understanding of your own capability and academic level.

Note on applying to Oxford and Cambridge (Oxbridge): When you apply to Oxford or Cambridge, as well as applying for a specific course you also need to apply to a specific college. You therefore need to spend time on deciding which college is more appropriate for you before applying as they can vary in their ethos and lifestyle offerings.

Applying

What do you know?

Test your basic understanding of applying to UK universities. Which of the following are true or false? Add your answers to the first part of Table 3.6 then check them in the second part of the table.

Table 3.6 Applying to UK universities – true or false?

Question No.	Question	True	False
1	You apply directly to most UK universities		
2	You have to have UK school qualifications to enter UK universities		
3	It is usual for UK universities to ask for IELTS scores for UG and PG programmes		
4	UK universities do not have to follow nationally set standards for entry to programmes		
5	Fees are not the same for the same or similar programmes at different universities		
6	It is logical that the best place to study your subject is at the best university in the league tables		
7	League table positions are useful because they are controlled by the UK Ministry of Education		
8	If I am an EU student I will pay the same fee as a British student for my programme		
9	To be classified as an EU student I just need to have an EU passport		
10	Personal statements are an opportunity to demonstrate how wonderful I am		

Answers

1	F	Most universities will want you to apply to them through UCAS. This is especially true for UG programmes. PG programmes can often be applied for directly

Table 3.6 continued

2	F	Most universities accept international qualifications for entry to programmes but this depends on how those qualifications compare to UK qualifications
3	T	This is the most common English level examination requirement. Many universities accept other exams such as the Test of English as a Foreign Language (TOEFL)
4	T	Each university is free to decide on its own entry criteria
5	T	Each university decides on its fee level for each programme
6	F	Universities may be high in the league table for a variety of reasons, but this does not mean that a university may be better than another in every subject
7	F	League tables are compiled by newspapers and different newspapers use different criteria to judge universities
8	T	If you are an EU resident you normally pay 'home student fees'
9	F	No. It is more complex than this – it may depend on where you were resident in the last three years
10	F	You should really write about what you have learned to date and your potential for learning. The reader should get a sense of who you really are!

Understanding and knowing the value of your national qualifications

UK universities accept national qualifications from all over the world, and most admissions officers in UK universities have a good idea of the requirements from each country in terms of their national qualifications. They tend to use the information provided by NARIC as a guide.

NARIC provides information such as the following. This example relates to the Bulgarian high-school leaving certificate:

Diploma za Sredno Obrazovanie (Diploma of Completed Secondary Education)	Is considered comparable to GCE Advanced Subsidiary (AS) level/ Scottish Higher standard

This means that a student with a specific grade in the 'DIPZO' (e.g. 4/6) may or may not be eligible for consideration for direct entry to Year 1 of a university UG programme. Universities vary on the grades they set for entry to each programme. To help you, most universities publish their entry criteria on their websites, often under 'country profiles'.

Accreditation of prior learning and accreditation of prior experiential learning

Universities will usually take into consideration any studies undertaken and credits achieved. Accreditation of Prior Learning (APL) may mean you can enter Year 2 or 3 of an UG programme. On a Masters programme you may be exempted from having to take some modules of the programme, and this may mean you are offered a tuition fee reduction. Accreditation of Prior Experiential Learning (APEL) may be used for mature students applying for programmes when they do not have certain university studies and qualifications but have work experience instead. Masters business programmes in particular may allow entry to applicants who have industry experience instead of academic qualifications.

Cultural note: Reporting your grades. Grades can be expressed in various ways throughout the world. They can be in the form of letters (A, B, C, D, E, F) or numerical, e.g. 1, 2, 3, 4, with integers such as 2.5. In some countries 1 may be the highest grade, or it might be the higher the number the lower the grade (e.g. Germany and the Abitur). In some countries, the higher the number, the better the grade, e.g. the French baccalaureate is marked out of 20 points, with a mark below 10 generally being seen as a fail. In other countries, verbal descriptors may be used (e.g. in Sweden, Pass (*godkänd or G*), Pass with distinction (*Väl godkänd or VG*) and Pass with special distinction (*Mycket väl godkänd or MVG*) are used). Other grade systems may use percentages (e.g. China). In the USA, particularly in higher education, use is made of the GPA (Grade Point Average), which is a score out of a total of 4, e.g. 2.3/4.0.

Exercise

Design a chart that will help explain the qualifications and grades you have. Complete the second column

Name of your high-school leaving certificate (in your own language, but in the Latin alphabet)	
Explanation of the schooling system you have undertaken with the number and range of subjects you have taken at senior secondary level	
Explanation of the grades you have received in your final high-school leaving certificate and/or national examinations (indicate what is considered a pass and a good score)	
Explanation of any other courses with certificates and grades that you have done	

Suggestion: It is very useful for UK university admissions officers to be given as much help and information as possible about what the qualification, scores and grades you have mean.

Advice on your CV: It is also important to send in a brief CV (there are many models of how to do a good CV on the Internet). This will show the assessor what you have been doing in any gaps between your studies. If these are not explained the application appears less convincing! If you were ill or unemployed it is better to say so than to leave this period unexplained.

English language levels

Universities also usually require students to supply the results of an independent English-language test to support their application (e.g. IELTS or TOEFL) – unless you have a recognised certificate for a curriculum that has been delivered in English (e.g. an international baccalaureate). Some universities are able to assess English levels themselves and may offer their own testing arrangements for this. Enquire if this is the case as it could save you some time and money.

UCAS tariff points: UK admissions officers may use the UCAS tariff points system to decide if candidates' grades and qualifications are sufficient for entry to each programme. In this case they may use conversion tables to match international student national examination results to these points.

Alternatively they may state the entry requirements in terms of UK qualifications. These are usually A levels and you need to work out the equivalent to these in terms of the qualifications you have from your country and your school system.

UK students typically take three A levels and these are graded from A–E with C being considered a satisfactory pass.

If a university uses tariff points, these are awarded for each grade at A level (A2 level) – exams that are usually taken at 18 years of age. Tariff points can also be given for some other exams, such as the lower-level AS level examination grades (also known as A1 level and usually taken at 17 years of age).

To help you understand and calculate tariff points use the conversion chart in Table 3.7.

Exercise

If a UK university states an offer as equivalent to 'A level grades BCC', what is the equivalent tariff score?

Answer: 260 UCAS points

Table 3.7 Converting and calculating UCAS tariff points

A level grade (normally taken at end of year 13 at 18 years of age)	UCAS tariff points
A*	140
A	120
B	100
C	80
D	60
E	40

AS level grade (normally taken at end of Year 12 at 17 years of age)	UCAS tariff points if AS level does not form part of the A level, i.e. is an additional subject
A	60
B	50
C	40
D	30
E	20

It may then be possible to find out from the university international application websites what this is equivalent to in terms of your own national qualifications and grades.

Useful website: http://www.ucas.com/he_staff/quals/ucas_tariff/quals

Applying through UCAS

Applying to UK universities is not complex. There are two ways of doing this, either through UCAS (Universities and Colleges Admissions Service) or directly to the universities. At UG level, home and EU students must usually apply via UCAS and international students are increasingly required to do so, although many universities still accept direct applications. At PG level, universities usually accept direct applications, although increasingly UCAS is used for this too.

UCAS codes

Each programme on offer in UK universities has a code, e.g. N102 is the code for Business or Business Studies. For the same or similar programme it is the same code across all universities.

Application fees: UK universities do not usually require an application fee with direct applications (unlike universities in the USA).

GMAT *(Graduate Management Admissions Test) and* **GRE** *(Graduate Record Examination):* Most UK universities and business schools are flexible about this criterion for their PG programmes and GMAT is not required. These tests are mostly used for applications in the USA. In the UK a good undergraduate degree from your country tends to be the key requirement.

The UCAS system

Useful website: http://www.ucas.co.uk

UCAS is managed by a private company, contracted by universities to undertake the admissions process for them. It allows students the opportunity to apply for up to five universities at the same time using the same application form. There is a small fee for using the service. When you register you are given an individual password and you can upload your details onto an online UCAS form (a data form that acts as an application form). Universities also have access to this. You can then track and manage the application, making choices as you progress. You are required to follow the steps of the application process and adhere to the dates and deadlines imposed by UCAS (Table 3.8).

Table 3.8 UCAS applications dates and deadlines

Date	Deadline
15 October	Oxford/Cambridge* (Oxbridge) and medical degrees
15 January	All other applications except art and design
24 March	Art and design applications
30 June	Last date for late applications

Note: You can only apply to Oxford or Cambridge but not both!

WARNING!

If you apply by the deadline of 15 January your application must be considered by the universities you apply to. If you apply afterwards, universities may reject you because their programmes are full. After the British A level results are published, *clearing* starts.

UCAS Extra

If you are unlucky enough not to receive any offers from any of your choices, or you have a change of heart and decide to decline any offers you do have, UCAS Extra comes into play at the end of February. This allows you to make a sixth choice of university. If you become eligible for UCAS Extra, UCAS will send you all the details you need, with courses at universities willing to consider UCAS Extra applications available on the UCAS website. You can then either use the UCAS website to make an application or contact a university directly. If you are made an offer, either unconditional or conditional, you can firmly accept or decline it just like any offer in the main UCAS scheme. If you don't get an offer (or decide to decline your offer), you can opt to make another UCAS Extra choice and so on, until either you get an offer or you run out of time (the scheme ends in early July).

UCAS Track

This is the name for the online UCAS system you use to see and manage the decisions that universities have made.

WARNING!

If you do not respond to the offers of universities as they come in you will automatically be rejected, so it is best to keep an eye on the state of your application by entering the UCAS site regularly to update yourself and respond to offers.

Towards the end of the process you will be required to select just two universities: one as the **first choice** and one as the reserve (**insurance**). If you get the necessary qualifications for your first choice you will go there, if not and if you get enough for your insurance choice you are committed to going to this one.

Clearing

For students who are late applying there is a final stage called 'clearing' which is basically a system whereby you are able to apply to universities who still have empty places, taking whatever offers they make. This is towards the end of the summer. To be sure of getting to a university you really want it is best not to go via clearing!

In clearing, each university has a list of courses still available on its website. Applicants must contact the university directly and check whether places are still available and if their qualifications are acceptable. If so, the university makes a verbal offer and based on this an applicant can add a clearing choice on UCAS Track.

Advice: It is a good idea to think seriously about the kind of programme you want to study at university *before* completing the UCAS form and entering the course codes for the programmes you select. Putting five completely unrelated study programmes down, from accounting to performing arts shows a well-rounded enthusiasm for knowledge in general, but it may be interpreted as a lack of seriousness by many admissions officers.

It is also sensible not to use all your UCAS choices on top 10 universities if you are not a top student in your school! Even if you are, it is sensible to choose a range of universities in terms of their ranking levels. Perhaps a sensible strategy if you are a good grades student is to have two top universities, two middle-ranking ones and one nearer the bottom of the tables as your UCAS choices. If you are rejected by the top ones you still have options. You also do not often know how you will perform in your school leaving exams and what grades you will actually get!

Deferred entry

There is also a system for deferring your entry to the following year, once you have been accepted. This may be useful if for unforeseen circumstances you are unable to go to the university that has accepted you as intended and have to delay entry.

The application process

Completing your UCAS form

You will need to complete a UCAS form online. It is important to complete all the necessary sections. Ensure that the name you use is the same as the name in your passport and also indicate if you are an overseas student liable for overseas fees and if you have any disabilities that the university needs to know about. Use the guide that is provided to complete the form.

Cultural note on disabilities

Disabilities can be mental and non-physical as well as physical. The UK identifies many disabilities – e.g. dyslexia, attention deficit hyperactivity disorder (ADHD), bipolar disorder, Asperger's syndrome, autism – that may not be recognised in other countries. These, however, are disabilities that can severely impact your learning, especially if they are not understood and catered for by the university. It is important to declare any such disabilities that you are aware of. Letting the university know about them will help you with your university study and life.

Entering your qualifications and grades

Make sure you complete both sections regarding your school certificates and grades. In the top right section put in the qualifications and grades you have already been awarded and write the full name of the qualifications in their original language (using roman script) – do not try to translate them. If the results you are putting in are simply those from the transcript of your current school year, e.g. Year 11 grades, and not the final grades, make this clear so that admissions officers are not confused and think that these are your final year school-leaving certificate grades.

In the bottom right section you are asked to put the exams you will be taking and one of your teachers or your school careers' guidance or placements' officer is expected to complete the section for your predicted grades along with the reference (do not use a family member or a friend for the reference!).

English language level information

Make sure you also enter information on your English language level: if you have taken an English language test (e.g. IELTS or TOEFL) or are going to take one add this information.

Note: If you do not enter the qualifications you have achieved or the ones you will be taking, your application is likely to be rejected.

Advice: Try to make the application as easy to understand and read for a UK admissions officer as possible. Do not expect the admissions officer to be able to guess any information you have not entered. Admissions officers have thousands of applications to process and cannot spend too much time on each one! If an application is incomplete or difficult to understand it may go to the bottom of their pile!

Personal statement

Advice: In the bottom left-hand section of the form you need to complete a personal statement. This should be a statement that explains what your motives are for wanting to study the programme you have selected, your strengths and the contribution you will make to the university community if you are accepted. Some universities take the personal statements very seriously and into consideration as part of your application, while others may be less concerned and focus mostly on the actual grades you have. Generally, the more popular the university and the more difficult it is to get in to, the more important will be your personal statement, which may the basis for calling you to interview. You should also use all of the space available for your personal statement – using less may be interpreted as a lack of seriousness or commitment.

WARNING!

Remember that with UCAS, the same statement will go to all the choices of university you have put down on the UCAS form. It is not sensible to make statements such as 'It has always been my lifelong ambition to live in Scotland' if you are also applying to English universities! The same applies for different pro-grammes: 'It has been my deepest wish to help children and work with them' may not be suitable if the early years programme you selected does not offer you a place and the statement is then read by the Business School!

Table 3.9 The application process

Step	Requirement
1	Complete the UCAS form/university direct application form
2	Send in any photocopies of any certificates or other evidence (e.g. a DVD of audition for musical performance ability) or undertake telephone or Skype interview
3	Wait for university offer
4	Meet any conditions that are set (e.g. payment of tuition fee deposit*, IELTS score, exam results). Provisionally book university accommodation
5	Wait for CAS† (if overseas TIER 4 student) or for Unconditional Acceptance letter
6	Apply for any visa necessary or for any grants/loans or other funding
7	Make final choice and send in acceptance of offer
8	Make deposit payment* for accommodation
9	Book airline ticket

*Many universities offer an incentive for you to make the full tuition fee and accommodation fee payment before arrival. This can be in the form of a percentage reduction in the total fee. Also note that deposits are refunded by universities to students who are refused their visas.

†Confirmation for Acceptance for Studies

Suggestion: you may want to post or scan an additional personal statement for each university to help with your application and make the statement more relevant. It is best to check with the university's international admissions office first to see if this is OK.

Payment of fees and currency exchange rates

WARNING!

It is difficult to know when it is best to pay for your fees. If you think the exchange rate will get better for you (i.e. your national currency will get stronger compared to the pound sterling), it makes sense not to pay all the fees upfront, but to use any instalment scheme the university offers. You should be able to find this information on the university's web pages. On the other hand, if you think your currency will get weaker it is best to pay as much as possible upfront!

Application stages

If you are successful with your application you will receive offers from the universities. When you apply via UCAS you will go through various stages in the application process. Different codes are used to describe the stages of application.

Table 3.10 UCAS application codes

Code	Wording	Meaning
CO	Conditional Offer	You are accepted and have a place if you meet (achieve) the conditions stated
CF	Conditional Firm	You accept the conditional offer
UO	Unconditional Offer	You are accepted without having to meet any further conditions
UF	Unconditional Firm	You accept the unconditional offer

Note on accepting offers: Once you have received responses from all the institutions you applied to *you must respond* by accepting up to two choices: one of these is a Firm Acceptance and the other one is called the Insurance Acceptance. The others are then declined. There are only four possible offer combinations:

1	UF	Unconditional Firm, no Insurance offer
2	CF	Conditional Firm, no Insurance offer
3	CF + UI	Conditional Firm + Unconditional Insurance
4	CF + CI	Conditional Firm + Conditional Insurance

Note on insurance offers: Many institutions may consider accepting you if you narrowly miss your conditional offer – so long as there are enough places on the programme remaining. However, if they don't offer you a place and you have achieved the conditions for the Insurance offer (or if this offer is unconditional), then you will be admitted to the Insurance course.

Interviews

Some programmes require more for consideration for entry than the completion of a simple application form. You may be required to complete questionnaires, send in DVDs of performances or attend interviews. Increasingly universities are offering telephone or Skype interviews to international students.

Booking accommodation

Do not forget to book your university accommodation as soon as possible. Most universities have an online booking system and it is often possible to reserve accommodation at the CO/CF stage.

WARNING!

Accommodation offices have a cut off deadline after which accommodation is not guaranteed!

UKBA requirements for visas

The UK Border Agency (UKBA) sets the requirements for entry to the UK for overseas students that universities have to follow.

Note: You do not require a visa if you are an EU, EEA or Swiss national.

Universities that follow the visa requirements of the UKBA are awarded Highly Trusted Status (HTS). They are allowed to issue a CAS number (Confirmation for Acceptance for Studies) to an overseas student applicant who has fulfilled the entry requirements of the university.

Note: Every overseas 'visa national' student must apply for either a General Student Tier 4 Visa (GSV) or a Student Visitor Visa to gain 'entry clearance' to the UK.

A Tier 4 visa is a points-based visa whereby if a student has a CAS and also the necessary finances to pay for the tuition fees and living costs while in the UK, they accumulate the necessary points to be issued the visa. You apply for the visa at the British Embassy or British Consulate or at a Visa Application Centre in your country.

All information on visas for students to study in the UK is available at the UK Border Agency website:

Useful website: http://www.ukba.homeoffice.gov.uk

Advice: You should read the information available at the UKBA website for 'studying in the UK'. Table 3.11 outlines some of the issues you need to consider when applying for a visa. Use the website to find answers to the following questions:

Table 3.11 Issues to consider when applying for an overseas student visa

Issue	Answer Yes/No
Are you a visa national?	
Is it best or necessary for you to get a TIER 4 Student Visa or Student Visitor Visa?	
Do you understand the difference between a Student Visitor Visa and a Tier 4 Visa?	
Do you know how much the two visas cost?	
Do you know where to go in your country to apply for your visa?	

Are you from an 'English-speaking majority country'?	
If not, do you know what English test you can take and the level of English you need to satisfy UKBA requirements?*	
Do you know where you can book a Secure English Language Test (SELT), how much it costs and how long it takes to get the result?	
Do you know how much money you need to have available and how to show this when you apply for the visa?	
Will you need to obtain a biometric residence permit?	
If so, do you know where to do this and what you need to do to get this?	
If you are a PG research student in science, engineering or technology, do you need an Academic Technology Approval Scheme (ATAS) certificate?	
Are you from a country that means you are required to have a tuberculosis screening certificate?	
Are you from a country that will require you to register with the police once you are in the UK?	
Have you worked out a timetable for applying for and obtaining your visa in time?	
Have you realised that you cannot extend or renew a Student Visitor Visa in the UK, but you can apply for another TIER 4 visa in the UK?	
Depending on the visa you obtain, do you know how long you are allowed to stay in the UK after finishing your programme of study?	
Do you know how long before your programme of study starts you are allowed to arrive in the UK?	

*Note that the website informs you of the various Common European Framework of Reference (CEFR) levels of English you need to attain in the SELT for various levels of programme.

Advice: Universities are able to offer their own assessment of a student's level, so it is worth asking if this is the case with the university you are applying to. If they do not offer this facility you will need to take a SELT such as IELTS.

Note on the CEFR (Common European Framework of Reference): The Common European Framework divides learners into three broad divisions which can be divided into six levels, as shown in Table 3.12.

Table 3.12 CEFR levels for language ability

A Basic speaker	
A1	Breakthrough or beginner
A2	Waystage or elementary

B Independent speaker	
B1	Threshold or pre-intermediate
B2	Vantage or intermediate

C Proficient speaker	
C1	Effective operational proficiency or upper intermediate
C2	Mastery or advanced

Applying for a visa

You can obtain a visa application form from the UKBA website. Make sure you follow the guidance notes for completing each section.

Note: You can only apply for a visa up to three months before the beginning of the course you want to study.

You will need to supply certain things with a TIER 4 visa application – use the tick boxes in Table 3.13 to ensure you have these ready.

With a Tier 4 visa, you have certain rights and restrictions.

Table 3.13 What do I need for a TIER 4 visa application?

Item	✓
The original certificates of all the qualifications stated as required by your chosen sponsor	
Your passport	
Your visa fee	
Your CAS reference number	
Your biometric details (all your fingers scanned and a full-face digital photograph)	
A recent colour passport sized photograph (45mm × 35mm)	
Proof from your bank that you have sufficient funds to cover your tuition fees and living expenses	

Exercise

Find answers to the following from the UKBA website

Question	Answer
Can you apply to extend your stay when in the UK?	
Can you bring dependents (partner and children) with you?	
How many hours can you work per week during the course of your study? What about vacations?	
How long before the beginning of your programme can you arrive in the UK?	
How long can you stay after your programme ends?	

Note:
- Dependants will be granted permission to work only if the student will be following a degree programme
- A CAS expires after six months

You may want to try and do the application yourself – if so make sure you read and follow all the UKBA information from the website carefully and that you follow the instructions carefully regarding completing the visa application form (Form VAF9 – PBS migrant).

Using professional help

In some countries the UKBA works with a local company that will help with the processing of your visa. These are called Visa Application Centres (VACs). The VAC will make sure you have all the right documents and completed forms and will be responsible for the application from then on.

Applying using an education agency

Many students apply to study in the UK via the services of an education agency. These can be very helpful and reduce the complexity of the application and visa process.

There are advantages and disadvantages to using agencies.

Exercise

Look at the following exercise and decide which are positive and which are negative factors in using the services of an agency?

Factor	Positive ✓
Undertake the paperwork	
May charge for their services	
Know how to prepare the visa application	
May direct you only to universities they have contracts with	
May make you lazy and detached from dealing with your application	
Know the programmes and the entry requirements	
May not know as much as they should about each university programme	
Can talk to university admissions officers and have personal contact	
May take over the UCAS application procedure	

Comment: Most education agencies make their living through promoting university programmes to interested potential students. They are paid a commission by universities for recruiting students to them and in this way they can often offer a free service to the student clients. This can be a very attractive service as it reduces the complexity and hard work of applying by oneself. The problem is that an agency might be more interested in promoting the universities they have contracts with than the one that might best suit you. The agency may, however, agree to help you with an application for a university that they do not have a contract with – but on the basis of charging you a consultancy and processing fee. If this is the case, ensure you know how much this will be and what service terms this involves.

WARNING!

Another potential problem you may have is that many agencies wish to retain control over the application process, and may want to complete the UCAS application for you and retain the UCAS password used for your application themselves. This effectively undermines your freedom to manage UCAS Track yourself. It is not right if an agency gets involved with helping you with your personal statement. There is an important difference between advising you on the process of the application and actually doing the application for you.

WARNING!

If a university suspects that you have not completed your own UCAS application form they will see this as fraud and will reject your application.

Chapter 4

Arrival and the early days

Once you have been accepted by your university of choice you need to think of the practical issues of getting there. You should have booked university accommodation and have the destination address and the expected arrival time – so all you need to do is buy an airline ticket and think about how you are to get from the airport to the university.

Flights

The main airports for the South of England are Gatwick, Heathrow, Stansted and Luton. They are all a short distance from Central London and the main railway and bus stations. There are other international airports that service the rest of the UK.

Useful website: http://www.airport-maps.co.uk/uk-airport-directory
University websites or pre-departure booklets usually explain carefully how to get to the universities from the main airports.

Tip: It is best to have sorted out your onward transportation from the airport before your arrival (see Table 4.1). Do not arrive and contract a taxi at the airport to take you to your final destination. You will pay far too much for this!

Useful websites: http://www.nationalexpress.com/coach/index.cfm
http://www.nationalrail.co.uk
http://ukairportcarhire.net

Note: Of course the easiest and cheapest way to get from the airport to your university accommodation is if the university offers a free airport pick-up service. Many universities even employ students to meet and greet new students at airports! Check if this is the case.

Table 4.1 Transportation options

Method	Advantage	Advice
Local taxi company	You will be met and can relax. UK airport service taxis are not too expensive over long distances	Ask the university if they have a booking service and if they can do this for you. The taxi driver will have a name card for you.
Coach	Coach companies are reasonably priced and have extensive networks. Some coach companies like National Express have coaches from airports directly to university cities. Otherwise you change at Victoria coach station, London. You can prepay for your ticket online.	Always book a coach ticket that gives you good time to clear customs and pick up your baggage. I suggest a minimum of 90 minutes. Many university campuses are out of city centres so you may need to use a local bus or taxi from the city coach station to the university. These should not be too expensive.
Trains	Each major airport has a useful link train to the city. For London there is the Gatwick Express to Victoria Station, the Heathrow Express to Paddington Station and the Stansted Express to Liverpool Street Station. They are fast and convenient and unlike buses are not held up by traffic jams. National trains can be a little expensive, however.	Check the timetables for these services online. You can also check the cost of a train ticket from the airport to your final city destination and prepay this online. You may find a pre-booked taxi is not much more, or is even less, expensive!
Rent a car	There are many airport car hire services. You can book a car online for the same day. You will need to leave it at the nearest local airport, but this may be a good solution after you have dropped off your luggage at your accommodation. You can get an airport bus back to town!	If you are a confident driver and like a challenge (remember in the UK you drive on the left) this may well be a very cheap and convenient solution. Check your driving licence is valid for the UK! It may not be a good idea if you are tired from a long-haul flight though.

Settling into your accommodation

The most important thing with university accommodation is getting on well with your flat-/housemates (the other students sharing the accommodation block and facilities with you).

Decide which of the items in Table 4.2 are what to do ✓ and which items are what not to do ✗!

Table 4.2 Getting on with your housemates – dos and donts

	Behaviour	✓ or ✗
1	Use the shared bathroom for over an hour in the morning when everyone is getting up	
2	Play loud music late at night when people are trying to study or sleep	
3	Introduce yourself to the others and make conversation with them	
4	Use other people's food without asking them if it is OK to borrow some	
5	Always wash up your own dishes and utensils after use and put them away	
6	Buy really smelly food such as fish and leave it out in the communal area	
7	When you cook it, offer some of your national food to the others to try	
8	Offer to help organise and participate in any parties and birthday celebrations the others are having	
9	Leave all your clothes and belongings cluttering up the communal space	

Basically it should be obvious you need to be considerate (do not do 1, 2, 6) and respectful of others' space and possessions (do not do 4 and 9, but do 5) and friendly and helpful (do 3, 7, 8).

There is lots of advice on the Internet for how to get on in your first few days at university. The following website, for example, has lots of useful advice:

Useful website: http://www.thestudentroom.co.uk/wiki/Fresher's_Week_Tips

You should also expect your housemates to be the same with you. If any of them are not, it is sensible to do the following:

1   Have a friendly word with them explaining the problem.
    If the problem persists . . .
2   Have a more serious word with them explaining that if things do not improve you will have to 'take it further' (report them).
    If that does not work . . .
3   See the accommodation warden and report the problem.

Advice: Remember you should not put up with behaviour that will ruin your studies or depress you. You must not try and ignore problems like this as in the end it will just get worse. An English saying is 'to nip problems in the bud', which means solve problems early on when it is easier.

Note: Many young British students may be away from home for the fist time and may be rather noisy and out to have a good time. That of course is fine so long as their good time is not at your expense!

Homestay accommodation (living with a British family)

Some of you may be coming to the UK for short courses or may have to be in homestay accommodation for a while if all the university accommodation is booked out at the beginning of term as you wait for university accommodation to become free (as some students leave or drop out).

This can be a nice experience, but it can also be a hard experience culturally. Unlike university accommodation, you have less freedom to do what you want in your own room! It is important to have clear rules for what you can and can't do.

Exercise

Rule-setting for homestay accommodation – find out early on what the rules are for the following:

Issue	Questions
Heating	Can you use an electric heater if you are cold? When will the heating in your room be on?
Ventilation	Is it OK to leave your window open when you are out?*
Use of the kitchen	Is it OK for you to use the kitchen to make coffee or tea or even little meals? Can you leave food in the fridge?
Use of the bathroom	When is it OK to use the bathroom for showers or baths? What is the best time of day for you to use the bathroom?
Use of phone or Internet service	Does the household have Internet access and can you use it? If so, when and for how long? Can you use the phone for local calls?
Use of the living room and TV	Is it OK if you use the living room? Can you watch TV? If so, make sure you are not using the TV when members of the family would like to use it
Friends visiting	Is it OK if your friends call round to visit you? Can they use the living room too?
Washing clothes	How often and how many clothes washes can you expect to be done for you? If you wear three shirts a day expect to use the nearest launderette!

Shoes in the house	Many British people wear shoes indoors – but some families prefer you to take shoes off and walk in socks or slippers on new carpets. Ask about this
Use of toilet	Which toilet in the house should you use?

* Homestay families will not be happy to see an electric heater or other heating on and the window wide open. This is because heating is very expensive in the UK

Advice: If you are in doubt about how you should behave or what the rules are, ask!

Gifts for homestay family members

In many cultures gift-giving is expected. In the UK this is not the case. Gifts, of course, will be happily received if you do have them, but don't worry if you don't. Something from your country, e.g. packet of tea, a small book (keep it small for your suitcase!) is fine.

Orientation/Freshers' Week

Most universities have an orientation week organised by both the university student support team and the student union. This is also called 'Freshers' Week' (a fresher is a new student). This is to both inform and entertain new students so that they have activities to participate in and get to know other students socially and generally feel welcomed to their new university environment. The Student Union will often organise a student fair too, in which all the university clubs participate and try to enrol you for membership in their clubs.

Advice: Participate! Get to know what options there are. If you are invited out to an event, it is a good idea to be open and go – it gives you the chance to meet others in the same situation as you! If you don't like it you do not have to go again.

Note: If you do not drink alcohol, note that not all the activities will have to involve drinking alcohol but be aware than many students in this period do tend to drink a lot.

The real English language

WARNING!

'The English of local English people is not the English I have learnt!' Many students feel very frustrated and depressed with their English when they actually try to understand English people when they are speaking. It may help to know that many English people also find it difficult to understand each other as well! This is because the English language varies greatly in the UK in terms of pronunciation and also vocabulary. British people express their identity (the region they are from – be it Scotland or Liverpool, and the class they are from – working or middle class) by the way they speak. The English language is also a stress-timed language which means that many words are reduced in sound and run into each other. This is normal and correct, but can be difficult for students who have not learnt about this and expect every word to be pronounced fully! For example, the phrase 'Isn't it a nice day today!' will often sound 'Izn tita nice day t'day?' Or 'What did you say?' will sound 'Wa'dya say?'

Note: For this reason international students often find the English of other international students easier to understand than that of the local British people, especially the local British students.

Getting work and work permits

Most international students will probably want to take up part-time work at some stage in their studies, for extra pocket money or for the experience.

Useful website: http://www.ukcisa.org.uk/student/working_during.php

Note: Once you start working you will need to apply for a National Insurance number. Use the website below for this.

Useful website: http://www.hmrc.gov.uk/ni/intro/number.htm

Note: EEA and Bulgarian and Romanian students

Useful website: http://www.ukcisa.org.uk/student/eea_work.php

All EEA and Swiss national students can work in the UK without the need to register; however, the latest EU entrant country students (Bulgarians and Romanians) must currently obtain work authorisation before they can begin working. This means applying for a Registration Certificate before working using a BR1 form.

Romanian and Bulgarian students should check with the following website before leaving their country:

Useful website: http://www.ukba.homeoffice.gov.uk (type in BR1 in search)

It is sensible to download the form and note what documentation you need to send in with the form and what details you need to have in order to complete the form.

WARNING!

The Home Office can take many months to process a BR1 form and this may mean that Bulgarian and Romanian students will have to wait before they can legally work.

Advice: Registration Certificates can be issued immediately if you apply in person at the Home Office's Public Enquiry Office in Croydon. You need to make an appointment in advance and it is best to do this soon after arriving in the UK. Alternatively, you can apply by post.

Useful website: http://www.homeoffice.gov.uk

For EU students it is a good idea to bring both your passport and ID card to the UK with you as you need to submit one of them. You can still travel using the other document in the meanwhile. You can also ask the Home Office to return your passport if you need to travel, but it is recommended you make sure that you allow plenty of time (at least two weeks) for the passport to be located and sent back to you before your travel.

Staying fit

One of the first things you should do is register with a doctor (GP, i.e. General Practitioner). The university should explain where to do this in their orientation.

Note: In the UK the GP is the person you make an appointment to see for all ailments (illnesses). The GP will assess if you need more specialised treatment and book this for you if necessary. GPs have their practices in surgeries, which have receptionists and booking facilities. If the surgery is closed (out of hours, weekend or Bank Holiday), the answer machine at the surgery should provide you with an emergency telephone number you can use. You can always go to the Accident and Emergency (A&E) department of the local hospital too – but this should be for emergencies only.

Advice: Make sure you get the name of your GP and the telephone number for the surgery he or she practices in securely stored for future use.

Information: prescriptions

In the UK, medicine is not free. Instead you are given a prescription by your GP. This is then taken to a chemist or pharmacy, where you will be given the medicine prescribed and charged a small prescription fee for the medicine. The prescription fee is a standard fee.

Health insurance

Advice: EU/EEA students should remember to carry their European Health Insurance Card (EHIC) – this normally allows holders to free NHS treatment while in the UK.

For overseas students, insurance should also be taken out to cover any period you stay on in the UK after your course/programme has finished. If you have not taken out medical insurance in your home country to cover your period of study abroad you can visit the Endsleigh website and arrange cover in the UK.

Useful website:
http://www.endsleigh.co.uk/Travel/Pages/international-student-insurance.aspx

Chapter 5

Understanding the teaching and learning methods

Introduction

This chapter looks at the academic experience you will face at a UK university. It is designed to help you analyse the kinds of teaching methods and learning experiences that are typical at a UK university. You are encouraged to think about how to adapt your approach to learning so that you can get the best advantage from the experience. The chapter includes:

- analysing and understanding your own expectations
- understanding the UK approach to teaching and learning at university
- developing an understanding of your teachers and fellow students and the roles they play in your education
- understanding and adapting to the teaching approach and teaching methods used.

Exercise

To begin this section do the following exercise, which is designed for you to investigate your attitude and approach to learning. You will be asked to do this again at the end of this section to compare your answers and see if you have changed your view in any way. There is a commentary at the end which should help you understand how your attitude will fit with the approach to education typical in UK universities

Cultural note: Depending on the education you have received so far in your life (the educational culture you have experienced), you will have developed certain views and expectations about learning and teaching and your and your teachers' roles concerning this. To investigate this look at the statements in the questionnaire and tick the ones you agree with:

Questionnaire: Your current beliefs and attitude to learning

1   It is the job of the teachers to be experts in the subjects they teach
    and to tell students what they need to know.   ❏

2   The main job of a teacher is to show students how to discover
    ideas for themselves and to give them the opportunity to do so.   ❏

3   There are no right and wrong answers to questions: facts are not
    fixed but rather interpretations. 'Correct' answers are therefore,
    in reality, simply good arguments.   ❏

4   It is the job of students to listen to teachers' ideas, take notes from
    the teachers, learn the ideas and then repeat them in exams.   ❏

5   Learning is about being given the right facts and memorising them.   ❏

6   The real aim of a university education is to show students how to
    find things out rather than to tell them what to know.   ❏

7   When students fail a course it is because they do not work hard
    enough.   ❏

Instruction: Keep a note of your answers – you will revisit this exercise at the end of this section.

Responsibility for learning

There can be two extreme views about who is responsible for a student learning successfully: the student or the teacher. In the UK it is not really correct to see either extreme as right. Learning is a *shared* responsibility requiring *honesty* and *interaction* between teachers and students. A teacher is responsible for students' learning and so must teach effectively, a student is also responsible for learning and must put in time and effort to learn.

Educational approach: learning by thinking and doing

It is important for you to understand the educational philosophy of learning that is common in UK universities. This is explained in Figure 5.1. If you understand this you will certainly know how to get the best from the learning experience offered to you.

Important beliefs in education in the UK are that learners need to be active in their own learning and need to be able to apply what they learn to the real world. For these reasons programmes often aim to have a balance between 'theory' (ideas) and 'practice' (doing). A good learning experience needs to link these together.

Suggestion: Look at the university programme you are interested in and assess the balance between theory and practice. Is the programme simply theoretical or are you encouraged to experiment with ideas in real-life situations?

The learning spiral

Learning is seen as a process. Look at the six stages of the learning process presented in Figure 5.1.

Explanation: In *Stage 1* you need to make yourself open to as many new ideas and ways of seeing things as possible. You need to expose yourself to as many ideas as possible. Of course you cannot take on all these ideas and theories: some will seem more relevant and meaningful to you than others . . . and so you enter *Stage 2*, where you notice links between the new ideas and your background experience and understanding. *Stage 3* is the practical stage where you have the opportunity to test the new ideas out in the real world. It is the 'Just do it!' stage. *Stage 4* involves you reflecting on and assessing the way the new ideas and theories actually worked in the real world. Did they work well or did they fail? Can you think why? This leads to *Stage 5* where you reject or accept the ideas (theory) or partly accept them and think of ways of adapting them to make them better fit your experience

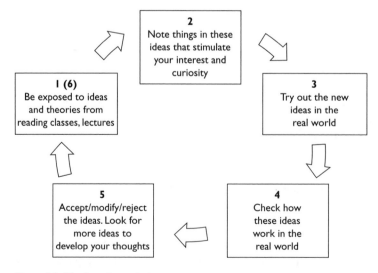

Figure 5.1 The learning spiral.

and view of reality. *Stage 6* is the beginning of the cycle again, only this time you are more focused on certain ideas that you want to develop, so you search out more related ideas that interest you to help develop the previous tried and tested ones!

Information: your role in each stage of the learning spiral

Self-test: Because the learning spiral is so important to understand, complete the exercise in Table 5.1 to see how well you have understood it. Look again at the stages of the learning spiral. What do you need to do at each stage?

What was your score? If you got some answers wrong go back and reread the information again!

Table 5.1 Five actions in the learning spiral

Stage of learning spiral	Learning actions	
1	A.	Refine the information you have to develop your ideas further
2	B.	Be prepared to try out and test new ideas in real-life contexts. Be ready to experiment and investigate these new ideas
3	C.	Gather information and ideas from all sources: key texts, lectures, classes, the library and the Internet
4	D.	Collect data (quantitative and/or qualitative, see pp. 111–15 for further information on researching) and develop a method for analysing the data
5	E.	Develop decision-making skills and be ready to act upon these decisions
6	F.	Take notes from the information you gather and note ideas that interest or challenge you

Answers: 1, C; 2, F; 3, B; 4, D; 5, E; 6, A

Interaction with teachers

This explanation of the philosophy of education should help you to understand certain teacher to student interaction patterns that you may experience. These may be different to what you expect.

Look at the following two possible interactions:

Example A

Student: Why are honey bee populations in the USA dying out so rapidly?
Teacher: Because certain new pesticides weaken their immune systems making them vulnerable to parasitic infestations.

The pattern here is SQ – TA (Student Question – Teacher Answer)

Example B

Student: Why are honey bee populations in the USA dying out so rapidly?
Teacher: What do you think the reason is?
Student: I read somewhere it is to do with a new generation of pesticides.
Teacher: Yes, I have heard that too. I think you need to investigate that line of thought – it sounds like a possibility.

This pattern is SQ – TQ – SA – TC (Teacher Comment)

Reflective questions:

- Which of these patterns are you most used to?
- Which one are you most comfortable with? Why?
- Why do you think in Example B the teacher does not give the answer?

Comment: In Example A the student treats the teacher as the information provider. In Example B the teacher makes the student reflect and think for him/herself and then gives a comment on the student's thinking. Example A does not require much effort from the student, but Example B does. Example B is a common pattern in UK university education and particularly at PG and PhD levels. You need to be aware of this and ready for it.

Anecdote: An international student completing a PhD told me that she found having her questions met with questions hard and confusing at first. Surely the supervisor is there to give the right answers, she thought. Because she thought this, the first few times she met a question to her question she felt confused because she was expecting an answer. She was also embarrassed that she was expected to give an answer as she didn't have one. It was an uncomfortable experience. But the student developed a technique for adapting to this new pattern of interaction: she learnt it was best to think ahead before she asked a question and to have a possible answer ready before she asked. This helped and made her learning much less uncomfortable.

Another aspect of student to teacher interaction you may notice is the following example:

Example C

Student: Why are honey bee populations in the USA dying out so rapidly?
Teacher: I don't know. Let's think about how we can try and find out . . .

Reflective question:

- How do you feel in this situation as a student? Why?

Comment: Maybe you feel that a teacher is someone who should know everything in their subject. If a teacher says 'I don't know' will you lose confidence in him/ her?

Question: Is it really possible for a teacher to know everything? You may feel disappointed to discover that a teacher is not all-knowing and perfect. On the other hand, it may be encouraging to see that the teacher is honest with you and prepared to show human weakness to you!

Staff and students: getting to know who your teachers and classmates are

The people who teach you

The people who teach you have a number of names at university. When you have tutorials this person is referred to as a tutor. This is also true of the person who may be assigned to you as the person you can go to with any problems you are having with your studies (or university life in general) – this person is your 'personal tutor'. When you are attending a seminar or a class this person may be referred to as your 'programme or module or course or class teacher'. In a lecture this person is normally referred to as the lecturer. Also, you will be studying on a specific named programme, e.g. accountancy or law, and this programme will be coordinated and led by a Programme/Course Director. Sometimes the programme director will be your class teacher, but often you will be taught by many different teachers. You may also be taught by postgraduate research students (students at your university studying for doctorates) who are specialists in the different areas your programme covers. Confused? Well, in this book, to keep things simple, we will refer to the people who teach you as 'teachers' for most situations!

Note: personal tutor: In UK universities you are normally given (assigned) a personal tutor. This is a person who should look after you and make sure you are OK. You should be able to talk to your personal tutor about any study or personal problems you are experiencing and that you need advice on. Personal problems can, of course, greatly affect your studies. You may be homesick (missing your family and friends or girlfriend/boyfriend) or you may be confused or unhappy about something to do with university life or your studies and the teaching. Talking problems through with an experienced personal tutor should help you.

Often your personal tutor is not the same person as your academic tutor. It may be a person who does not teach you at all. This is because this person is someone you should feel you can talk to freely about problems you may be having with your studies. Your personal tutor may be able to help you or may suggest where you should go and who you meet in the university to talk further about any problems you have.

Advice: Getting to know your teachers. It is a very good idea to make sure you know who your teachers are. Learn their names, their responsibilities and their specialist areas of knowledge. It is surprising how often students do not know the names of their teachers, their specialisms or their roles. This often means students are not sure who to go to with problems or who to refer to when they have a problem in their learning and want to discuss this with support staff. This is even more the case when a student is studying a combined or joint/modular degree programme.

Suggestion: Complete your own chart, following the example of that given in Table 5.2. Do this as early on in your studies as possible.

Table 5.2 Identifying your teachers

Role title	Name with any title (e.g. Dr, Professor)	Responsibility to you	Location (office number) and contact details (e-mail and telephone)
Personal tutor		The person in your department or faculty who is responsible for your well-being	
Academic tutor(s)		The individual(s) who will be responsible for running your group/ personal tutorials	
Programme director(s)		The person(s) in overall charge of the programme(s) you are studying. These are two people for a combined programme!	
Course/ module teachers		The names of the academic teachers who are responsible for the course/ modules you undertake as part of your programme	
Lecturer(s)		The person giving a lecture on a specific topic. Lecturers may be people who are specialists in their fields	

Information: a note on titles

When you write to an academic or mention an academic to another academic it is best to use the person's title, e.g. 'Dr Johnson' or 'Professor Livingston'. A doctor is someone who has completed a PhD (doctorate) and is therefore considered an expert in a special area of research. A professor is someone who has a senior status in a university being well known in a field of work. The title is an honorary one, however, as you do not always need a formal qualification such as a doctorate to be a professor.

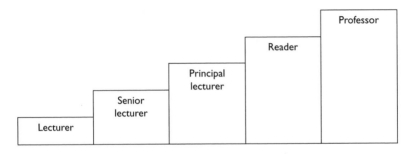

Figure 5.2 The normal hierarchy (rank) of university teachers.

Note: Talking about the people who study with you: the usual way to refer to these people is either 'fellow students' or 'fellow class members'.

Advice: Getting to knowing your fellow students. When you study in the UK you will be expected to interact (speak and work) with your fellow students. You are expected to learn though interaction, so it is a good idea to get to know your fellow students, learn their names and have an idea of their past experience, interests and expertise. Your fellow students can act as an important support for you with your learning. It is good to make sure you find out about them and understand their strengths and weaknesses. Not to do this is to waste this opportunity.

Suggestion: Early on you can draw up a chart about your fellow classmates like the one below:

Name	Experience	Area of interest/expertise	Notes
1. Rebecca	Five years working for Cathay Pacific as an air stewardess	Speaks basic Cantonese Chinese and is interested in Chinese culture	Talks more than listens and doesn't like to compromise. Difficult to work with
2. Mohammed	Helps his father and brothers run a family business in Morocco	Interested in Berber history	Is quiet and observant. Good in group work
Etc.			

Cultural note: Students' names. Names are not simple things! In the UK, students will simply introduce themselves with their first names (Christian names). It would be unusual for students to introduce themselves with their last name (surname) as this would seem too formal. On the other hand, a Chinese student may well introduce herself by giving her last name first followed by her first name, e.g. Li, Yuping, or she may adopt a 'Western name' such as 'Candy'. The important thing is to find out which name the other students are comfortable with you using. This will normally be the name they tell you. If Candy wants you to call her Candy it is because she is comfortable with this rather than Li Yuping. This is like a British student saying 'My name is Michael, but you can call me Mike.'

An explanation of university teaching methods

Explanation: In this section we will analyse the usual teaching methods used in UK universities, focusing on the approaches used to teach the programme of study.

Exercise

To see what you already understand about teaching methods complete the exercise in Table 5.3 by trying to match the teaching method names to the definitions

Table 5.3 Teaching methods and definitions

I	Tutorial	A	A large gathering of students (often from various classes) at which the students listen to a presentation on a subject by an academic
2	Seminar	B	A small number of students who are required to work together to research a topic, usually in order to present this later to the rest of the class
3	Lecture	C	The regular meeting between the study members of a year group (cohort) and their subject teacher
4	Class	D	Time spent out of a class studying by yourself. This is usually in a library and involves reading background material on the key subjects you are studying
5	Group work preparation	E	A programme that is delivered through the use of the Internet. This may also be accompanied by materials sent through the post such as course books and DVDs
6	Self-study	F	Learning support provided through the use of the university intranet (e.g. using Blackboard, an online site where lessons and materials are posted for students). This is often used to supplement and support face-to-face teaching

| 7 | Blended learning | G | A small number of students focusing on a particular subject. Everyone present is required to participate actively |
| 8 | Distance learning | H | A session with just one or possibly a few students in which the teacher gives individual attention to the student(s) |

Answers: I, H; 2, G; 3, A; 4, C; 5, B; 6, D; 7, F; 8, E

Exercise

Self-analysis regarding learning methods

You may find that you are comfortable with certain methods of teaching and learning. Look at the kinds of teaching methods listed in Table 5.3 and then do the following self-analysis

Method	What are the good points for you?	What are the bad points for you?
Tutorial		
Seminar		
Lecture		
Class		
Group work preparation		
Self-study		
Blended learning		
Distance learning		

Stop and think: Which do you think is your favourite method of learning? Why? Which is your least favourite method? Why?

Example: Table 5.4 is an example of a similar chart completed by an international student. Read it and then think about the questions that follow in relation to yourself.

Table 5.4 An example analysis of teaching methods by an international student

Method	Student X – the good points	Student X – the bad points
Tutorial	This is very relevant and I can ask about things I am not sure about. I can learn at my own speed and check I understand everything	If I am tired or have not prepared properly this can be very hard work and quite embarrassing
Seminar	It is interesting to listen to other students' views. I find it easier to discuss and argue these with them than with the lecturer	The quality of the other students' presentations may not be good, so I don't feel I am learning. I wonder if I am wasting my time sometimes
Lecture	I can snooze in the back row if tired, or skip it without causing any trouble! My friend can pass me his notes if I don't attend	I get tired of listening to academic English quite quickly and the lecturer speaks fast and uses jokes and examples that I don't understand
Class	I like being able to contribute when I have something to say, but also to be able to sit back and listen if I don't	Sometimes there are certain students in class who impose their views on the rest of us. This is annoying because I prefer to hear the view of the teacher!
Group work preparation	I have made good friends with a Chinese student by having to work with her. She knows a lot more than I do on the subject and is very organised and hard-working	I sometimes feel a bit useless because my English is not good. I can see the others get bored when I speak. One student does not put in his fair share of work. This makes me stressed
Self-study	I like to choose books in the library and have the freedom to study and learn things that interest me. The library is a nice environment	I sometimes find my concentration wanders a lot. I can spend lots of time looking out the library window!

Question: Do you think you will have similar feelings? If so, which of the following understandings in Table 5.5 below do you think you need to work on in order to get the best learning experience?

Exercise

Look at the following ideas; how important (I = not at all; 5 = very) is each idea for your learning?

Table 5.5 Ideas for learning and their importance for me

Idea	Importance Score 1–5
Learning from all the people in a classroom, not just the teacher	

Table 5.5 continued

Understanding that the tutor does not like to waste valuable time

Planning which nights you go out socialising

Listening for ideas and not worrying if the English is not perfect

Listening for the gist (main ideas) and taking notes to follow up on things you do not at first understand

Reading through the lecturer's notes on the virtual learning environment (VLE) before a lecture so that you know the main ideas and vocabulary

Setting yourself targets for reading and timing yourself for these

Not getting put off by other students. Believing that if you have done your best, that is good enough

Not to impose your views or let yourself be dominated by the views of other people in class too much

Learning to negotiate workloads when doing group work

Accepting that there will be other students in a group who do not work as hard as others and not letting this affect your motivation

Note: All methods are designed to help you learn in different ways and require and develop different skills. You need to focus on the methods you are less comfortable with and analyse what it is about your personality or beliefs that may hold you back. To understand yourself more do the following exercise.

Exercise

This exercise looks at the fact that because of your cultural/educational upbringing you will probably have developed certain beliefs about teaching and learning. You may have quite fixed beliefs about what is correct and good for learning and what is not. These are your educational values. It is useful to understand that certain things you may be required to do on your programme of study in a UK university may not fit with and may challenge these values. The following exercise is designed to help you bring to consciousness these beliefs and values. Once you identify them you are encouraged to question them. This is to help develop your receptivity to learning in different ways. You may wish to come back to this exercise at different points in your studies. Read the instructions in the first chart and then look at the worked example before trying this yourself.

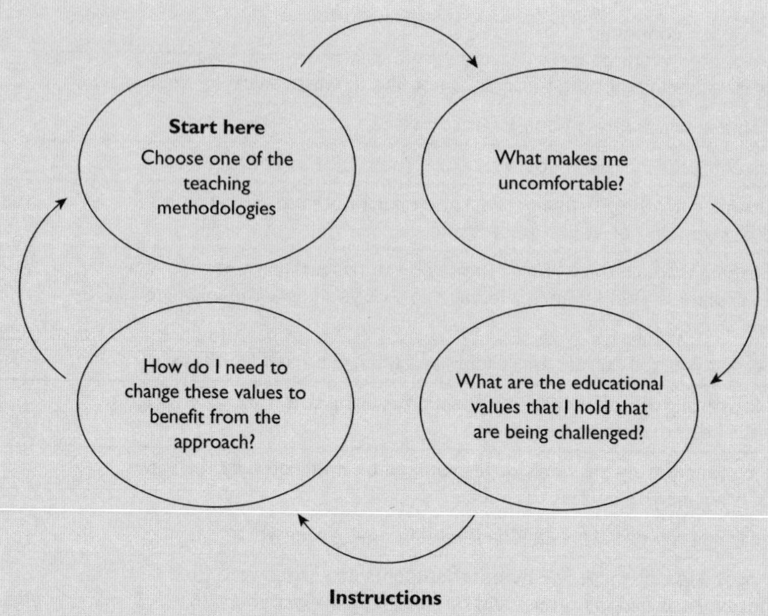

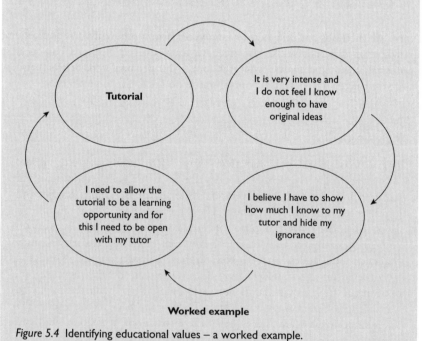

Start here
Choose one of the teaching methodologies

What makes me uncomfortable?

How do I need to change these values to benefit from the approach?

What are the educational values that I hold that are being challenged?

Instructions

Figure 5.3 Identifying my educational values.

Tutorial

It is very intense and I do not feel I know enough to have original ideas

I need to allow the tutorial to be a learning opportunity and for this I need to be open with my tutor

I believe I have to show how much I know to my tutor and hide my ignorance

Worked example

Figure 5.4 Identifying educational values – a worked example.

In the rest of this chapter we will look at each learning method in turn and try to understand your role as a student and what the teacher's expectations are of you.

Stop and think: How true are the following in your opinion?

- True learning hurts! Learning can be a painful experience. This is because real learning takes you beyond your current comfort zone.
- The more you learn, the more you realise the more you need to learn, and the more you realise how little you know.
- Real learning is a very satisfying experience. Exercising your mind is like exercising a muscle in the gym – you can feel it grow.
- The hardest criticism to take comes from a teacher you respect. This is because you know he/she is right! Criticism from someone you do not respect is easier to ignore.
- Getting bad grades or being criticised can make you feel angry at first. But on reflection you probably realise that this is your pride getting in the way.
- Tutors are human beings with their own doubts and problems. They too are emotional and have feelings that you need to consider.

Table 5.5 Roles and expectations for a tutorial

The tutorial	
Role of student	*Role of tutor*
To be prepared to talk about the topic, having read about it by doing the recommended reading. To have questions arising from this reading and to be prepared to express critical opinions	To know the topic well and to try to develop the critical thought processes of the student. This is done by questioning and posing problems for the student to try and solve. At times the tutor may push students so that they undertake deeper analysis
Expectations of the student	*Expectations of the tutor*
The tutor will be knowledgeable about the topic, will have a great depth of reading and be able to guide the student to key texts	The student will have done the necessary background reading for the tutorial. This shows respect for the tutor's valuable time
The tutor will respect the student's viewpoints and work with these to question and develop them	The student will engage with the tutor's questioning and will approach the tutorial from a position of curiosity, realising that there are important things to learn
The tutor will have read any student work handed in by the student before the tutorial and refer to it	Students will give in any written work for the tutorial in advance so that the tutor has time to read it

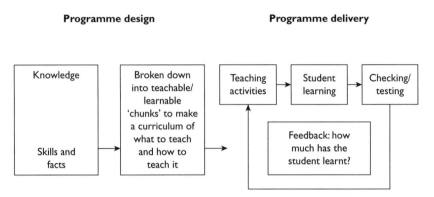

Programme design   **Programme delivery**

Figure 5.5 The curriculum delivery feedback loop.

Note: Feedback and the feedback loop. An important part of education is the 'feedback loop'. This is the way that a teacher checks if a student is learning. Figure 5.5 shows the basic stages of learning and the role of feedback.

Feedback is two things: information from the learner (student) to the teacher about what he/she know and information from the teacher to the learner on how he/she is doing. This is vital information. Feedback is used in three different ways: for diagnostic purposes, for formative purposes and for summative purposes.

Exercise

It is important to understand the purpose of feedback, so try to match the three feedback purposes in Table 5.7 to their definitions.

Table 5.7 Purposes of feedback

Type of feedback		Use
A	Diagnostic	1 To see how much a student has learnt and therefore what grade and award to give the student (usually at the end of the study process).
B	Formative	2 To see what the student already knows and doesn't know, to help determine what help is needed at the beginning of teaching a subject/topic.
C	Summative	3 To see how a student is progressing and where there are areas of weakness that still need focusing on.

Answers: A, 2; B, 3; C, 1

Information: giving and receiving feedback

Anecdote: Imagine the following kind of tutorial: A student has handed in his first essay at the beginning of the year to his tutor. He has then gone to a tutorial with another student. On entering the tutor's study both students are asked to sit down. The tutor picks up the two essays handed in by the students and tears them up in front of them. He then turns his back on the students, gives a big sigh and stares out of his window for five minutes before saying: 'Right, I expect these to be handed in again first thing next Monday morning.'

Question: What would be your reaction to this if you were one of the students? How would you feel?

You might agree this is probably an example of how a tutor should not give feedback to a student. It is easy to see how this could damage the students' motivation and self-confidence and possibly make him angry and upset. What is more, it is unhelpful as there is no explanation of what was not good, what needed improving – or indeed if any of the work already done showed promise. There are other and better ways of giving feedback!

Information: the feedback sandwich

I am sure you know what a sandwich is: a slice of bread on top – something interesting in the middle – then another slice of bread underneath. The important part of a sandwich is therefore the filling. A common device used by many UK university teachers to tell you what they think of your work (i.e. it is not perfect yet and there is room for improvement) is to use the following sandwich feedback technique:

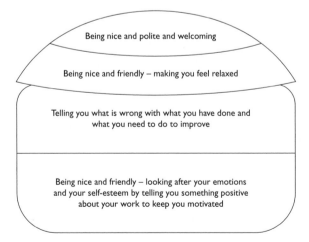

Figure 5.6 The feedback sandwich.

Example: Look at the following feedback by a female tutor and identify the top slice, the filling and the bottom slice:

T: Hello . . . Come in, sit down and make yourself comfortable. I love that top you have there – you look lovely in it. Is it from home?

S: Thank you. Yes it is from my county.

T: How have you been?

S: Oh OK . . .

T: It's a tiring time isn't it? Now let me see. Right. Well this is a valiant effort. It shows potential and I am sure if we work on certain problem areas we will be fine. Firstly you know it is important to reread yourr work before you hand it in. Also you must always have in your mind the 'So what?' question all the time.

S: What do you mean?

T: Think why you are doing what you are doing all the time. Why am I referencing this book or this person now? How is this helping my main argument? Look at this example . . . [etc.] . . . Basically don't add irrelevant references in!

S: It is difficult.

T: Yes it is – come on, don't look so sad! Your writing style is really coming along well. You have some excellent turns of academic phrase now. All you really need to work on now is keeping the main argument sustained in your paragraphs. Just remember: reread and ask yourself 'So what?' each time you provide examples or a quotation.

Now imagine if the tutor was not skilled at giving feedback and did the following:

T: Hello . . . come in, sit down and make yourself comfortable. Firstly you know it really is important to reread you work before you hand it in and to have in your mind the 'So what?' question all the time. Keep this uppermost in your mind. Think – Why am I referencing this book? Why am I referring to this person now? How is this helping my main argument? Is it helping my main argument? If not, it fails the 'So What?' test, doesn't it? I mean look here, you are making your main point, I believe, but then you add in another idea here. This is totally irrelevant to your main argument – it undermines your essay altogether and this is why you have scored so badly this time. You really must keep your main argument going and sustain and back it with quotes and references or even anecdotes.

Question: How different would you feel if you had received the second feedback instead of the first? Would it be demotivating for you, even if essentially the message is the same? For most British students the second feedback style is too direct!

Tutorial pitfalls

Taking offence and getting emotionally angry

You may react this way with a tutor who tells you your ideas are not good enough. Remember you are at university to learn and it is of course obvious that you do not know all there is to know about a topic. Remember that a tutor has probably heard most ideas and arguments before, even if they are new for you! As a student and in order to learn, you certainly need to be able to take criticism constructively. Especially at PhD level, academia can, and should, be an intellectually challenging experience and you need to learn how to accept criticism while at the same time keeping faith in your own ability. This can be difficult!

The fear of not knowing

Tutorials are quite intense in that there is nowhere to hide. There are no other students to shield you as in a classroom! You cannot hope that you will slip by unnoticed as you may in a lecture. In reality a good tutorial should be a place where you do not feel you need to hide your ignorance. It should be an enjoyable experience with the tutor not trying to catch you out but helping you to build on what you already know.

Note: the concept of give and take: It is important to develop the right relationship with your tutor – one in which you are able to learn positively. For this to happen the tutor needs the student to be able to accept constructive criticism. It also requires the student to be prepared to offer ideas and thoughts without fear of them being wrong.

Confusing the boundary between tutor and friend

This relationship can be an intense one and the boundary between friendship and the tutor–student relationship should be kept clear. You may like a tutor and a tutor may like you, but this should have no bearing on the tutor–tutee relationship which is primarily about your intellectual development and your ideas.

Cultural note: Feedback and culture. Cultures may vary in their concepts of how acceptable it is to be direct when giving feedback. UK lecturers operate in the UK's cultural environment and will be following their cultural norms in this respect. Generally you can expect feedback not to be too direct in the UK. Sometimes, for students used to direct feedback, this can be confusing.

However, in many UK universities you may meet tutors from many different cultural backgrounds, all with their own personal and culturally acquired styles of giving feedback. These styles may or may not fit with the way you expect feedback to happen – as you too are a cultural being with certain expectations in this regard.

If you believe in directness, you may not like the UK sandwich method – even seeing it as vaguely dishonest. On the other hand, if you are from a culture where it is rude to be too direct, you may find direct criticism upsetting and unnecessarily aggressive!

In fact it is good to remember that a tutor has a difficult job – that of both teaching and assessing you. In other words, of looking after your motivation and self-esteem and letting you know how good your work is! It may be that the British feel a need to attend to what they think is your self-esteem by saying that your work is 'fine' or 'good' – this may be because they worry about your feelings or they may want to appear to be kind and considerate. But this can be confusing: one minute you are told you are doing fine and then the tutor awards you a low mark for your work. I have often been asked by international students why their tutor didn't tell them 'the truth'. 'If the tutor had told me what she really thought of my work, then I would have worked harder on it!'

WARNING!

This situation may lead to a breakdown of trust in the relationship, which is damaging for you. You need to be careful that you hear the main message – which is the filling in the sandwich!

In some cultures it is not expected that a tutor will attend to your feelings very much, and students expect quite harsh criticism. This is the 'sandwich without any bread' method of feedback! A tutor in such a culture is seen as a serious tutor and a person who one should respect if she or he is strict. This may well be reassuring for students! You may feel you know your role and where you are with such a tutor if this is your expectation. If you do expect a tutor to be harsh, you may think that a UK tutor who says nice things is not being honest or has some other goal!

On the other hand, in other cultures it is not expected that a tutor will be very harsh. This is seen as unnecessary and cruel. A tutor in such a culture must be seen to be concerned with students' feelings. This is because education and an educator is seen in such cultures as someone who must try to bring out the best in each student – i.e. to help each student realise his/her full potential. It may be felt that criticising learners is counter-productive for this because it may lower the students' self-esteem and motivation by making students feel negative about their ability.

Expectations about grades

Cultural anecdote: As a teacher in Morocco, I recall that if I gave high grades for any work students generally didn't believe me and perhaps felt I was doing something dishonest. Maybe the students also then didn't feel I was taking my teaching role as seriously as I should have. This was because of the grades culture in Morocco, which is inherited from the French education system: a good grade in this system was 12/20, so if I gave 17/20 this was confusing for the students and for the other Moroccan teachers in the system. In my UK grades culture of the time it was expected that I should use the full grade range. On the other hand, when I taught in a private school in the Dominican Republic modelled on the US school system, I became aware of serious discontent among US students if they received a C or even B grade average (which by British standards is perfectly acceptable). The students were in a system of 'grade inflation', where even a B was seen as negative.

Question: What is your expectation about grades? What grades are you used to receiving?

Advice: Check out what normal grades are in the UK university system. Ask students who are in Years 2 or 3 what to expect. For example, is 70 per cent a good grade or a common grade? Should you be happy with this grade?

Table 5.8 Roles and expectations for a seminar

The seminar	
Role of student	*Role of teacher*
There are two clear roles: • presenter of information to other students • listener and active questioner of information provided by other students. In both roles it is important that you treat other students in your seminar group with respect and realise that learning happens from active interaction, by listening to and discussing issues with them. If you are presenting information in a group you need to make sure that you present this information in a way that is clear and interesting for other students. If you are doing a group presentation make sure you have: • researched your part thoroughly • practiced the presentation beforehand with your fellow students as a group. You should have divided up the presentation between yourselves clearly and follow an agreed structure. Remember, a seminar is a particularly good opportunity to learn from your peers.	The teacher takes more of a back seat in seminars as these are led by students. The teacher's job is to set up the conditions for the seminar. This means: • managing students into groups • explaining the research task they need to do and the type of presentation they need to give • explaining the assessment procedures both for groups and for individuals. During the seminar the teacher will: • act as timekeeper and general manager of the seminar session • act as a prompt to ask important questions, if these are not raised by other students during the seminar. The teacher should make it clear that your audience is the other students and not just the teacher. At the end of the seminar the teacher will normally give feedback on the presentations, usually covering the depth of the information presented and its relevance and also the skill shown in the presentation itself as an act of communication.

Table 5.8 continued

The seminar	
Role of student	*Role of teacher*
Do other groups show skills in their presentation that you can learn from? Do they work better as a group? Why? It is a good idea to keep a learning diary/ log. Think about what you have learned from the other students and make notes in your log.	
Expectations of the student	*Expectations of the tutor*
To have clear guidance on the subject area of a presentation and be provided with the necessary reading lists to be able to successfully research the topics. To have information on the type of presentation wanted: its length (time), the depth of its content. To have information on the way the presentation will be assessed. If the method of preparation of a topic is by group you need to know how any grades that may be awarded are to be given to individuals in a group.	Students will work cooperatively and maturely in mixed-culture groups. They will be understanding of each other, show each other respect and will divide up the work fairly. They will be democratic about the workload and about who does the presenting. (A person who ignores the rest of the group or who does not function as a team member will not be looked upon favourably!) Students will spend time doing the necessary research and presentation together and they will practice (rehearse) the presentation beforehand.

Note: The importance of understanding group work. It is clear that in order to successfully participate in seminars as a student you need to understand how to participate in group work and how to debate ideas. These are two important skills and are not as easy as they may initially seem. One problem with group work is that both students and teachers may have unrealistic expectations about the ease with which people with different personalities and from different cultural backgrounds will understand each other and find a way to work together positively. Because working in a group is a skill that you need to develop, you may at first find the experience quite stressful. Apart from the fact that group work may be new to you and to others in your group, the problem may also be that you have not been prepared for this sufficiently as a class by your teacher. You may not have understood the purpose of group work or been trained in how to approach it.

Cultural note: Discussing and debating. Traditionally in UK schools, students are introduced to the idea of arguing ideas in an open and public way. Controversial topical issues may be chosen for debates. When this occurs half the class may be required to argue *for* a motion and half the class *against* the same motion. A motion is a statement such as: 'Euthanasia should be legalised' or 'Drug taking should be de-criminalised.' Students prepare their arguments in the two groups which are either 'for' or 'against' the motion. The students are then given the opportunity to have an open debate on the issue and are judged by the teacher on the skill with which they can argue and defend their ideas against each other or attack and successfully undermine the oppositions' arguments.

Intercultural note: Remember, teaching and learning styles vary greatly across the world. Because of this students from different cultures bring different communication and learning styles to group work when they study together in groups on UK university programmes. For example, it may be that one person believes that you should not really express an opinion about something in a classroom or learning situation unless you have first thought the ideas through and come to a conclusion. On the other hand, another person may have a learning and communication style which is the opposite: they may feel that you learn by talking ideas through and that to initiate this you can express any half-formed idea as a starting point and then debate and argue about it with your fellow students.

This can be summarised as:

THINKING and then TALKING *versus* TALKING to THINK

Which best explains your approach?

In the UK, the culture of debating means that it is considered OK to experiment in debates and discussions with ideas – in fact it is expected. So even if you do not have a clear idea of where you stand on an issue, you need to understand that it is through debate that you end up with a clearer idea. Indeed you may discover that the experience of debating means you change your mind on an issue. This is fine, as it is important to realise that there is often not one correct answer or attitude that you should have, but that many different points of view are correct so long as they can be well argued.

WARNING!

Some people may think that they are not in a debate to listen, but to try to make everyone else agree that their point of view is right! A debate, however, should be seen as an opportunity, through discussion, for you to develop your ideas on a subject. It is also an opportunity to refine your skills at arguing a position and convincing others that this position is valid.

Group work as a learning methodology is based on the idea that you need to discuss ideas and reach certain conclusions through doing so. It is not expected that you should hold back with ideas until you are sure of them. This may be hard to do if you are not used to it, but it is worth trying. Staying silent may be seen as not contributing to the group and not being helpful to the others!

In order to fully take advantage of lectures you need to develop certain skills. These are highlighted and looked at next.

Table 5.9 Roles and expectations for a lecture

The lecture	
Role of student	Role of tutor
• To do the key reading before the lecture. • To be attentive (not tired and distracted) and engaged with the ideas and perspectives offered on the subject by the lecturer. • To take notes of things that offer insight and new ideas for you to follow up after the lecture and on things you have not fully understood and need to investigate more. In other words, to be an *active listener*. Some lecturers may expect students to respond to various questions asked – this is to make the lecture a little more interactive. But it is not expected that you will be called on individually to answer questions, as you may be in a classroom situation.	• To provide the subject area to students before the lecture along with key reading text references that will help with the background to the lecture. Note: This information is usually provided in the timetable or through any VLE system in use in your department. The outline of the lecture is ideally also posted on the VLE along with notes and a bibliography. This is particularly useful for non-native English speaking international students as it offers them the opportunity to check their understanding and go though the ideas using the support of dictionaries for any new vocabulary. • To provide an analysis of the subject matter of the lecture and offer an interpretation of the subject, not just to repeat facts that can be read in books. • To maintain the attention of the audience – perhaps through variety of pace and the use of visuals (e.g. PowerPoint).
Expectations of the student	Expectations of the tutor
• The lecturer will speak about things that are relevant to the programme and the title of the lecture. • The lecturer will cover the subject matter stated and in the time given. • The lecturer will speak clearly and loudly enough for everyone to hear and will keep the listener's interest by using appropriate devices for this.	• The students will have done the basic reading so that the lecturer is not talking to a 'blank canvas' and can assume a common level of knowledge in the subject covered by the lecture. • The students will arrive on time and wait until the end to leave. They will be attentive and responsive to the ideas presented, showing this by taking notes. • Students will show feedback signs that they are engaging with the thoughts presented (i.e. not fall asleep, send text messages, eat their breakfast or read a newspaper!).

Advice: Note-taking. It is useful to understand how to undertake note-taking. It is wrong to think you should copy down everything that the lecturer says! If you try to do this you will become very frustrated because the lecturer is talking too fast and also you will miss the learning opportunity that a lecture provides – which is to engage your thoughts (through listening not writing). The main aim of the lecture is to both help you understand a subject more and to perhaps challenge you to think about the subject in new ways. You should therefore note down the new ideas that the lecture presents you with. These are the important points *for you*. The basic facts and figures on a subject should already be available from the lecture notes provided on the VLE or in handouts or the pre-reading you have done and you should not need to copy these down. You should also make notes about things you do not understand from the lecture and that you need to check up on later. When this happens, do not panic – noticing gaps in your knowledge should happen all the time! You should see this, when it occurs, as a learning opportunity, not something to be worried about!

Suggestion: Below is a short example from a lecture and a note-taking chart (Table 5.10) that has been filled in. This was done by a student attending a lecture on the issue of 'marketing opportunities in an economic downturn'. You may find that using a similar chart for your lectures is a useful tool for you.

Example
Lecture extract:

> Of course now that R&D funding is being cut back so severely across the globe because of the global recession, it is logical that companies that already have international reach, and for which international brand awareness exists, consolidate their sales in the markets they already feel confident in. I am of course referring to nothing new here, simply to the top box on the Ansoff matrix – further old product penetration in an already established and per-forming market. The costs of new market penetration are perhaps a luxury that cannot be indulged in by companies until they see which way the wind is blowing and how this will affect their bottom line over the next few years. Of course this perhaps opens up a nice space for venture capitalists from less affected BRIC countries to open up markets with new products in new markets without the usual cost of overcoming the competition from the established brands. While established companies' eyes are off the ball, others can slip in. So it is not all doom and gloom – more a question of a re-alignment. I personally am positive about the situation. We are just entering a paradigm shift with brand opportunity sliding from the West to the Rest and the East particularly . . .

Table 5.10 Example note-taking chart

Prompt	Thought
Big brands will consolidate sales in their existing markets because of cut backs in R&D funding	Is this true? Are all companies doing this or are some actually responding in a different way to the recession by banking on new product development to help them out of the current hole? I need to check this out – How? I could ask my tutor how I can check this.
Venture capitalist	Who are these people exactly? I need to get some names to understand who they are. I can ask Mohammed – he mentioned them the other day in a seminar.

Prompt	Missing knowledge
Ansoff matrix	I recall the name – but I cannot picture it. I need to check it and make sure I understand the quadrants. It is obviously considered a common piece of knowledge in business so I need to know it too.
BRIC countries	India, China, Russia – What country is B for? I need to check this too.

Stop and think: What problems do you think you may have with learning from attending lectures in a UK university?

Below are some common problems that international students tell me may occur.

The lecturer's use of British examples and anecdotes

This can lead to problems of understanding for international students. A lecturer may be unaware of the lack of knowledge of British culture of the students and use examples in their lecture based only on British culture. This is particularly a problem when perhaps 60 per cent of the student audience is non-British and has not lived in Britain (often the case on many Masters programmes). For example, if you heard a statement like the following in a lecture: 'To say it was crowded is an understatement! I mean it was like Stansted on the night before a bank holiday weekend, or getting round the M25 at 5:00 p.m. on a Friday!' How much of this do you understand? If not much, this is because it is full of local knowledge from the experience of living in the UK and has local meaning only.

The lecturer's use of humour

In some cultures it is not unusual for the lecturer to give very long lectures (these can be up to several hours long). In the UK, students would generally not be able to cope with this as they are not trained to learn in this way. British students expect to be engaged and kept interested in the subject by the lecturer. There is a basic belief that it is the teacher's job to make learning interesting for the student. In other cultures it may be that the lecturer and the learners may not share this responsibility in the same way. The attitude may be that it is up to the learners to listen and find their own interest in the subject and not for the lecturer to spend time keeping the listeners entertained or engaged.

Cultural note: The fact that British lecturers use jokes and visuals in lectures may be because of this sense of the need to entertain and keep the audience paying attention and engaged. International students, not used to this, may think that the lecturer is perhaps not as serious about their subject as they should be and is using up the lecture time in irrelevant and unnecessary ways!

An added problem from this use of humour is that humour is often very particular to culture. It may be the case that a lecturer uses British ironic humour in which the jokes can only be easily understood by someone who has been brought up in British culture.

The lecturer's use of idiomatic language

Lecturers who are not used to speaking to international students may use a lot of 'localisms' and idiomatic language in their presentations instead of easier-to-understand language for the international students. An example of this is where a lecturer may say: 'It's easy to get the wrong end of the stick', instead of saying: 'It is easy to misunderstand'; or: 'It's a storm in a teacup, I am sure there are clear blue skies ahead', instead of saying: 'It's not such a big problem as people may think, I believe the future will be better.'

Bad lecturing with no change of pace or activity

An unskilled lecturer may continue too long without a change of activity or without using visuals. It is generally estimated that people can concentrate for a maximum of 20 minutes on one subject in a lecture without a change of activity or pace. After this the natural habit is to stop listening and daydream to give the mind a break: this is especially true when listening in another language to your mother tongue, as this is more tiring!

WARNING!

Autonomous learners

In some cultures, it is acceptable for the students to chat to each other, look at their mobile phones or laptops (to look up words) during class, or maybe even leave the lecture theatre when they feel like it. This is seen as the students' choice – after all it is the students' problem if they do not listen or want to learn! If you are used to such an education system (one where students have autonomy to behave in this way), then you need to be aware that British lecturers would feel quite insulted if you decided to get up and leave a lecture before the end, or talked with your partner during a presentation or openly did something other than listen to the lecturer (such as play games on your mobile phone or do a sudoku). The lecturer may interpret this as a personal comment on their unimportance or effectiveness as a teacher.

WARNING!

Impassive listeners

It is also noticeable that British lecturers may also become disturbed if the students sit passively with neutral impassive faces that show little or no engagement or communication during lectures. In some cultures it is seen as good behaviour to listen in this way: it may even be seen as respectful. Instead of interpreting this as displaying respectfulness, however, British lecturers may interpret this as boredom or disengagement or even being upset. Be aware of this if you are from a culture where it is not expected that you do more than show respect by listening impassively.

Stop and think: What do you think are the ways that you can show engagement to a lecturer or teacher in a lecture or class?

Which of the following do you think are signs of engagement? Tick those you believe are acceptable behaviour for showing this:

Sign of engagement	✓
Making eye contact	
Staring into space	
Nodding your head	
Shaking your head	
Making agreement noises such as 'uhuh', 'mmm'	
Smiling at jokes	
Saying aloud 'I agree' or 'Yes'	
Writing down notes in your notebook	
Punching the air	

Comment: Making eye contact (but not for too long), nodding, smiling at jokes, making 'mmm mhum' noises occasionally and taking notes are all feedback mechanisms that British lecturers/teachers look for to show that their students are paying attention and listening and understanding what they are telling them. Staring into space, actually speaking out loud or being too physically active are not signs that they feel are acceptable to show this!

Cultural anecdote: Nodding versus shaking. When I first taught a Tamil student I was surprised and worried to notice the student 'shaking' her head at things I said. I began to wonder if I was offending the student in some way. I then found out that there are some cultures in the world where sending back positive signs of engagement to the speaker is shown by rocking the head from side to side rather than by gently nodding the head up and down, and this can appear to be like shaking the head.

Learning point: It is wise not to assume that your body language gives the same messages when you change cultures. You need to learn what the new body language is!

Classes

Note: The class situation is the most regular method of teaching/learning. It is quite usual for class size to be about 20 students. In fact one important measure used for positioning universities in league tables is called the 'staff–student ratio' (the number of students per member of teaching staff in the university). This can vary in UK universities from 10 to 25. Generally, if class sizes are bigger than 20, this is not very practical for interactive teaching. UK teachers like to personalise their classrooms as much as possible and part of this is learning the names of their students (however they may often then get these wrong or forget them!). Obviously learning students' names is more difficult to do if the class size is bigger and then the teaching becomes more impersonal.

Table 5.11 Roles and expectations for the classroom

Role of student	Role of tutor
To be flexible in their approach to learning and prepared to interact with all other students in a variety of ways, according to the instructions from the teacher.	The classroom teacher has two roles: • provider of information on a topic • organiser of student learning.
To approach pair and group work in a cooperative and democratic way so that all class members can benefit from these activities.	Both these aspects of a teacher's task are usually integrated so that there may be a mini-lecture period or a handout to read where information is provided (input) followed by some tasks/activities that are
To be aware of the classroom context and contribute to the class but not try to take over the class by focusing issues exclusively upon themselves.	undertaken by the students either individually or in pairs/groups. Students are then required to provide feedback from the tasks so that the teacher can monitor if learning is taking place.

Table 5.11 continued

Role of student	Role of tutor
To listen attentively to other students in the class and to address them, not just the teacher, when providing feedback.	The teacher needs to be prepared with the necessary input and also to have thought about and implemented the patterns of interaction among the students to accomplish the learning tasks in the time provided.

Expectations of the student	Expectations of the tutor
The teacher will help by providing clear instructions for tasks and by controlling the time spent on them. The teacher will monitor and clarify any points of confusion and also step in to help any pair or group that is not functioning.	Students will quickly develop and use the necessary interaction skills for working positively with other people in pairs and groups. Students will focus on the tasks in question and be ready to provide clear and relevant feedback for the whole class from their pair or group work.

Tip: It is useful to be prepared for the different kinds of interaction that you will be expected to undertake in the typical classroom. Below we look at each one briefly.

Individual work

The classroom is not an ideal environment for this and it would be unusual for this to be used much. The library and out-of-class time is best used for individual work. However, there may be tasks that require you to reflect on an issue and form your own initial opinion before seeing what other members of the class think about the issue.

Pair work

This provides the opportunity to get to know another student and his/her experience better and to discover his/her opinions and point of view. A good idea is to make sure you work with a different person in pair work as often as possible to broaden the range of experience and points of view you are exposed to. In pair work a skilled interactant will always be interested in your opinion but also be prepared to offer his/her opinion. However, both people should ideally be prepared to change their initial opinions through discussion.

Group work

A group is usually three or four students. The teacher, who often forms the groups, gives the groups tasks and sets a time limit for the groups to come up with their ideas and to report these back to the rest of the class. It is a good idea for the teacher to assign people to different groups each time this is used so that you get into the habit of working with different people each time.

The main benefit of group work is that in a class of 20 students every person in the class ideally has the chance to offer opinions and discuss the issues under consideration. This is particularly good for shy students or students worried about speaking English publicly. Such students do not find they can participate in a whole class discussion so easily, as they may often be dominated by the more self-confident and outward-going personalities in the class.

Teacher with whole class discussion

The teacher may approach the classroom teaching session as a mini-lecture. This is more informal than a timetabled lecture, and it is expected that there will be more interaction between the teacher, who is providing ideas and information, and the students. This means that there will be open questions asked by the teacher to the class. These are opportunities for students to respond. This routine may be an actual teaching methodology called the 'Socratic lecture' approach. This is an interactive approach with the teacher controlling the pace and focus of the session. The following is an example of the Socratic approach.

Example: The teacher stands in front of the class, in front of a whiteboard and has a whiteboard marker in her hand. She writes the title of the class on the board: 'Understanding the causes of anaemia'. She smiles and says: 'Anaemia. What does it mean?' A student raises his hand and says: 'It means you don't have enough red blood cells in your blood.' The teacher nods and then pauses and asks: 'Why is that bad?' A student then raises her hand and the teacher says: 'It's OK – Please just shout out your ideas at this stage and I'll write them up on the board for you.' Students then shout out their ideas and the teacher writes up the ones that she feels are useful and correct, commenting on each one or asking for clarification if the idea is not stated too well. One student, the comic in the class, says: 'It's not bad if you want to act in a vampire film!' Some students laugh and the teacher smiles and says: 'Well I don't think that will go on the board!' (Note that teachers will use different ways of soliciting answers – they may randomly ask students for their ideas, or they may ask for hands to go up or they may play the waiting game – which is to ask a question and then wait in silence refusing to go on until some suggestions have come from the class.) The teacher then stands back from the board and says: 'Okay. We've talked about why anaemia is not good, now let's think of the reasons why a person might be anaemic.'

Table 5.12 The Socratic lecture approach – good or bad?

The Socratic lecture approach ...	Agree ✓	Disagree ✓
Is an active and meaningful method for students in the class		
Builds on what students already know		
Is a participative approach to knowledge		
Is a democratic approach to learning		
Is exciting and fun		

Stop and think: Table 5.12 lists the good points of the Socratic teaching approach as seen in the example. Do you agree with these statements about it?

Reflection: One criticism of the method that I have heard from students is a feeling that questioning all the time seems pointless: some students may think that if teachers know an answer, why do they keep asking questions of people who presumably don't know? A student thinking this may feel irritated by not under-standing why the teacher simply does not tell the class the answer or 'the truth' – it would be so much quicker, after all!

Stop and think: How far do you think students should be expected to work things out for themselves and how far should teachers just tell students the facts?

Why do you think the Socratic method as a teaching approach does not believe in simply telling students what they need to know but instead uses probing questions to direct learners to answers?

Perhaps the following refrain is helpful to think about this?

I hear . . . I forget – I see . . . I remember – I do . . . I understand

Group work preparation

As mentioned already in this chapter, one of the common methodologies for learning in the UK system of higher education is group work. It is based on the idea that interaction with other students is good and that an individual learns by working on tasks with other learners. Many teachers believe that simply learning how to work with other people on tasks is a useful life skill in itself, particularly if this means working in intercultural groups to successfully undertake tasks with people from different countries and cultures.

This may well be true, but it is not easy, and if students are not used to this concept of learning – they may in the past have been trained to learn either indi-vidually (usually from reading books) or from listening to teachers telling them what to believe – then the group work methodology may not be particularly successful. For this reason it is best if teachers who introduce this way of learning in class – who ask students to work in groups on small research projects or to prepare a seminar presentation – explain the basic roles and approaches that are helpful for group work. This may not always happen, so the following exercise is designed to help you prepare for group work.

Exercise

Look at the following behaviours and attitudes for group work and decide if they are helpful and positive for group work to succeed or unhelpful and negative

Table 5.13 What is needed for positive group work

Action	Positive	Negative
Talk as much as possible and not listen to other students' contributions		
Believe that there is nothing to learn from fellow students, only from the teacher		
Actively try to include everyone in conversations		
Become angry when others do not follow or agree with your viewpoint		
Everyone talking at the same time		
Insist that you are right and argue forcefully for your point of view to be accepted		
Ask others in the group questions		
Not participate because it seems pointless or boring		
Be interested in the others as people and in their points of view		
Promote and accept group roles for working together (someone as secretary, timekeeper and spokesperson)		
Tell everyone else what they must do		
Not contribute as much as the others to the work of the group		
Contribute more than the others to the work of the group		
Be able to compromise and accept that your ideas are never perfect and will be modified through discussion		

Advice: If you have not had any training from your teacher and find yourself in a group it may be good to suggest you all do this exercise together at the beginning and discuss your findings. You may then be able to agree some group rules for working together that will help you all.

Tip: To function well it is sensible for each group to agree the following group member roles early on:

- **A secretary** – the person who will take notes or outline the group's findings on a large sheet of paper or overhead transparency, to help with the feedback of findings to the rest of the class.
- A **chair** – it is the chair's job to monitor the time and ensure that everyone in the group is involved in contributing their ideas.
- **A spokesperson** or **spokespeople** – the person or people who will provide the feedback to the rest of the class. It is best to decide these roles at the beginning of the task to avoid wasting time discussing or arguing over this towards the end.

Suggestion: Another good idea is for you to discuss your experience of group work and your expectations of it with the other members of your group. In this discussion you can see if you can all agree to sign up to the following principles (charter):

- The work should be shared evenly among all members of the group including the presentation itself.
- All opinions and ideas need to be discussed and gathered. Not to do this is to waste the group's potential.
- All of the group should also consider the statement that 'English language ability is not equal to intellectual ability.' It is, of course, easier for a person working in their own language to express ideas more quickly – but this doesn't mean that these ideas are better than those the group would come up with once all members have had time to consider and find the right words!

Suggestion: Group methodology for gathering ideas and thought sharing. It is perhaps a good idea to have a group methodology for gathering ideas (brainstorming). The following is a methodology that may help with this, especially in the early days of a group working together:

- *Materials:* a pack of 'PostIts', several large sheets of paper, a marker pen, an empty room, some blu tac, digital cameras.
- *Procedure:* hand out the PostIt notes to the members of the group and place a large sheet of paper on the wall using the blu tac. On the whiteboard write up the idea that is to be brainstormed, e.g. 'The best way to market a new antidepressant pharmaceutical drug'. For 10 minutes everyone individually posts up ideas associated with this (writes ideas on the PostIt notes and sticks

these on the paper). These can be as free-ranging as the person wants them to be. After this the group works together and looks at the ideas and in agreement groups them into similar themes. The group then decides on headings for these 'clusters', e.g. for the example here: 'ethical issues', 'competitive alternative treatments'. The work can then be photographed by all and uploaded onto computers to act as a summary of ideas for further work and a basis for assignment writing.

Information: the psychology of group formation

It is well known that groups go through distinct psychological stages in group formation, usually described as 'forming, storming, norming and performing'. This is not always a comfortable process, but it is a necessary one. It is a good idea to read up on this process so that you are prepared and understand what is happening. If you are aware of this process you will be better able to help contribute to your group and help it function well. Another useful thing to do is to analyse yourself and the people in your team from the point of view of typical team member types and the roles they prefer to take on in a group.

Exercise

Table 5.14 Matching team types with their definitions

Type	Description		
A	Plant	1	Gets contacts and opportunities and starts with enthusiasm
B	Resource investigator	2	Is a fair and logical judge of what is going on in the team. Moves slowly and analytically
C	Coordinator	3	Is a good diplomat and makes sure everyone gets on with each other
D	Shaper	4	Takes colleagues' suggestions and turns them into actions
E	Monitor evaluator	5	Is a perfectionist and wants everything to be just right
F	Team worker	6	Likes to be the knowledge provider
G	Implementer	7	Is an achiever who pursues objectives vigorously and wants the rest of the team to conform to his or her ends
H	Completer finisher	8	Act like a chairperson – is mature, sees the strengths of others and can delegate well
I	Specialist	9	Imaginative creator of new ideas

Answer: A, 9; B, 1; C, 8; D, 7; E, 2; F, 3; G, 4; H, 5; I, 6

Stop and think: Which one do you think you are?

Advice: The key to group work is not to despair! You need to be patient and understand that group formation is about negotiating roles between members of the group, and this takes some time before you settle down. It would be very unusual for a group of people to be able to work harmoniously immediately, especially a group of people from very different cultural backgrounds – which is the situation you are likely to be in on your university course. Developing an effective teamwork spirit in a group takes a lot of hard work from all the members of the team and if it happens is a great achievement itself!

Cultural note: In the UK, group work is a common approach to learning: training for this starts at primary school. UK students, and indeed UK teachers, may think this approach and the skills that it requires are widespread. They may not realise that it is a very new idea for many students from different parts of the world where this style of learning is not culturally usual or promoted.

WARNING!

The native English speaker trap

In groups where there is a mix of native English speakers and non-native-English speakers, the balance in contributions between the two types of participants may be lost.

It is obvious that a student working in his/her native language has certain advantages of expression over those working in a foreign language (with English as a second or third language). This ease of expression does not mean that this person has the best ideas! It can be too easy for a native speaker working with non-native speakers to forget this and begin to dominate the group work sessions – effectively becoming the unelected leader and spokesperson for the group. On the other hand it is also easy for a non-native speaker to assume that it is easier and more logical for the native speaker to be the person who leads the group as the spokesperson because of his/her ease with using the English language. Over-relying on native speakers can be a big mistake that may lead to under-performance and frustration in groups. Both native speakers and non-native speakers need to be aware of this trap.

Integrating practical learning with theoretical learning in UK university education

It has been emphasised in this chapter that UK higher education believes in being in touch with the real world and in linking theory to practice. This means there should be an important practical aspect to your learning. In Figure 5.1 (see p. 60)

Stage 3 is about 'trying out new ideas in the real world'. The next section looks at how this can be achieved.

Note: Being 'job ready'. Universities are increasingly expected to produce graduates who are able to work with little further training needed, i.e. they can start a job immediately. One of the important statistics for universities is the percentage of students who are in graduate-level work soon after graduating, and universities compile 'Destination of Learners from Higher Education' statistics which they publish.

Traditionally, in the past, practical skills-based training courses for school leavers were provided by polytechnics, but many of these became universities in 1992 and now these very practical courses tend to be offered in Further Education (FE) colleges. However, universities, and especially the New Universities (the former polytechnics of which there were 35), continue to aim to offer practical learning as part of their programmes. Indeed, two of the growing areas of education are part-time 'work-based learning' Foundation Degrees and distance learning programmes, where people already in jobs study at the same time as they work. In this way they are able to apply and test out new knowledge 'on the job'.

This practical approach is also noticeable at postgraduate research level in the UK, where generally it is important to see research as 'grounded' and 'empirical'. In other words, concepts and theory should be seen to have derived from observations in the real world and to interact and be tested against the real world.

Further Education (FE) colleges

In the UK, different programmes are designed with different learning objectives. A training programme may be designed to develop practical working skills. When this is the case, this is referred to as *vocational education*. Examples of this are programmes of study which prepare students for trades such as hairdressing, plumbing or car mechanics. The aim of these programmes is to develop students who can work in their chosen trade without the need for further training. Typical qualifications offered by FE colleges are National Vocational Qualification (NVQs or SVQs in Scotland), The Business and Technology Education Council (BTECs), City and Guilds, OCR Nationals, Higher National Certificates (HNCs) and Higher National Diplomas (HNDs).

Useful website: http://www.direct.gov.uk/en/EducationAndLearning/QualificationsExplained/DG_181951

The 'apprenticeship model' of learning is often used for those learning a trade. Undertaking an apprenticeship involves the learner observing, working with and learning from, skilled professionals. Theoretical knowledge is of course necessary to update the learner on new approaches and skills, but the emphasis is on developing practical skills, and apprenticeships are increasingly on offer as part of FE education.

Fact: The are over 350 FE colleges in England, 48 in Scotland, 20 in Wales and 16 in Northern Ireland.

Note on Higher National Diplomas: HNDs are a British Technology and Education Council (BTEC) qualification awarded in England, Wales and Northern Ireland. They are awarded in England by Edexcel and in Scotland by the Scottish Qualifications Authority (SQA). Many universities accept students who have completed an HND at an FE college. They can enter onto either a Level 5 (second year) or Level 6 (third and final year) of a degree programme. For many international students 'Year 3 entry' may often be referred to as a 'top-up' year. The decision as to whether a student with an HND or equivalent from their own country can enter into the final year or the second year of a degree programme depends on what subjects the student has studied and how these match the university degree programme content. Remember that in the UK each university designs its own degree programmes so they are all different. This is why one university may be able to accept an HND (or equivalent) for entry into Year 3 while another can only offer Year 2 entry.

Practical education in the university sector

University education, of course, goes beyond the aim of equipping students with practical skills to undertake a trade. However, theory by itself without reference to the real world is seen by many in the UK as too abstract and theoretical to be useful. For this reason an interaction between theory and practice on a programme is seen as a good thing. This is why UK university programmes are increasingly concerned with offering practical experience as part of the learning programme (this fits with the learning spiral idea explained). A recent example of this innovation in universities is the Foundation Degree offered in certain universities in England, Wales and Northern Ireland. This is a work-related, two-year Higher Education degree (offering two years of university credits). In many universities it can be converted into a full three-year degree.

Exercise

Decide which of the qualifications in Table 5.15 are more academic or vocational or a mixture of the two. Use a tick ✓:

Table 5.15 Academic and vocational qualifications

Qualification	Academic	Vocational
Bachelor of Arts (BA)		
HND		

Postgraduate taught (PGT)		
MBA		
BTEC		
PhD		
NVQ		
Foundation degree (FD)		

Answers: Academic: BA, PGT, PhD; Vocational: HND, BTEC, NVQ, FD; Mixed: MBA

Exercise

Look at the professions listed in Table 5.16 and decide ✓ if the education required is best obtained through a practical training programme or a programme that focuses more on theoretical, analytical skills. Note the reasons for your choice.

Table 5.16 Practical training versus theoretical learning

Type of career/profession	Practical skills training	Theoretical knowledge development	Reason:
Beauty therapist			
Hospitality manager			
Hotel receptionist			
Teacher			
Surgeon			
Engineer			
Bio-scientist			
Economist			
Painter (artist)			
Software designer			
IT technician			

Comment: You may have found it difficult to categorise all of these into one box or the other. It is good if this is the case as it shows you realise that there is a need for theory and practice in most learning. It may seem clear that a hairdresser best learns by cutting hair and it may seem clear that a designer needs to develop new ways of thinking and not just copy what is there already. However, a hairdresser needs to know the latest theories and techniques in hairdressing and a designer needs to know what is possible and practical to design!

Reflective exercise: What is it you want from your education? What is the best programme for you to achieve this – one which is mostly theoretical or mostly practical or an even mixture of both? If we take the case of a surgeon, we would all want to be operated on by someone who has a lot of practical expertise in undertaking operations, but we would also want to be operated on by someone who is up-to-date with the latest techniques, who is creative and confident in their thinking and able to find solutions to any unexpected problems as they occur during an operation!

Advice: It is important to make sure that the programme you choose to study is:

• the right level for what you want
• offers the necessary balance between theory and practice that you want.

Question: How do universities offer students practical skills and experience of the real world alongside their theoretical studies on the programmes they offer?

Exercise

Look at the list of approaches in Table 5.17 and match them to their definitions

Table 5.17 Approaches to gaining practical experience

Approach to including practical experience		Definition of activity
A Work experience (internships)	I	Students may be required to produce commercially valuable items and engage in their commercialisation as part of their studies, e.g. software programs, promotional films, running a newspaper or radio station
B Public performances and shows	2	The 'caring professions' such as teaching, social work and health-related professions
C On-the-job training in the real-life context usually with	3	Programmes with built-in consultancy services for the general public to use,

	the help and guidance of an experienced mentor		e.g. law students running a mediation clinic, business studies students offering free consultancies to local businesses
D	Offering of free services to the public	4	Researching a real-life issue and writing a report for commercial or social use, e.g. a biological study of river contamination or tourism students undertaking visitor needs analysis for the local city council
E	Shadowing and observing	5	This may be expected of students on arts programmes such as music, performing arts or fine art
F	Production of a commercial entity or item	6	Placement in a local business for a defined period of time. The student is expected to carry out day-to-day functions in the company at the necessary level of their training
G	Undertaking fieldwork	7	Undertaking experiments in controlled conditions to verify and discover new knowledge
H	Laboratory practicals	8	Access to skilled workers may be secured for students to observe and discuss practice with highly skilled practitioners, e.g. cardiology students observing heart surgery

Answers: A, 6; B, 5; C, 2; D, 3; E, 8; F, 1; G, 4; H, 7

Stop and think: If you were an employer, besides knowledge in the area of your sector, what are the main skills that you would expect and need any candidate for a job in your company to have? For example, you would probably want reassurance that the person is capable of undertaking teamwork. Before reading on, make a list of what you feel are important skills that a graduate should develop during his/her studies to be flexible and effective in the modern job market.

Information: key transferable skills and generic skills development

At FE colleges, programmes are designed so that students acquire and are assessed in the following:

1 Communication
2 Application of number
3 Information technology

4   Working with others
5   Improving your own learning and performance
6   Problem solving.

These are referred to as *key transferable skills.*

At UK universities programmes are designed to conform to QAA guidelines. These guidelines state that any graduate from a UK university must have demonstrated sufficient ability in seven 'generic skills' (see Table 5.18) to be able to graduate.

All undergraduate programmes in the UK should develop these skills and examine them throughout the programmes. This means that any future employer should be confident that any successful UK graduate is competent in these areas.

Table 5.18 The seven generic skills of undergraduate learning

Generic skill	Usual method of checking and examining
Written communication	Assignments
Oral communication	Presentations
Critical and analytical thinking	Tasks, assignments
Problem solving	Product design
Teamwork	Group presentations
Independent learning	Evidence of referencing ideas in assignments
Information literacy	Undertaking a research task (library, Internet)

Information: the skills-based approach to further and higher education

Flexibility through skills

It is recognised that graduates from any FE or HE college or university may enter into any number of careers and jobs and that these may not be directly related to the content knowledge of the degree programme a person has studied. In the modern world people are less and less likely to have one lifelong career. Economic circumstances change fast and the speed of innovation, especially with the Internet, means old professions become less meaningful. Globalisation means that what was once a stable industry in one country may disappear overnight as cheaper competition from other countries undercuts it. What university education can offer, however, is a set of skills that are useful and can be adapted to most working environments.

Question: How far did your list of the necessary skills from the above stop and think exercise match those used in UK FE and HE? Is there any other skill that is missing? Personally, I believe one important skill you will develop by studying as an international student in a UK university is the ability to communicate and work interculturally. This, I believe, is an increasingly important skill to have.

Self-study

So far, we have looked at the delivery of learning through working with others. Another important part of learning, especially for developing reflective ability, is individual study. This may be the method you at first feel most comfortable with as it may be the one you are most used to from your school experience. When you study by yourself, you do not have to interact with anyone and you can interrupt it whenever you like! In this section we will look at important aspects of self-study that you need to consider. This will involve looking at how you find out information by yourself for your studies, i.e. it will help you to develop research skills. It includes information on using the library, using the Internet and accessing and using the university VLE to support the work you do with your tutors and teachers.

Exercise

Which of the following tactics do you consider good advice?

Tactic	✓
Find a comfortable, quiet place to study where you feel peaceful	
Make sure you know how to find the necessary information using the Internet	
Make sure you clear your mind of worries before beginning to study	
Don't study for more than a couple of hours at one stretch	
Set objectives for your study before you begin (what you want to find out)	
Read any comments on previous work from your teacher and follow these up	
Have a learning log and make notes on key ideas you discover	
Always ensure you reference where you have found any quotes or ideas	
Follow a routine for study – i.e. a timetable for study	
Make sure you have a block of uninterrupted free time for studying	

Tip: Developing your memory. One of the big problems of private study is that of developing an effective revision method. It is very good for learning to recall what you have studied and test yourself regularly to see if you can recall the key ideas and references from your previous study before moving on to new areas of study. Memory needs training!

Explanation: In order to develop your own theoretical understanding of your subject area, you need to be organised and self-aware. One of the key aims of a UK university education is to develop independent and critical thinkers. Demonstrating this independence and critical ability is key to obtaining good grades. The following section looks at how you can organise your learning and how you can present this in a critical manner.

Organising your learning and developing your ideas

Throughout your university programme the emphasis is on you developing your ideas. These ideas do not have to be the same as anyone else's – if they were, that would be rather strange – as we all naturally have different experiences and views on things. During your programme you will be assessed on how you present your ideas and show what you have learned. It is a good idea whenever you are studying to think about the learning points that are occurring for you as you study.

Advice: Rather than just reading or listening to a lecture and then hoping that somehow you will learn something from this activity, and that you will remember it, it is best to be more active and systematic about your learning. One activity that may be of help is that of keeping a learning journal that maps out your thoughts.

Example: Learning maps. One way to get ideas on paper that are then easy to access for revision and when you need to write an assignment, is to draw 'ideas maps'. These can be made while reading a book, an article, listening to a radio or TV programme, a lecture or from a class discussion. You can use these as quick revision keys for information topics you need to know about – an ideas map is much quicker to use than reading through pages of random notes or highlighted text in photocopied articles and book pages. The example in Figure 5.7 is taken from an environmental biology student interested in recalling the main points about the life of the Death's-head Hawkmoth.

Tip: Learning log. Organising your learning is important and to do this it is a good idea to keep a learning log/diary. This is a notebook in which you record your main ideas as you attend classes, lectures, tutorials or practicums on your course. It is very important to recognise and note where your ideas come from, as you will probably need to reference or 'acknowledge your sources' when you come to present your ideas later in an assignment, presentation or examination. One example of how you may design your learning log pages is shown on pp. 101–2:

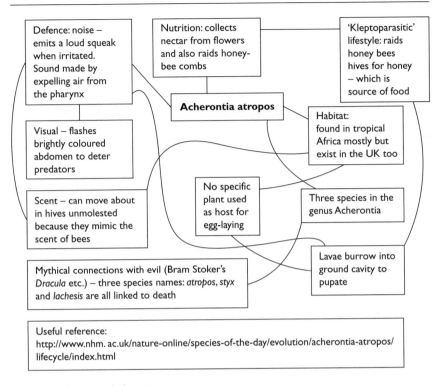

Figure 5.7 An example learning map.

Date:		
Event:		
Idea	Origin	References

For example:

Date: 20 April 2011

Event: Group work discussion about the kinds of teeth filling materials available for dentists to use

Idea	Origin	References
Cosmetic dentistry is becoming mainstream in the West. More and more NHS patients ask for white fillings even if this means a surcharge.	Jaime saying that in his country (Spain) no one wants to have metal in their mouths as it makes them look ugly and that therefore white fillings are standard practice.	Need to find and note here any articles that discuss the growing cosmetic demands of clients in dental studios in the public health sector.
		Refs: http://www. cosmeticdentistryguide. co.uk

Tip: It is often the case that you may read an interesting idea somewhere, and this becomes something that you want to mention in a later assignment or presentation. In order to do this properly you will need to reference this idea. If you haven't made a note of where you got your idea from you may be tempted to do the following:

• Pretend the idea is yours
• Leave the idea out altogether.

Both of these 'solutions' are problematic because you may be accused of *plagiarism* in the first case, or you may be losing the opportunity to develop interesting and original ideas in the second case.

Understanding plagiarism

You have probably been told or heard about plagiarism and realise that it is a serious 'crime' in the academic world to commit plagiarism. But are you really sure what plagiarism is and how you can avoid it?

Reflective exercise: You can do this exercise with a fellow student, in a group or individually. Complete the following chart as best you can:

Plagiarism is . . .	You avoid it by . . .

Look at the following and decide if your definition covered these ideas as plagiarism:

- Copying text from a book and presenting it without a reference, so that it appears as your idea.
- Copying text from a book and presenting it in a slightly changed way (different words), so that it appears as your idea.
- Reading an idea and then presenting that idea in your own words, but not referencing where the original idea came from.

Pitfall!

Borrow, don't steal! All of the above tactics are plagiarism. This is because they are really about stealing other people's ideas. If you *reference* the ideas or text then they are 'borrowed' ideas and are no longer 'stolen'.

To avoid plagiarism you need to be honest about where your ideas have come from. This means referencing these ideas. Not to do this and to pretend other people's ideas are yours. Simply copy other people's work (including published texts) is a serious offence at university. *You need to make sure you understand this and don't fall into this trap by accident.* You may fail your programme of study and be told you cannot continue on your course if you are accused of plagiarism. Be aware that many universities use software such as 'Turnitin' to check texts for plagiarism!

Cultural note: Some universities recognise that for cultural reasons international students may not fully understand plagiarism and need support to avoid it. It is a good idea to check if your university has a plagiarism policy and read and understand it. Seek clarification from your tutor or from the student study support centre if you are not clear.

WARNING!

If an examiner (or marker of an assignment) suspects plagiarism there is a university disciplinary procedure that will be followed – this procedure should be available to you as a student. It will inform you of the steps that will be taken and what your rights are.

Reasons for plagiarism among international students

Exercise

Table 5.18 lists reasons that can cause plagiarism. Tick them if you too feel they may be a danger for you

Table 5.18 Possible reasons for plagiarism

Reason	Possible danger for me ✓
My lack of confidence in English: feeling that my English is not good enough to explain the ideas, especially as well as the article/book I am reading	
Being in a rush and laziness: it is so much easier to cut and paste ideas	
Wanting to show off: I feel my own expressions and language are not academic enough so it makes my work look better to use other people's words	
Feeling inferior: I don't feel I am able to come up with ideas as good as those in the articles and books I read. My ideas seem unimportant	

Cultural note: In some cultures, copying and repeating other people's ideas is not seen as a bad thing. In fact, in many education systems, copying teachers' notes or learning and copying ideas from the accepted intellectual leaders' books is expected. In such educational cultures these ideas are to be learnt and repeated if you are to be successful. In such a culture, memory and memorisation is seen as an important ability. This may be particularly true in societies where religious text or political text is to be learnt and followed as guidance for people. If you have been trained to learn in this way you may find the UK approach to learning, where you are expected to critically analyse and personally respond to the ideas of accepted 'great thinkers', rather than simply repeat them, strange or perhaps even dangerous.

Comment: This is a reasonable point, but it is important and necessary for you to understand the UK concept of *critical analysis*. In reality, ideas can only progress and help society if they are developed, contested, changed, rejected or adapted by others. We cannot, for example, expect the ideas and beliefs of the Middle Ages to have much day-to-day relevance for modern societies. Just think of the changes in medicine that have occurred. It takes courage to put forward your own ideas: after all, Galileo paid a heavy price for arguing a heliocentric view of the universe!

Having an angle

The important thing for you to understand and demonstrate to your teachers is that you do not unquestioningly accept ideas as right and relevant to you without first questioning them. This is what is meant by having a critical approach to your studies. You also need to show in your work that you are referring to and using other people's ideas *for your purposes*, i.e. to support a particular point of view *you* are arguing for. I call this showing that you 'have an angle'. It may be that a particular thinker is someone who you agree with and this person's ideas therefore support your point of view (angle), or it may be that another one has ideas that you do not support or cannot see as relevant to your argument. You need to reference these people to show that you have undertaken background reading in the area you are discussing and that you can present an argument linked to this background reading. Most reading will be suggested to you by your teachers in bibliographies.

Tip: The important thing is that you need to have an argument and a purpose *before you start writing.* If you do not have an argument you may well just end up repeating what other people say and then you fall into the possible trap of plagiarism.

Finding an angle

The following is an example of how to plan an assignment from a Business Studies programme: 'An analysis of the operations management of a business of my choice' (2,000 words).

One way to approach this would be to concentrate on analysing the business by using some established models of operations management from the programme literature. You may then want to argue that the business you have chosen when assessed against these models has good and bad points with regards to its operations management. You may then want to make recommendations for improvements. This is a plan! You now have an angle!

Tips: Planning the assignment. You could use the approach outlined in Box 5.1 each time you write an assignment, ticking the steps off as you go.

Box 5.1

Step	Words (2,000)	Step completed ✓
1 Do a 'thoughts map' to capture the main ideas you have and want to cover in the plan	X	
2 Find references that will back up the points you are making as you follow your plan and note these on the thoughts map	X	
3 Divide the plan up into sections and assign words from the total wordage for each section	X	
4 Ensure you have an introduction explaining your approach to the topic	200	
5 Describe your reason for doing this (e.g. type of company chosen and rationale for choice of company)	300	
6 Introduce your theoretical models (one or two should be sufficient – explain why these models are helpful for your analysis)	300	
7 Analyse the object of the study using the models (e.g. use them to highlight strengths and weaknesses of the company). You can pull in some other references from the literature at this point	600	
8 Make suggestions for improvements, each time with a rationale and any references for ideas you have borrowed	400	
9 Conclude summarising your overall findings and clearly stating your point of view on the company and what needs doing	200	
10 Bibliography – to include all books and articles you have referred to in the assignment	Not in word count	
11 Appendices – examples or evidence of anything you refer to in the main text. Use appendices to back up your points	Not in word count	

The 'So what?' test

When you reread anything you have written (or indeed that others have written) it is useful, after each paragraph, to ask yourself the 'So what?' question. You can ask yourself:

- How does this paragraph help the general argument I am making?
- How does it link to the paragraph before it and after it?
- How does the information I am providing help the reader understand my point?

If you cannot answer this it is probably best to cut it out – it may be you are putting in irrelevant information, or going off theme and confusing the reader.

Exercise

Look at the following and undertake the 'So what?' test. As part of some social research a student has decided to undertake a piece of small-scale research to find out from fellow students *if there is a marked gender divide over their television viewing habits undertaken in the evenings*. He designs a questionnaire with the following questions. Analyse his questionnaire design using the 'So what?' test:

Question	Does this pass the 'So what?' test	Yes/no + Comment
Name		
Nationality		
Age		
Gender		
Number of hours of TV viewing per day		
Type of programmes watched starting with most watched (list three)		

Question: What conclusions do you draw from running the 'So what?' test over his questionnaire design?

Comment: The student is collecting data that is true, but the student's stated angle (their interest and what they want to find out) is if gender influences TV viewing habits. Let's look at the questions that are being asked: Name? Why are names being collected as data? This is only useful if the student wants to find them again for more follow-up questions. Nationality? Again how does this pass the 'So what?' test? It does not! The research project does not state it is investigating nationality as a variable for viewing habit – so why collect this information? In fact the only identity tag that needs to be collected is 'gender'. This is essential for the aims of the research! The final two questions are also relevant and pass the 'So what?' test.

The process of academic writing

Exercise

The points in Table 5.19 may help you with understanding the process of academic writing at university level in the UK. Put them in the correct order

Table 5.19 The process of academic writing at university level in the UK

1	Write a draft of the assignment making sure that each time you make claims about facts or make recommendations or criticisms you have a reference to an idea that supports you
2	Read and analyse the title of the assignment you have been given by your teacher, making sure you understand the key words and concepts in the title
3	Re-read the assignment correcting mistakes, and using the 'So what?' test. This may lead to rearranging sections – cutting and pasting or deleting parts that are not relevant
4	Plan your assignment (maybe doing a thought map) and think of the balance of words from the word count and the logical line of thought you will employ to structure it
5	Undertake reading in the topic area, making sure you look at key recommended texts
6	Think of a position that you want to argue or an approach to the subject that you will follow (find an angle)
7	Take notes on key ideas that the reading suggests to you and make sure you note where you read the ideas so that you can later reference them

Suggested order: 5, 7, 2, 6, 4, 1, 3

Tip: Fresh eyes. It is a good idea to have someone else read your draft assignment before you write up the final version. This is perfectly valid. Why not form a self-help group with other students so that you can read each others' drafts and comment on each others' work?

Note: Using tutors to check assignments. It is not generally fair to present your teacher with a draft version for comment, especially if this is not something offered to all students on a programme. The teacher, after all, is the person who assesses (judges) your work and grades it. You should have had enough guidance and input from lectures, seminars, classes, discussions and bibliographies to do the assignment.

Referencing

Question: Are you using your sources or are your sources using you? Who is in control?

Stop and think: Look at the following statements. To what extent do you agree with them?

- 'There is no such thing as an original idea: all "new" ideas are based on other ideas that have influenced you.'
- 'Originality is mostly about putting old ideas together in new ways.'
- 'All art is 1% inspiration and 99% perspiration.'

Note: If you do agree with any of these statements, then you see why you need to reference ideas!

Exercise

Look at the following piece of text that you have read from an article published in 2008 by Dr Abigail Spok entitled: 'Internet communications, customer perceptions of quality and the need for speed of response in high involvement purchase contexts'. It is from a collection of articles in an edited book called *'The E-consumer: New Demands on old Systems'* by Roger Galloway and Peter Benetti:

> The internet potentially allows for personalisation and customisation. In high involvement purchases, such as an international education, potential customers (i.e. prospects) increasingly demand to be individually catered for and be involved in personalised two-way communication as part of the decision making process for purchase. New technology allows for this demand to grow. Simply being offered a prospectus or a webpage to browse does not satisfy this demand. A noticeable trend in university customer relations' departments is, therefore, an increasing number of enquiries from prospects arriving by e-mail. This puts additional strain on university communications' systems (p. 203).

Reading this you have noted the new idea that increasing e-mail use in the world is putting non-personalised information presentation methods under strain. You want to be honest about where you got this idea from, to show that you have read relevant literature and also to cite others as this strengthens your point.

Question: How can you go about referencing this idea?

There are two ways:

You can do a *primary reference* in the following way:

> The use of e-mail is putting new demands on customer relationship systems (CRM), as Spok states:
>
> The internet potentially allows for personalisation and customisation. In high involvement purchases, such as an international education, potential customers (i.e. prospects) increasingly demand to be individually catered for and be involved in personalised two-way communication as part of the decision making process for purchase.
>
> (Spok, A. 2008, p. 203)

Or you can do a *secondary reference*, which sums up what someone else says:

> The use of e-mail is putting new demands on CRM systems. As Spok (2008, p. 203) points out, customers expect tailored responses to their enquiries about the products, especially for complex and expensive products.

Tip: Secondary references have the advantage of taking up fewer words, show that you have read and digested ideas and are using them for your own purpose and also ensure that you use your own words.

WARNING!

Primary references involve copying other people's words and run the danger of including irrelevant words and ideas, being too long and of not using your own words – which runs a risk of plagiarism if not done skilfully.

Advice: Try to use more secondary references than primary references and if you do use primary references, make sure they are not longer than three lines in length.

Information: referencing and the bibliography

Here are the rules of what *not* to do. Transform each one into a rule for what to do!

- Put all the books you have read on the subject in the bibliography even if you do not refer to them in your work
- Only write the following information: names of authors, dates of publication and titles of the works read
- Forget to put a work cited in your assignment in the bibliography
- Do not follow the conventions for referencing required by your teachers on your course (e.g. the Harvard system)
- Add a few books into the bibliography by some famous and relevant authors you have not read, to make the bibliography look good
- Do not have the works cited placed in alphabetical order

Advice: To keep your understanding of the main things you must do when undertaking an assignment it is useful to bear in mind the six concepts in Table 5.20.

Exercise

Table 5.20 The right question for the right concept

Concept		Question to ask yourself	
1	Focus	A	Do you support and back up your claims?
2	Practice	B	Are you citing works and using a bibliography accurately and carefully?
3	Signposting	C	Do you help the reader to follow your argument by using guidance language?
4	Evidence	D	Have you learnt, understood and used key expected models or calculations?
5	Referencing	E	Have you read through and corrected your work?
6	Proofreading	F	Are you answering the question asked?

Answers: 1, F; 2, D; 3, C; 4, A; 5, B; 6, E

Research and research skills

When you work by yourself, a lot of what you do is finding out information by yourself. This is called 'developing your research skills'. This section is particularly important for you if you are coming onto a research programme or if you have to undertake a piece of research on your programme. This might be at a later stage in your programme, maybe in Year 3 on an undergraduate programme or the final stage of a Masters. You may wish to read this section later on in your studies when this is the case.

Stop and think: People often talk of research skills. Let's think about what this means. Look at the following two definitions:

1. Any gathering of data, information and facts for the advancement of knowledge.
2. Performing a methodical study in order to prove a hypothesis (a statement of fact) or answer a specific question. Finding a definitive answer is the central goal of any experimental process.

Do you agree with both of these? Which definition do you most agree with?

Comment: You will find that the first definition is a general one that fits with most approaches to research across all disciplines. The second one is more specific to scientific research.

Exercise

Look at the list of skills for undertaking research in Table 5.21 and do a self-audit (analysis of which ones you are already good at and which ones you need to develop). Use a tick ✓ to assess your level for each skill. You will then first need to attend to and develop Level 1 then Level 2 and finally refine your Level 3 competences (skills).

Table 5.21 Assessing my skills level

Skill	Level 1 (need to find out about)	Level 2 (can benefit from some improvement)	Level 3 (competent)
Using a university library			
Understanding and using bibliographies			
Using the Internet to search for information			
Skim reading to find relevant information in books/articles			
Note-taking and record keeping			

Understanding the research process and following a research plan			
Gathering information from people (interviewing)			
Questionnaire design			
Understanding statistics			
Using statistical software packages			
Time management			
Getting help from tutors/supervisors			
Understanding your own ideological outlook			

Stop and think: How would you identify yourself as a researcher? Read the following explanation.

Research traditionally falls into two approaches: *qualitative research* or *quantitative research*. Qualitative research is often used to find out people's subjective opinions and feelings – things that cannot be reduced to numbers (numeric data) easily. Quantitative research is used when dealing with numbers which can then be analysed using statistical methods. In fact both approaches are considered useful and can be used together (this is called *mixed methods*). This is because qualitative research can provide information about people's motivation and perspectives – i.e. the 'big picture' – and can help with the interpretation of data, and quantitative research methods and analysis can serve to make findings generalisable (less context-dependent). Quantitative research methods are important for science, which seeks general truths about the universe, but are not adequate for social research which may be about understanding a unique social situation and context and about the attitudes and perspectives of the people being researched. Research into unique contexts is often referred to as *case study* research.

WARNING!

When you are undertaking research at any level of study and especially if you are studying for a research degree (e.g. a postgraduate research qualification such as a doctorate), you will find that you tend towards a particular view of the nature of reality. Look at the two points of view expressed in Figure 5.8 – the 'voice of the positivist' and 'voice of the relativist'. You may be more sympathetic to one of them than the other. It is crucially important that you choose supervisors with whom you have a basic understanding and agreement on this ideological issue. If you agree with a positivistic view you will not enjoy being supervised by a supervisor with a relativistic view and vice versa! It is for this reason that you need to understand and be able to explain your basic stance (outlook) on this issue in any research proposal you put forward.

At PhD level it is also essential to ensure that ideologically sympathetic external and internal examiners are selected for assessing and judging your dissertation submission and conducting your viva voce! Your supervisors should help you with this selection.

Tip: How can you check if a potential supervisor is compatible with your views?

A very important way is for you to do your own research on the proposed supervisors (you will have two, the most important one being the first, but the second can be vital for you too if you find you do not get on with the first supervisor at some stage). Every PhD supervisor will have had to publish research work in academic journals or will have written academic books, otherwise they are unlikely to be appointed as a doctoral level research supervisor. Read some of what they have published and see if you are sympathetic to the approach they have taken in their research.

Question: Who do you feel more in sympathy with: the positivist or the relativist? Or do you find this more complex? Do you think that maybe both have good points? Look at the extreme positions of each of them expressed in Figure 5.8.

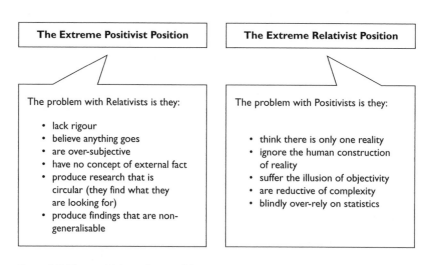

Figure 5.8 The positivist–relativist debate.

Note: As explained above – for all students, even those not undertaking a postgraduate research degree, a major part of self-study depends on the skill of accessing the right information for your studies. This is a key research skill and it needs to be developed by all university level students.

Stop and think: Where can you find information relevant to your programme of study?

Exercise

Use of information sources. Here is a list of possible sources of useful information for your programme. In each case decide if you know how to use the source well ✓, or if you need training ✓

Information source	Understand and can use	Need training
Library		
Internet		
Course handbook and recommended reading lists		
Course tutor(s)/teacher(s)		
Virtual learning environment (VLE)		

Information: using the library

It is probably true that many students do not learn how to use the library on the university campus properly. A library may seem a confusing, complex and frightening place! You should not however, feel intimidated and embarrassed if you do not know how to use the library. For many students a UK university is the first time that they have had a big library to use and it is normal to feel confused and worried when you have to use a new system for the first time. University libraries offer introductory tours and have helpdesks with people trained to show you how to use them. This is their job and you should make sure you approach these people to help you fully understand how to use your library as early as possible in your studies.

Library pitfalls

- Loan periods: you take out books on short loans (three-day or seven-day), don't realise this and then get fined for being late in returning them.

Solution: Always make sure you check the loan period when you take out books and note the date to return the books in your diary/on your mobile phone.

- Key texts (important books) are all out on loan: in order to secure the important books you need to read, you need to understand and use the library booking system for reserving them.

Solution: Think ahead so that you reserve these books in time. If a key book is not available use the university inter-library loan system and check and understand your rights for using other university libraries in the country.

Cultural note: Librarians tend to be people who are very careful to treat everyone the same. When you have a fine to pay there is little possibility for the librarian to excuse (waive) the fine, no matter how good your excuse is!

Information: using the Internet

Doing searches on the Internet using key words can be extremely useful to gather ideas and new leads for finding further information. The Internet is a wonderful resource.

Internet pitfall

- The main problem with the Internet is also its strength: it is open to anyone to put up their ideas on all subjects. The difference between this and published texts is that such opinions have not usually been tested by others (by qualified peers) and so the information may be incorrect. A good example of Internet knowledge is Wikipedia where people can post whatever they know – this does not mean that this knowledge has been rigorously tested and may be nothing more than opinion. You will probably find that your teachers are not too keen on you using many Internet references in your work for this reason.

Information: using the course/programme handbook and recommended reading lists

Advice: Read the information you are provided with. Handbooks usually contain very useful information about what to do in various situations that may occur to you and how to generally get more out of your studies by using the various facilities the university offers you – facilities you may not otherwise find out about and fail to use.

Tip: One of the problems is the timing of when you first receive this information, which is usually at the beginning of your programme when you have just arrived: new students do tend to suffer from information overload in the first week when starting university. If it is too much to read in the first few days, make sure you find an hour one evening to read it through early in your studies. It will contain a lot of very useful and relevant information.

Reading lists

Reading lists can sometimes be rather long and off-putting. A good reading list from your programme director should break the recommended books down into 'key texts' and then more peripheral 'added interest' texts. If it is not clear what the 'must read' (essential) books are for your programme, make sure you get this information sorted out with your teacher by highlighting them on your list.

Advice: Although you should be able to obtain a copy of most of the books on the reading list in your university library, it is a good idea to buy the key texts (if you can afford to do so). With your own copies you can highlight sections and make notes in them, which is very helpful for assignment writing and for revising for exams.

Information: using tutors and lecturers

UK university teachers like to think of themselves as accessible and in contact with their students. Compared to many other university teachers and lecturers operating in university systems in the world this is generally true. An open door policy is a nice idea – but you do need to check what the reality of this offer of accessibility is. For example, is it clear how often you should or can reasonably take advantage of the open door? After all, university teaching staff are busy people and have a lot of academic and administrative functions to attend to.

Advice: Some programme handbooks may explain carefully exactly how much individual access you can expect from your programme teachers and where you should go for other help in the university (academic or welfare support). If you do not have clear information then it is best to ask your tutor(s)/teacher(s) so that you are clear about this and do not feel uncomfortable about this issue. The ground rules in Box 5.2 are useful for you to find out about and resolve. Try to fill in the resolutions (answers) early on in your studies!

Box 5.2	
Ground rule issue for using teacher support	*Resolution*
What is accepted as a reasonable amount of time for visiting programme teachers beyond timetabled slots?	
What sorts of issues are acceptable for you to use this access for?	
What level of help you can expect from a programme teacher?	
How can you make appointments – is this by e-mail, telephone or dropping in?	

Stop and think: Staff–student relationships. Ask yourself the following questions:

Question	Your thoughts
Is it right for your teacher to be your friend?	
Should you give gifts to your university teachers?	
To what extent is learning a shared responsibility between teacher and student?	

Culture note: friendship

WARNING!

There can be a problem if a relationship between a university teacher and a student goes beyond the professional contract of a teacher–student relationship. The main problem is that of 'equity' (equality of treatment for all students that the teacher teaches). This means a teacher must avoid favouritism and hence accusations of corruption. Because of this many universities have policies about this. Here is an example of a typical policy:

> *Guidelines on Personal Relationships between Students and Teachers, and Staff and Staff*
> The University does not wish to, nor can it, legislate against the development of personal relationships between staff and students, or staff and staff. However, two key principles must govern all such relationships:
>
> a)   there is no abuse of a position of power
> b)   all teaching or staff management must be (and be seen to be) unbiased.

WARNING!

Because staff and students are legally adults, they are free according to law to form the relationships they wish, however, professionally there is an expectation that this will be avoided. This is because of the issue of how the other students on a programme may feel if they know that their teacher is in a relationship with one of their fellow students. In other words, there are risks to the development of anything beyond a professional relationship, especially for staff.

A university may decide to investigate a staff member for professional misconduct if it is felt that the relationship has led to any form of bias (treating one student better than another) or if a staff member's position of power has been used to influence a relationship. The rules are in place for a reason: to ensure all students feel they get fair treatment.

Culture note: gift giving

WARNING!

In many cultures gift giving is accepted as part of the social way of doing things. In some cultures it is normal for students to give gifts to their teachers at the end of the academic year. In the UK, gift giving is complicated by the fact that it is often thought of as linked to bribery and corruption. In other words if a gift is given, then it is felt this is because something is expected in return. If a student gives a teacher a gift, the suspicion is that this is done because the student thinks that by doing this the teacher will be nicer when marking the student's work. Staff may feel this is a kind of emotional pressure being put on them by the student and feel uncomfortable with this.

Advice: The simplest thing to do is not give a gift. If you wish to express gratitude for a teacher's support and help, then the best way to do this is to send a card or a letter. Most universities also have a policy on the giving and receiving of gifts by their employees and provide guidance based on the fact that a gift must mean that it will not influence any decision by a member of staff. Here is an example of policy from a UK university:

> It is an offence under the Prevention of Corruption Act 1906 for members of staff to accept corruptly any gift or consideration as an inducement or reward for doing, or refraining from doing, anything in an official capacity or showing favour or disfavour to any person in an official capacity.

Common sense suggests that this is unlikely if the gift is a pen or a book compared to a free holiday for the lecturer and family on a tropical island owned by a student's parents, for example.

Learning point: If a staff member politely refuses a gift you offer, despite your intentions being honest, reading this explanation should mean that you will hopefully not be insulted or upset by this.

Using the virtual learning environment (VLE)

When you come to the UK to study in a university you will find that most university programmes combine face-to-face teaching with support from a VLE. This is the use of a software package such as Blackboard which is accessed by students and their teachers. You will be given a student computing ID and password to access the VLE and it is a good idea to make sure you understand and can use all the features of the VLE to support your programme of study. There will probably be training sessions offered for this by your department or the university. A study programme may mix face-to-face teaching with a VLE and when this occurs this is referred to as a 'blended approach'. When most of the programme, or even all of it, is delivered through a VLE, this is referred to as 'distance learning' (DL).

Exercise

VLE checklist. Box 5.3 contains a list of the features that a VLE may offer. Tick each one that your programme's VLE offers and tick each one you do not fully understand how to use. For the latter, make sure you receive training early in your programme so that you are able to take advantage of the features.

Box 5.3

Feature	Feature offered ✓	Training need ✓
The syllabus for the course with the relevant credit information and necessary reading lists		
Administrative information such as the programme timetable and information on how to get help		
Use of a notice board providing up-to-date course information		
The essential teaching materials. (These may be the complete content of the course in PDF format, or copies of lecture notes)		
Student registration and tracking facilities, showing your grades for courses/modules completed. (This may include course payment information and options)		
Additional resources: this may be extra reading materials and links to outside resources on the Internet and to virtual libraries		
Self-assessment tests for you to monitor your understanding and progress. These are usually scored automatically		

Explanation of the formal assessment procedures used to assess your work, with marking criteria		
Electronic communication support, including e-mail, threaded discussions (message boards) and a chat room		
Production of documentation and statistics on the course. This may show how your scores compare to the group average		

Information: distance learning

Distance learning (DL) is a method of programme delivery that is growing in popularity with many UK universities. Certain universities in the UK have a lot of expertise in DL provision: for example the University of London has been offering DL since 1858 and the Open University, the largest university in the UK, founded in 1969, is a world leader in this method of teaching and learning – using mixed media and Internet delivery. The programmes offered by these and other university providers are available at a distance in many countries.

Useful website: As an example of what is available visit the following site of the Open University: http://www3.open.ac.uk/study

WARNING!

Distance learning is not an easy option and it is not a suitable way of learning for everyone. It is a good idea to make sure what it involves and if it is right for you before you enroll on a DL programme. To help you with this look at the following exercise.

Exercise

Look at the aspects of DL listed in Box 5.4 and decide which are advantages (+) and which are disadvantages (−) for you

Box 5.4

Aspect of DL as a methodology for my learning	+ or −
Individualisation: it is a methodology that can allow you to focus on your own particular specialist areas of interest	
You need to be very organised, disciplined and self-motivated	
Flexibility: you can study and continue in your job at the same time. It is up to you to decide when you study	
You can combine family life with studying	
You do not have the social aspect that face-to-face learning provides	
You may be required to attend special testing centres to undertake examinations in controlled settings	
Language: you can study without worrying about your spoken English as you have time to look up words and grammatical phrases	
You are required to have an up-to-date Internet connection and laptop, especially for any type of synchronous activity (e.g. web-conferencing, in which you and your fellow DL students are required all to be present at the same time)	
Cost: the programme is cheaper because you can study from home without the costs of travel, visas, accommodation and food that face-to-face tuition requires	
Materials: many of the materials are up to date and coordinated because the programmes and materials are designed by specialists	
You will probably not have easy access to a fully stocked library with all the key texts in it, but will have to find a local library or buy texts online and use the DL provider's virtual online library	

You need to be proficient and confident with the Internet and other new technologies	
You do not have the personal contact with your tutors and other students that face-to-face teaching offers. It can be very lonely!	

Note: DL can be a tough form of learning because you need to be self-sufficient and disciplined to be able to maintain your motivation and put in the necessary hours of study each week. You will usually be provided with a tutor and your relationship with your tutor is very important, as this may be your main source of motivation. You may find that an e-mail relationship is not as easy to develop as a face-to-face one and there is room for misunderstanding people's tone and intentions with e-mails. Skyping may be better as you can see the facial expressions of the other person. You may also find that it is difficult to have open discussions with your fellow students if you do not know them personally in any way: everyone may be cautious about expressing their views as they do not really know each other and whether anyone will take offence at anything said. People may be worried about 'flaming' – hostile and aggressive Internet messages occurring because of emotional reactions. Your tutor, who may act as the discussion board moderator, needs to be quite skilled to maintain useful discussions among the different students in order to develop interesting and worthwhile conversations among them and this does not always occur.

Suggestion: Why not form a self-help group with any other students who are also doing the DL programme and who live in your region? It is very reassuring to discover that the problems and issues you have are also shared by others!

Thinking it through again

You completed this exercise at the beginning of this chapter. It is repeated here for you to see if your views have changed in any way from having undertaken the reading and exercises in this chapter. Cultural values can be very deeply held and so it may be that you still have the same outlook as previously. On the other hand, this chapter may have made you reassess those values. The important thing is that you should now be aware of these values and views and be better placed to understand the challenges that the UK university education system may present you with.

Look at the following views and tick the ones you agree with:

1   It is the job of the teachers to be experts in the subjects they teach and to tell students what they need to know.   ❏

2   The main job of a teacher is to show students how to discover facts for themselves and to give them the opportunity to do so.   ❏

3   There are no right and wrong answers to questions: facts are not fixed but rather interpretations. 'Correct' answers are therefore, in reality, simply good arguments.   ❏

4   It is the job of students to listen to teachers' ideas, take notes from the teachers, learn the ideas and then repeat them in exams.   ❏

5   Learning is about being given the right facts and memorising them.   ❏

6   The real aim of a university education is to show students how to find things out rather than to tell them what to know.   ❏

7   When students fail a course it is because they do not work hard enough.   ❏

Commentary: If you have ticked any of boxes 1, 4 and 5 you may have problems understanding the general UK approach to learning. Your beliefs are for a traditional approach to learning – often referred to in teaching as the 'jug and glass method' – with the teacher being a jug pouring water (knowledge) into an empty glass (the student). Many teachers do not believe in this and believe that learning is something that occurs when learners are active themselves and seek their own knowledge. There is a belief that a learner is never an empty glass and that it is important to build on the knowledge a learner already has. There is also no belief in modern education that there is a right set of answers to everything – rather there is a belief that there are many possible different right answers to questions, so teaching one set of answers would be restrictive and not justified.

If you have ticked boxes 2, 3 and 6 then you are probably more in tune with the philosophy of education you will encounter in the UK – although probably not all the time and not with every subject teacher – variety exists! However, you will be able to better understand the reason for research and argument and the general lack of value placed on rote learning and memorisation. It is true that some subjects seem to offer themselves better to the 'right and wrong answer' approach – natural science subjects and medicine may seem to lend themselves more to this – but of course, if that were the whole story there would be no advances and no new research to make those advances. The history of science and medicine is that of proving current theories wrong. This is not to say that basic facts need to be rediscovered in each class, but that a spirit of critical thinking and enquiry needs to be developed in all learners for future progress in the discipline to happen.

Chapter 6

Understanding the university academic structure and system

Introduction

It would be unusual to purchase an expensive new car without understanding how it works or having a guide as to what the different functions of the car are and how to use them. However, many international students purchase a UK university education without ever really understanding how the university works, why it works in the way it does, what is available to them, and when and where to go for help.

This section of the guide is designed to help you, as an international student, understand the basic academic structure of a British university and how you fit into and can use this.

Note: All universities differ: for example, some may be structured into faculties and departments, others into schools and colleges.

Faculties are administrative groupings of similar or related departments. A common faculty title is: 'Faculty of Arts and Humanities'. Within this there may a number of departments such as the Department of Modern Languages or the Department of Music. Each faculty has a Head of Faculty to which each Head of Department reports. The Head of Faculty often oversees the departmental finances. In a university that has a college system, such as the University of Oxford, each college is an independent unit within the umbrella of the university and runs its own academic and administrative systems. A school, such as the school of business, is also a semi-independent unit within a university. The heads of the various faculties, colleges and schools form what is called the University Senate or Senior Management team. They hold meetings (often in Senate House) to discuss and plan the overall management of the university and its policies.

In fact, different words are often used to refer to basically the same things. Universities all have the same basic features. This chapter introduces you to these. By understanding how the academic side of the university is designed and functions, you will be in a better position to better understand your studies.

Academic structure and systems

This section begins by explaining the general approach (ethos) to university study and education normally found in UK universities. It then looks at the structure of the education you receive, from practical timetabling to explaining how the teaching programme is designed and delivered to you. It also explains how you are assessed.

General ethos of UK university study

Creating independent, self-motivated learners

A major challenge for many students when they enter a university in the UK is that of becoming a self-motivated and self-directed student. Responsibility for learning and for planning your studies lies largely with you! If you are used to being told exactly what to study for homework and when and where to study each day, you may, at first, find a lack of structure (someone telling you and controlling this) difficult. Learning to be in charge of your own learning and planning when you study can be challenging if you are expecting this control and direction from someone else. It is also difficult to know what books you should read and what ideas you should present in your assessed assignments. Again, although you will be given a booklist of recommended books, you will not be told exactly which books you should read and what quotes and ideas you should present in the assignments – this again is up to you. In other words, you are the person who needs to decide what ideas you are to develop and present.

Not realising that you are alone in this, and thinking that you will be controlled and directed can lead to problems. It means that at first you may feel that university study in the UK is too easy: instead of going to classes from 9:00 a.m. to 5:00 p.m. each day, you only have several hours of class to attend. No one seems to be too worried if you skip (miss) a class either (apart from reasons of control for your visa conditions).

WARNING!

This of course is a false conclusion to draw, because if you allow time to pass without keeping on top of the reading, the class discussions and the work you should be doing under your own direction, you will fall behind and not have the time to catch up later. Remember that because university study in the UK involves continuous assessment and not just final exams each year, you cannot relax during the term and think you will be able to 'cram' study in a couple of weeks to catch up before the end of year exams. You usually need to be studying continuously and handing in assignments throughout the year!

To be successful in your studies at a UK university you *must* be in control of your own learning and your own motivation. In other words, your motivation must be internal (intrinsic).

<table>
<tr><td colspan="2">Reflective exercise: Look at the following statements and decide which are true for you:</td></tr>
<tr><td>Statement</td><td>✓</td></tr>
<tr><td>I expect my teacher to tell me what to read, when to read it and what to say about what I have read</td><td></td></tr>
<tr><td>I expect to be in class most of the day and to be told off by the teacher if I do not go class</td><td></td></tr>
<tr><td>I do not feel comfortable if I am told that it is up to me what I read and how I feel personally about what I have read</td><td></td></tr>
<tr><td>I do not like being told what I should read and what I should think about what I have read</td><td></td></tr>
<tr><td>I prefer to plan my own day of study and to set up meetings with colleagues and tutors according to my own need</td><td></td></tr>
<tr><td>I like to experiment with new ideas and new ways of learning. I realise that doing this means I may at times get things wrong</td><td></td></tr>
</table>

Commentary: If you ticked the first three statements you will need to think about how you adapt to the UK university view of studying, which is more in line with the final three statements. Of course this may vary according to subject and the level of study you are undertaking.

Note: Levels of study. HE Level 1 is the first year of university study (known officially as NQF Level 4). At this level you are introduced to key theories and ideas: i.e. to fundamental and accepted theories and approaches in your subject. As you progress to Level 2 (NQF Level 5) and Level 3 (NQF Level 6), you are expected to become increasingly self-directed and critical in your thinking. This means you do not simply accept and apply key theories, but evaluate them yourself and question their relevance to various situations.

Note: Passing or failing your programme of study. One of the biggest worries and sources of stress for students is the fear of failing their studies. There should be some reassurance for you in knowing that in the UK it is generally expected that once a student has been accepted into a university, the university will do what it can to ensure the student does not fail. High failure rates in a university are seen as a bad sign for a university – it may indicate that the university doesn't recruit the right kind of students, or does not provide the right kind of support or care for its students. Academics whose students are failing may worry that their teaching is not effective. Indeed the Quality Assurance Agency (QAA) would look seriously at a university that had a higher than average failure rate (students not passing) or drop-out rate (students not continuing at the university) among its students.

Cultural issue: Intercultural competence of teachers. It is important for you to realise that a university has a responsibility to you if it has accepted you as an international student onto one of its programmes. A good university, with interculturally experienced and competent lecturers, understands that you, as an international student, will not immediately fully understand what is expected of you, and that you will have different approaches to learning and points of view to British students. This is because of your educationally distinct background and culture. They will realise you need to go through a period of learning and adjustment because of this. For this reason you may be invited onto a pre-sessional study skills course before your main programme begins. This is designed to help you with this adjustment. Alternatively you may be offered a module called 'Study skills' to study alongside your main study programme.

Lecturers with little experience of international students, or lecturers who are not interculturally competent, may expect you to react to and understand everything from the same point of view as the British or any other groups of students they are used to teaching. They may not realise and understand the need for this period of adjustment.

Advice: It is essential that you let your tutor know if you do not understand something important. This is much better than pretending that you understand and that everything is fine. The earlier you make this clear, the better.

Always remember that the university offered you a place based on your previous study profile and that you are therefore considered by the university to be intellectually suitable for the programme you are on. You should not begin to doubt yourself or lose your motivation if you are unfortunate enough to have an inexperienced or culturally insensitive teacher. Remember teachers are also human and need to learn about other cultures too.

Note: External verification of grades. Teachers cannot, of course, pass students who do not perform to required educational standards (who do not achieve the stated learning outcomes for the level of study of the programme being offered) as monitored by the QAA. Universities that do this will be subject to government investigation and possible sanctions (financial penalties). To check that a university is not awarding passes or good grades to students who do not merit these grades, every programme awards its end-of-year grades to students through an exam board. A key member of the exam board is the external examiner(s), whose job it is to ensure that grades are being awarded in line with external criteria and in a manner comparable to other universities teaching the same courses on similar programmes. The external examiner is usually an academic teaching in the same field of study. This person writes a report for the university on their findings, with recommendations for improvement. The external examiner will often want to meet and talk to students to gather their perspectives on the programme. The recommendations presented in the external examiner's report need to be acted upon and shown to have been acted upon by the department concerned, as this will be checked by any future QAA inspection team.

The external examiner is also sent a sample of students' work for a particular course of a programme: this is usually 10 per cent of the work and represents the top grades awarded and the bottom grades awarded, plus any borderline cases. If marks are seen to be too high or low compared to the general university sector standard, there may then be a process of adjustment of grades. For this reason you should always consider that the grade you are at first given by your teacher may not necessarily be the final official grade! It is likely to be, but it may legally be changed at an exam board. You grades are only official after they have been approved by the exam board (which convenes at the end of each year's examination period).

Note: World approaches to education. There are many different philosophies and approaches to education in the world. Perhaps the biggest difference that can be observed can be explained by the concepts of the 'pyramid' and 'box' approaches to university education.

The pyramid system

Explanation: The pyramid. This is a university system in which anyone with the necessary school leaving examination grades is allowed into a state university to study. However, the process is one of survival of the fittest, with a high percentage of students being failed in Year 1 and in Year 2. This leads to high drop-out rates. Students who fail usually leave with no formal qualification to show for their studies and time. Characteristics of the pyramid are:

- lecture teaching mode with lecturers lecturing to hundreds of students at a time (especially in Year 1)

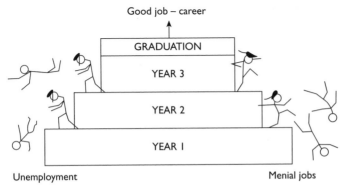

Figure 6.1 The pyramid system of higher education.

- students are required to learn and not question the 'received wisdom' of the lecturer
- little interaction between students and academic teachers
- little group work and shared learning experiences
- an attitude that responsibility for learning rests only with the student
- little learning support provided to the student
- libraries tend to be small and badly furnished
- students are expected to buy their own course books
- student failure is seen as the students' problem.

The box system

Explanation: The box. This is a system in which universities tend to control whom they select – as well as stating various entry grades, they may require interviews and use these to judge who to accept onto programmes. Once students are in the university and studying, they are monitored for signs of difficulty and study support is provided if necessary. At the end of each year it is expected that there will be little more than 5 per cent of students dropping out or failing in total (this is called 'natural' attrition). Students who fail modules and hence the academic year of study can take resits before the next year begins to have a second chance to continue without having to repeat the year. Some universities may offer two resit opportunities!

Universities may also offer concessions for students who are ill or are experiencing other life problems. This means that these circumstances are taken into consideration and exam results may be adjusted accordingly. In the box university system there is usually a big emphasis on library services and student support systems, as well as a system of personal tutors. There is usually also a system of

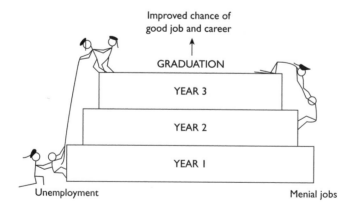

Figure 6.2 The box system of higher education.

diagnostic and formative testing to spot any problems students may have and be able to intervene and help them. In such systems big lectures are not as frequent as classes and classes tend to be small. Seminars and tutorials are also common. Teachers (academics) get to know their students and interaction between teachers and students is normal.

Note: Of course education systems can be a mix of the box and the pyramid – it is unlikely that a university system is exclusively one or the other. It is also true that the more money you pay for your studies, the more likely you are to enter the box system and the less likely you are to be content with entering a pyramid system.

Flexibility of study and study pathway

Another difference in approaches to university education that can cause confusion for students coming to the UK is that of the relative flexibility of their studies. In other words, the extent to which students can select what they study and when they can study various subjects, or the extent to which they are controlled as to what they can study and when they can study by the university system they are in.

WARNING!

In the UK, learning programmes are often designed with fairly tight controls, so that you can only study Y after you have studied X. This is because programmes are designed with learning outcomes (statements about what you have proved you can do after studying on a programme). These are assessed. Only once you have proven you have achieved the learning outcomes for X can you then undertake Y! It is also often the case that in Year 1 you need to study a course that forms the basis of the second part of the same course in Year 2. This means that you cannot do the Year 2 course before the Year 1 course (i.e. the Year 1 course is called a prerequisite for the Year 2 course).

Of course universities will vary again as to how they generally structure learning on their courses: some will be very rigid about the order of study of subjects, the order of the levels of study and the content of various modules that are accepted as part of a given degree award.

Note: UK universities also have strict rules over the number of times a student can repeat a part of a year (a course or module) and how long a degree can last. This emphasis on the progression of learning and the tight control of the order and content of study of a programme means that UK programmes are not as flexible as many other university programmes in the world. In many countries, and especially with the European Credit Transfer System (ECTS) that is developing in the European Higher Education Area (EHEA), the order of study is not seen as so rigidly important. Rather, a student accumulates a certain number of credits each year to be able to graduate. In such a system the student can elect to do a variety of programmes each year, or repeat courses over a number of years to build up the credits for the final award.

Teaching block approach (semesters or terms)

Many UK universities operate a system of terms rather than semesters. Some operate a dual system of semesters and terms.

In a semester system there are two main blocks of study (semesters) in a year. At the end of each semester there is a system of assessment (usually exams) and students are awarded credits for half a year of study. An undergraduate programme is typically comprised of six semesters' worth of study. The EHEA system of study (often referred to as 'the Bologna Process') requires that in each semester there should be an offer of 30 ECTS credits worth of study. Any programmes that a student fails and does not get credits for can be retaken – often in the next semester so that the missing credits can be obtained. It is not a prerequisite to obtain all 30 ECTS (pass all courses) in semester 1 to be allowed to study programmes in semester 2. In some universities using this system, students can also do more than 30 ECTS credits in a semester if they wish to and can often take courses from different semester blocks at the same time and finish their studies quicker – or, alternatively, they may decide to take longer and work at the same time or interrupt their studies to travel. This is a very flexible system. Not many universities in the UK structure their studies to allow for such flexibility. In the UK the approach is more 'lock-step' – in that all students are expected to progress and study the same things at the same time.

Typical UK division of undergraduate academic year (30–32 weeks of study) by terms

September–December	January–March	April–June
Term 1 (12 weeks)	Term 2 (10–12 weeks)	Term 3 (8–10 weeks)
Continuous assessment plus end-of-year exams for 120 UK credits (60 ECTS)		

Typical division of undergraduate academic year by semesters

September*–January	February–June
Semester 1 (15–16 weeks)	Semester 2 (15–16 weeks)
Continuous assessment and end of semester exams for 60 UK credits (30 ECTS)	Continuous assessment and end of semester exams for 60 UK credits (30 ECTS)

*Some universities may prefer to begin their first semester of the academic year in August so that there is no interruption of studies for the Christmas break in December). Semester 2 may then end earlier for the summer vacation.

Usual academic breaks

Christmas holidays	Easter holidays	Summer holidays
Mid-December–early January (3–4 weeks)	Varies: usually end of March and first part of April (2–3 weeks)	Mid-June–late September (12–14 weeks)

Note: *Reading weeks.* As well as the above three holiday periods, there is often a reading week (a week without timetabled classes) half way through each term or semester.

Understanding your study programme

When you enrol on a programme of study you will find that there are various words that describe different parts of the programme. It is important to know how to talk about and understand what these parts of your study programme are.

When you choose to study something you first choose a *subject* area, e.g. 'engineering' or 'law'. You then choose a specific aspect of this, e.g. civil or mechanical engineering or international or contract law. This is then called your *programme of study.*

As well as words to describe what you study, you will also come across words to describe how your study is organised into smaller units, e.g. *module, session, course* or *programme.* This can be a little confusing and so the next exercise is designed to help you understand these terms.

Exercise

Programme of study – vocabulary exercise. Read the following paragraph and place the words in bold from below in the right spaces. You can use the glossary at the end of the book to help you.

A _____ is an area of study (e.g. sociology or business studies). A _____ is an aspect of this, e.g. marketing, which can be studied to achieve an award, e.g. BA, BSc. A _____ is an assessed part of this, which carries a set amount of credits, e.g. internet marketing, these may be joined together and be taught as a _____ and this is taught either intensively over a short time (as a block) or over the whole academic year (a strand) as a regular timetabled slot. When you are studying you will need to go to classes and each timetabled slot/period is referred to as a _____ .

Figure 6.3 The vocabulary of study programmes.

Answers: subject; programme; course; module; session.

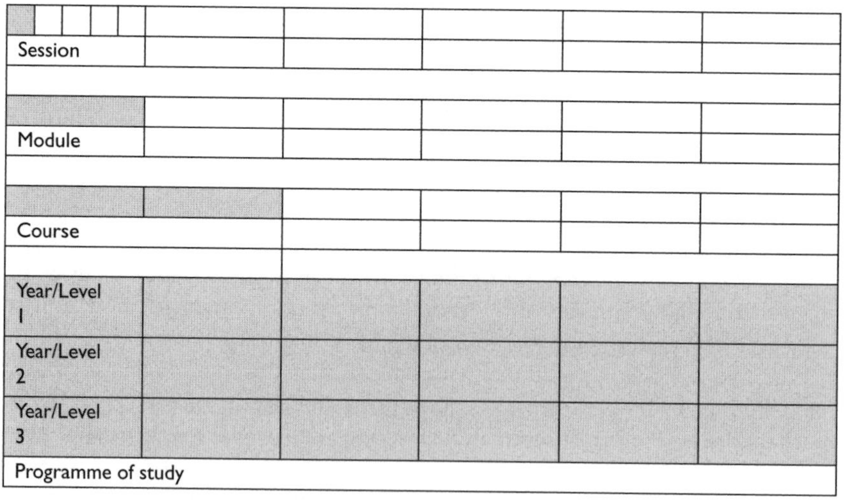

Session					
Module					
Course					
Year/Level 1					
Year/Level 2					
Year/Level 3					
Programme of study					

Figure 6.4 How units of study are combined.

Note: A problem is that many people mix these terms up!

Planning your day and managing your time: introduction

One very important skill that as a student you need to develop is the ability to organise yourself independently and plan the use of your time well (you need 'time management' skills). Responsibility for this is left to you. You should not expect someone to give you a clear guide about how you spend your time as this is up to you. This may be very different from what you have been used to before and you may feel a bit lost at first as it seems you do not have a clear timetable and structure to follow. In fact, much learning in UK universities is based on the idea of self-directed learning and not timetabled classroom time. This section looks at how you can manage your university time.

Look at the typical weekly timetable for a university programme in Figure 6.5.

Explanation: There are various methods of study used in UK universities. These can be lectures, classes, seminars and tutorials. (These are explained in greater depth in Chapter 5.) For practical and experience-based courses there may also be laboratory practicums, or placement days in professional organisations outside the university.

Stop and think: Count up the total number of timetabled study hours in your week. The example shows 15 hours per week. It is quite usual not to have more than this. The question is whether this means that you only study 15 hours per week? The answer is a clear 'No': it is estimated that you need to study outside of

	9:00–11:00	11:00–1:00		2:00–4:00	4:00–6:00	6:00–8:00
Monday	Seminar			Class		
Tuesday		Group tutorial	L U N C H T I M E			
Wednesday	Individual tutorial	Class			Class	
Thursday				Group work		
Friday		Lecture				

Figure 6.5 A typical weekly undergraduate timetable.

	9:00–11:00		11:00–1:00		2:00–4:00	4:00–6:00	6:00–8:00
Monday	Seminar		Researching vocabulary in the library		Class		Academic English support class
Tuesday	Self-study in library preparing for group tutorial		Group tutorial	L U N C H T I M E	Going to study support centre to run through last assignment		Reading in room
Wednesday	Individual tutorial	Running through tutorial notes	Class		Researching my assignment in the library		Class
Thursday	Writing my assignment				Group work	Preparing my part of presentation for seminar	
Friday	Re-meeting with classmates to run through group presentation		Lecture				

Figure 6.6 An extended typical weekly undergraduate timetable.

class even more hours than you study in class. Look at the same timetable in Figure 6.6 now that self-directed time is included.

Question: You now have a 36-hour study week! What do you think is missing from this week for a balanced student life? Have a look at the timetable again.

	9:00–11:00		11:00–1:00		2:00–4:00	4:00–6:00	7:00–9:00
Monday	Seminar		Researching vocabulary in the library		Class	Gym visit	Academic English support class
Tuesday	Self-study in library preparing for group tutorial		Group tutorial	L U N C H T I M E	Going to study support centre to run through last assignment		Reading in room
Wednesday	Individual tutorial	Running through tutorial notes	Class		Researching my assignment in the library		Class
Thursday	Writing my assignment				Group work	Preparing my part of presentation for seminar	
Friday	Re-meeting with classmates to run through group presentation		Lecture		Football practice		Working in student bar 7:30–11:00

Figure 6.7 The final weekly undergraduate timetable.

You should also think of keeping fit and perhaps earning some extra pocket money. Have another look at the timetable. Is there something still missing from your university experience? To help you consider, think about the following English expression: 'All work and no play made Jack a dull boy' (and the same applies to Jill!).

Advice: When you first looked at your timetable it seemed you had a lot of spare time. But now that you have added in the self-study and extra-curricular activities the question is when can you relax and have fun? To be happy at university it is important to balance your study time with social activities. It is a good idea to build your social life into your timetable. You can start by deciding which night(s) it is sensible to go out and party. Many students try to keep Friday and Saturday nights free for this. Looking at the final timetable above, why do you think it is not a good idea to go out late on Tuesday night?

Suggestion: One of the first things you should do at university is design a timetable and pin it on your notice board in your room. A key to happiness at university and to successful study is effective time management and this is a vital first step!

Information: assessment methods

There are two main ways of assessing your work. These are coursework and examinations. Coursework is the work you do during the year: usually through handing in assignments that are marked. Most programmes award a mix of credits for both methods of assessment.

Stop and think: Which method of assessment do you prefer? Which do you do better at? Why?

Look at the following comments from international students:

Student A: I prefer examinations because I don't like having to continually produce work for assessment throughout the year. I like to have rest periods where I just read or do other things. Coursework is not good for my work–life balance! I prefer to cram for examinations. I'm prepared to sit up all night memorising important ideas and concepts for exams. I have a good memory and I need to have the adrenalin of exam conditions to push me to do my best.

Student B: I prefer coursework because I get very nervous if I have to do sit-down exams. My mind goes blank and I panic. It is not fair. I like to take my own time to do work and check things carefully before I hand it in.

Reflective question: Are you more like student A or B?

Have you checked how you will be assessed on your programme of study? It may be important for you to know this! Many programmes combine both types of assessment – coursework and examinations – and many programmes balance this at 50/50. Check what the balance is for your programme. It is better to be prepared than unpleasantly surprised!

Information: types of assignments

Exercise

Match the assessment type to the definition in Box 6.1 and then rate each one according to how much you like it as a method.

Box 6.1		
Assessment type	Definition	Rating 10 = love it! 0 = hate it!
1 The essay	A This is usually undertaken on a PhD, when a piece of work is questioned and you need to 'defend' it by answering the questions	
2 The review	B A piece of written work usually on a general topic with a word limit – often of 2,000 words	
3 Oral examination (viva voce)	C A particular style of writing that presents some findings from an analysis or investigation and may suggest some solutions or ways forward to a problem	

4 The report	D A summary of the main points or ideas contained in another piece of work, or in a whole area of knowledge	
5 The dissertation	E A verbal summary or presentation of particular ideas related to a particular topic	
6 The presentation	F A long piece of written work, usually based on reporting some form of research	
7 The project portfolio	G This is either doing a performance (music, drama) or presenting work done before in a final show (art)	
8 The product	H This is a finished, designed object (e.g. a usable test, a computer software package, or an architect's design)	
9 Performance or show	I The collection of various pieces of work and evidence related to a particular topic area undertaken over a defined time period	

Answers: 1,B; 2, D; 3, A; 4, C; 5, F; 6, E; 7, I; 8, H; 9, G

Understanding your grades

Undergraduate degree classifications

In the UK there is not normally a system of Grade Point Average (e.g. GPA 2.3/4.0) to show how well you have done in your undergraduate studies. GPA is the system used in the USA. In the UK, the following system is used, as shown in Table 6.1.

Table 6.1 Degree classifications awarded

Classification	Common name
First class honours	First
Upper second class honours	Two-one (2:1)
Lower second class honours	Two-two (2:2)
Third class honours	Third
Ordinary degree	Pass
Unclassified	Fail

Table 6.2 outlines the usual percentage averages that these classifications correspond to. The table also includes the US GPA that roughly corresponds to these classifications.

Table 6.2 Understanding classifications

UK classification	Percentage	US GPA
First	70+	3.8–4.0
Upper second	60–69	3.3–3.79
Lower second	50–59	3.0–3.29
Third	40–49	2.29 and below

Note: Scotland. In Scotland, an Ordinary Degree is awarded for a three-year programme whereas a four-year programme is referred to as an Honours Degree programme.

Note: Progressing from an undergraduate degree to a Masters degree. Students in the UK can progress to Masters level degrees upon completion of an undergraduate degree. Top universities will require students to have been awarded a First or at least a 2:1. Each university will vary on its requirements. Candidates with a 2:2, a Third or an Ordinary Degree may sometimes be accepted onto some Masters programmes, provided they have also acquired satisfactory professional experience.

Note: Transferring between universities. One of the key strengths of having a state-regulated HE system is that graduates from any state university in the UK can be confident that their degree and their degree classification will be accepted by other universities. You may have studied at UG level in a university that is in the lower range of the league tables' rankings, but this does not mean that you will not be accepted by a higher-ranking university for a PG programme if you have a First or a 2:1. Note that it is also quite accepted practice for students to transfer between universities at undergraduate level too. You may study your first year at a low-ranking university and transfer to a higher-ranking one for your second year, provided you have the necessary credits and grades. This, however, depends on a similar programme of study being offered at the second university to the first university.

Note: Medical degrees. In the UK, medicine is taught as an undergraduate programme. If you are successful you are awarded a Bachelor of Medicine, officially known as Bachelor of Medicine, Bachelor of Surgery. University medical degrees are marked as Pass, Fail or Merit (which is the equivalent of a First in most other degrees).

Note: British humour. UK students have lots of names for the types of degrees that they are awarded. These can be amusing. For example, a 2:2 is sometimes referred to as a 'drinking man's degree' and a third as a 'gentlemen's degree'. Can you think why?

It is to do with the fact that if a person is not too serious about studying and does not spend their three years in the library, then that person has probably enjoyed university social life – sometimes perhaps to the cost of their studies!

Note: Rhyming slang. This is a feature of the language of the working class from the East End of London. The rule is as follows: find a famous person's name (first name and surname). If the surname rhymes with the degree title then refer to the degree by the person's first name. (This is one common pattern for rhyming slang.)

Exercise

Try to match the degree qualification to the name and then to the slang title for the degree. The first one is done for you.

Degree classification	Famous person's name	Slang for degree class
First	Attila the Hun	A Damien
2:1	Douglas Hurd	
2:2	Damien Hirst	
Third	Dan Quayle	
Fail	Desmond Tutu	

Answers: Find a UK student to help you if you are stuck. The odd one out is the Fail as you have to refer to the person's full name for this one!

Marking of students' work

One of the main concerns of students is the issue of who marks your work and how you know this is done fairly.

Exercise

Imagine a situation in which a marker just reads your work and then simply thinking of who you are and what you have written decides to award a percentage grade, with perhaps a one-line comment (e.g. 'satisfactory'). What are the problems associated with this way of marking?

Comment: If a marker marks in this way, the danger is it is unfair because it is very *subjective*. It may allow personal preferences and prejudices to interfere in the scoring. The other major problem is that you have learnt very little from the experience. You do not know why your work is either good or not so good, and so how you can improve it for the next assignment? In other words, there is no feedback provided for you.

Question: How can marking be made fairer and more *objective*? One answer is machine marking such as with multiple choice tests – however, a lot of knowledge cannot successfully be examined by multiple choice. Such marking is really only summative as there is little feedback.

Exercise

The methods in Table 6.3 are for making marking objective and fair

Table 6.3 Making marking objective: matching exercise

Method	Explanation
1 Blind (anonymous) marking	A At the end of each academic year all teachers on a programme hand in their marks for each student and a decision is made at a meeting amongst them as to the overall grade achieved by each student. This information is then sent to the Registry. The external examiner is present to check all is done correctly

2	Second marking	B	Testing people in different ways, not always by written work, but through other methods such as oral presentations. This allows people with different communication styles and strengths a chance to do well
3	Published criteria	C	If you are concerned about prejudice or personality clashes, it is unlikely that all markers will hold a similar prejudice. A range of different markers marking your work can be seen as more reliable
4	Variety of first markers	D	Work is marked again by another marker who does not know you, or the score the first marker gave. Markers then agree the score together. This is often done for a sample of work
5	Variety of assessment methods	E	All programmes have to be checked by an academic from outside the university. This person looks at students' work to ensure that grades are being given out correctly (not graded too high or low) and to general university sector standards
6	Exam boards	F	Student names are not on the work – instead they have numbers. This way the marker does not know whose work is being marked
7	External examiner	G	Your work is assessed against publicly available standards that you can check and use to understand the markers' comments and reasons for the grades awarded for a piece of work

Answers: 1, F; 2, D; 3, G; 4, C; 5, B; 6, A; 7, E

Note: Marking criteria. University teachers will mark your work by using published criteria (you should be given a copy of these in your programme handbook or have them available on the VLE). These are descriptors that explain what you need to have done to obtain the percentage you are given. The markers' comments will often refer to these, and point out if you have not done something you are supposed to have done, according to the criteria. The following is a brief example of marking criteria.

Real-life example

Table 6.4 Marking criteria from a UK university

Overall rating	Criteria	Mark range
First class exceptional 80% +	Comprehensive awareness of the issues. A soundly argued answer which shows significant independent thought, originality and critical judgement. Clear evidence of reading and knowledge beyond the course content. A well-structured and very well-written answer of literary quality.	80–100
First class excellent 70% +	Comprehensive awareness of the issues. A soundly argued answer which shows evidence of independence of thought, originality and critical judgement. Clear evidence of reading and knowledge beyond the course content or of critical or analytical ability. A well-written answer.	70–79
Upper second 60% +	A good pass. Sound awareness of the issues, factually correct and well organised. A good understanding of course material. Evidence of some reading and knowledge beyond course content or of critical or analytical ability.	60–69
Lower second 50% +	A satisfactory pass. An adequate answer with fair understanding of the course material. An awareness of the main issues. No outside material and arguments not strongly presented. Many omissions.	50–59
Third class 40% +	Acceptable answer but weak in material content and understanding of the course material. Significant omissions and inaccuracies but some relevant knowledge.	40–49
Poor	Appreciates the objective of the question, and provides some positive material but significant inaccuracies with limited understanding of the topic. Insufficient knowledge.	30–39
Weak answer	Some recognition of the meaning of the question but little understanding. Knowledge vague, skimpy and inaccurate.	25–29
Very weak answer	Few points relevant to the answer. The majority of the answer is either irrelevant or a misunderstanding of the material.	12–24
Of little merit	Complete failure to appreciate the question. Little material of value to the question set.	1–11
Irrelevant	Nothing of relevance to the question.	0

Explanation: Understanding key concepts – language exercise. In Table 6.5 key words have been copied from the descriptors underlined above. Understanding these words is essential for understanding what markers are looking for. Match the key words to their definitions.

Table 6.5 The language of criterion descriptors: working out their meaning

Key word or phrase		Explanation	
1	Comprehensive awareness	A	The main points of view are presented and your point of view is clearly and rationally set out
2	Soundly argued	B	Not accepting standard ideas and theories but subjecting them to questioning
3	Independent thought, originality	C	Showing you can use a questioning approach
4	Critical judgement	D	Demonstrating enough knowledge to show you know the general area, but nothing more
5	Critical or analytical ability	E	All-round understanding of relevant information referring to the topic
6	Satisfactory, adequate, fair understanding	F	Things you should have mentioned but either forgot to or didn't know about
7	Knowledge vague, skimpy	G	You are not simply following standard arguments, but putting forward your own
8	Omissions	H	Lack of clear definitions and superficial treatment of concepts

Answers: 1, E; 2, A; 3, G; 4, B; 5, C; 6, D; 7, H; 8, F

Information: contributions of yearly marks to final degree classification (weightings)

Different universities count the assignments and exams you do each year in different ways towards your end of year grade – giving more or less importance towards the overall final degree classification. This is called 'weighting'. Table 6.6 is an example of how a university might divide up your assessment.

Advice: Make sure you find out what your university does with your grades from each year.

Table 6.6 How marks add up for a degree

Examined course work	Contribution to yearly total	Sit-down examinations
Assignment 1 (2,000 words)	0%	
Assignment 2 (2,500 words)	10%	
Assignment 3 (Presentation)	10%	60% 40%
Assignment 4 (3,000 words)	20%	
Assignment 5 (Group presentation)	20%	
Portfolio	40%	

Comment: Marking is an important part of a teacher's job. However, for marking to be a useful function for the students it needs to be done in a certain way and needs the cooperation of the student.

Exercise

Look at the following scenarios and make a list of rules for good and useful marking and feedback:

Scenario A: Teacher X would write comments in red pen on the students' work. The handwriting was difficult to read and the comments were cryptic and difficult to understand. Sometimes teacher X would underline a paragraph and simply put a big red exclamation mark by the side of it in the margin, or several question marks or at times even write *NO!* The teacher did not provide any feedback related to any marking criteria to show how the final grade was arrived at but wrote a general summative paragraph at the end of the piece of work. The teacher seemed to pay particular attention to any spelling or grammar fault in the work, spending time on this and correcting the same mistake time and again, rather than commenting on the ideas that were being presented, even if by, at times, faulty grammar. The students did not receive their marked first assignment back before their second one had to be handed in. If a student got a low or fail grade there was no offer from the teacher to meet with the student to discuss the work.

Scenario B: Student Y had never bothered to read the marking criteria that was in the handbook for the programme of study. When a piece of work was handed back student Y would not bother to read the detailed comments that the teacher had made on the work in the margin (these were done by typed inserted comments as the work was sent in and sent back electronically). The only point of interest for the student was the grade given for the work. The student was happy if the grade was better than those given to colleagues and upset if it was worse. The student often handed the work in late and the student never made an appointment with the teacher to discuss the grade given.

Look at the following table of good practices (Table 6.7) and see if you agree with them.

Table 6.7 Good practices in marking and submission of work

Teacher (marker)	
Practice	I thought of it ✓
Comments should be easy to read (typed is best)	
Comments should be easy to understand	
Explanations should be provided (just '?' or '!' or 'NO!' is unhelpful)	
Feedback should relate to marking criteria	
The content ideas of what a student is presenting should not be overlooked because of a problem with grammar (as long as the meaning is still clear)	
Students must have feedback from their first (or previous) assignment in good time before they begin to write their next assignment	
Teachers should offer to meet with a student for a feedback tutorial, if the student is having problems	
Student	
Practice	I thought of it ✓
You should make sure you read and understand the marking criteria for the piece of work you are handing in	
It is important to spend time reading the detailed comments from your teacher. This is a very important individualised learning opportunity	
The grade itself is less important than understanding how the grade was determined	
You should compare your grade with your own previous work and progress, not with other students	
You should make an appointment to discuss your work with the teacher if you do not understand something or are worried about your work	
You should hand in your work in good time to give the teacher time to mark it properly	

Information: core modules and options and electives

As already explained, a programme is the name for the collection of modules (courses) that you study. There may be several programmes in a subject area, e.g. a subject area like business studies may offer programmes in finance and accounting, retail management, marketing or human resource management – and sometimes the same modules will be studied by students on these different programmes (so at times you may have classes and lectures with students on different programmes). Some modules on each programme may be obligatory to study and pass, others may be called *electives* or *options* (you choose to do them instead of others – this allows you to specialise in what you prefer).

WARNING!

Which modules must I pass?

Different universities have different regulations: in some universities you must pass all modules with a minimum pass mark (usually 40 per cent) to pass the year of study and progress to the next year. In other universities you may only have to pass the *core modules* and achieve an overall average of 40 per cent as a modules' average grade. Other universities state you can fail one module and no more.

Advice: Make sure you check this at your university so that you are clear about how this works. This information should be available in your programme handbook.

Information: credits

UK universities manage your learning by awarding you credits. This is best thought of as academic money that you earn.

Undergraduate

For each undergraduate year you usually need to earn 120 credits from the Credit Accumulation Transfer System (CATS). So you need 360 credits to be awarded a UK Bachelor's Degree. Each year's study period is divided up into modules and each university may do this in different ways. It is quite usual, for example, to have to do six modules of 20 credits each in a year. The modules may be taught as blocks (intensively over several weeks) or as strands (a couple of hours per week) over the whole year.

Credits are awarded at each level of study. You need to collect 120 credits at HE Level 1, 120 at HE Level 2 and 120 at HE Level 3 of an undergraduate programme in order to pass. Each level has learning outcomes, i.e. statements about what a student who passes a level can do, e.g. at Level 3 it is usual to say that a student can engage in critical thinking and undertake a piece of self-directed research. This would not be expected at Level 1. In other words, learning in the UK is about progressing from one level to the next.

Postgraduate programme and credit structure

Masters programmes are awarded once 180 M-Level credits have been accumulated. A Masters programme usually lasts one full year (12 months) and is often

Table 6.8 Types of taught postgraduate qualification

Postgraduate Certificate	PGCert
Postgraduate Diploma	PGDip
Postgraduate Certificate in Education	PGCE
Master of Arts	MA
Master of Science	MSc
Master of Law	LLM
Master of Education	MEd
Master of Business Administration	MBA
Master of Philosophy	MPhil

divided into three stages: the PG Certificate stage of 60 credits, a PG Diploma stage of a further 60 credits (total 120 credits) and a dissertation stage which often attracts a further 60 credits. The dissertation (which can be 8,000–12,000 words long) is usually completed over 3–6 months.

Note: The diploma stage is often the more practical and 'applied' stage of the programme (learning how to do something and relating it to the outside world) and the dissertation stage is about developing and using research skills at an advanced level.

Information: Postgraduate Research Programmes (PGR)

The following are the usual programmes that can be taken as research degrees in the UK.

Table 6.9 Types of research degree and their duration

Types of research degree	Duration
Master of Philosophy (MPhil)	Two or more years
Master of Research (MRes)	Generally one year
Professional/taught doctorates (DEng, DMus, DEd, DBA, DClinPsych	Variable
New Route Doctorate of Philosophy (PhD)	Three or more years
Doctorate of Philosophy (PhD or DPhil)	Three or more years

Note: The research programme 'New Route PhD' is a programme that combines research and classes/seminars and the development of professional competences. It is a PhD designed to link the development of high-level research skills with employment potential.

Table 6.10 Abbreviations for doctorates

Doctor of Engineering	DEng
Doctor of Music	DMus
Doctor of Clinical Psychology	DClinPsych
Doctor of Education	DEd
Doctor of Business Administration	DBA

Research Excellence Framework ratings

UK universities are currently ranked in their research achievements by a four-star rating system which is shown in Table 6.11. The data is gathered every five years from universities by a panel of experts asking them to submit the research profiles of their academic staff in the different disciplines (subject areas) that are offered. The number of staff publications and amount of research activity engaged in by staff is assessed and star awards made. The last was undertaken in December 2008. By visiting the website listed below you can look up the research awards for the UK universities in the subject areas you may be interested in.

Useful website: http://www.rae.ac.uk

Table 6.11 The university star rating system

Rating	Description
4*	Quality that is world-leading in terms of originality, significance and rigour
3*	Quality that is internationally excellent in terms of originality, significance and rigour but which nonetheless falls short of the highest standards of excellence
2*	Quality that is recognised internationally in terms of originality, significance and rigour
1*	Quality that is recognised nationally in terms of originality, significance and rigour
Unclassified	Quality that falls below the standard of nationally recognised work or work which does not meet the published definition of research for the purposes of this assessment

The structure of doctoral studies

UK doctorates (PhDs) are traditionally undertaken by research, although increasingly parts of a PhD, such as research methods and ethics, may be offered for part of a PhD as taught courses that attract credits. These are usually undertaken in the first year of the PhD.

To be accepted for a PhD you need to complete a proposal and find a supervisor (a university professor, senior lecturer or reader) who is willing to become your first supervisor. Many academics in universities tender (make an offer) for research projects (to get the funding for these) and when they are successful with such a bid (a competitive offer) they then often advertise for PhD students to undertake the necessary research under their guidance as part of the project.

Advice: An important issue for a potential PhD student, apart from finding a source of funding for a research project, is to make sure that a suitable and sympathetic supervisor is found as the first supervisor.

As well as a first supervisor a second supervisor is allocated to you (usually, but not always, from the same university as the first supervisor). You meet on a regular basis with these people to discuss and guide your progress. You will also have a chairperson whose job it is to administer an annual review of your work. The annual review is a check to ensure you are making sufficient progress in your research. After two years your annual review is referred to as the 'upgrade' and if you are successful you progress to the final stage of the PhD, which is to complete the research and write up the thesis.

You may successfully terminate your studies after the first two years and not be upgraded to the final PhD stage. In this case you may be awarded an MPhil (Master of Philosophy). By the end of the third year of study you should be in a position to hand in your first draft of your thesis to your supervisors. It is then normal to take a year to write up the final draft and have it bound and ready for the viva, which is the presentation and defence of your thesis to an external and internal examiner. A viva usually lasts several hours. You will be told at the viva if you have passed. There are various categories of award: Pass, Pass with minor corrections (you are usually awarded three months to do these and hand in the thesis to the internal examiner); rewrite (you are usually given a year to complete this and it needs to be seen by the internal and external examiner again with a possible second viva being seen as necessary); or, unusually, you may be awarded a Fail.

Note: A fail is not just seen as a fail for the student but also for the supervisors! Students should not get to the final stage of a PhD if they are to fail.

Useful websites: http://www.findaphd.com/student/study/study-1.asp
http://www.newroutephd.ac.uk

European Higher Education Area: ECTS and Bologna

Led by the Council of Europe, there is a movement to both standardise and make higher education more unified across the various countries that form membership of the European Higher Education Area (EHEA). To do this several ideas are now being put into practice. In 1999, 29 European countries came to an agreement called the 'Bologna Process'. Since then, other countries beyond the EU have also signed up to this agreement.

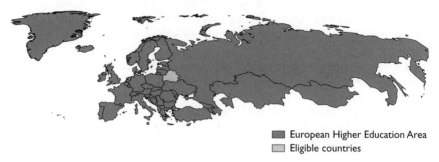

European Higher Education Area
Eligible countries

Figure 6.8 The European higher education area.

There is a basic framework for higher education to which the membership countries must conform, which divides studies at university level into three cycles:

- First cycle: typically 180–240 ECTS credits, which usually leads to the award of a Bachelor's degree.
- Second cycle: typically 90–120 ECTS credits, which usually leads to the award of a Master's degree.
- Third cycle: Doctoral degree for which no ECTS range is given.

The names for the various degrees vary across countries but the idea is that first-level studies take three years, second-level studies two years and third-level studies three years. For this reason the basic Bologna framework is referred to as 3:2:3

Within this framework, one academic year ideally aims to correspond to 60 ECTS credits. This is equivalent to about 1,500–1,800 hours of study.

The development of the Bologna Accord

Increasingly, other states in the world are looking to the Bologna Process to also standardise the delivery of their own country's higher education. The main aim is to make it easier for students to study and undertake research in different countries. It is also part of the process of making it easier for graduates of the member countries to find employment in each others' countries with these awards. The main principles of Bologna are therefore as follows:

- To have a standard transferable credit system. Each year of HE study should offer 60 ECTS.
- To offer students a standard transcript that clearly explains their achievements in the national HE system they have studied in (this is called a 'Diploma Supplement' and should be available to you at a UK university).
- To divide higher education studies into the separate cycles and awards: undergraduate, postgraduate and doctoral level studies.
- In order to allow students to experience education across the EHEA, universities

are expected to make entry into their study programmes easier through acceptance of the credit accumulation system and the use of semesters. A driving force for developing this is the Erasmus student exchange programme (see below).

- Universities are encouraged and expected to offer all students work experience and industrial placements as part of their study programme. This is to increase the employability of graduates. Typically one semester may be dedicated to this.
- Universities are encouraged to develop bilateral agreements with other universities in the EU to promote student exchange on various schemes, e.g. The Socrates Erasmus scheme.

The UK and Bologna

The UK has always had a clear distinction between first and second cycle studies (UG and PG programmes). However, the usual pattern is UG three years (although longer for engineering, medicine or veterinary sciences), and one year for most Masters, and these Masters usually only accumulate 90 ECTS. Many universities have not switched to a semester system, making semester exchange and ECTS credit accumulation difficult, and the system of assessment is through learning outcomes, i.e. 'can-do' statements as outcomes for each HE level (year) of study, rather than through shorter semester-based credits awarded for passing end of semester examinations. While many of the arguments from UK universities for not developing their systems in line with Bologna may have a theoretical and cultural legitimacy, there is also a problem of resistance to change and at times there may appear to be an underlying assumption and belief in the superiority of the UK system. The danger is that this lack of willingness to meaningfully develop the UK HE system in partnership with other EHEA countries could isolate UK students by making it more difficult for them to undertake periods of mobility abroad as part of their studies. Universities vary greatly in the extent to which they have embraced Bologna.

Reflective question: What do you think are the benefits of the Bologna approach to higher education? What are the benefits of the traditional UK approach to higher education? Which do you prefer and why?

Note that many EHEA countries are currently undergoing radical change to fit with the Bologna ECTS system (e.g. Russia, Spain, Italy). Previously, in these countries, there were no three-year undergraduate degrees but five- or six-year post-secondary school diploma programmes. These countries are changing their systems to fit with the Bologna Accord by dividing these five or six years into a system of three (or four) plus two (i.e. six or eight semesters for an initial Bachelor's degree) at which point students can stop studying or follow it with a further four semesters at Masters level.

Exercise

From reading the above explanation of UK university programme design, tick the scenarios you think will be problematic. What problems do you think the following students will have with their study plans at a UK university?

Box 6.2	
No. *Scenario*	✓
1 Marie has been studying law in a Swedish university for two years and has accumulated 120 ECTS. She wants to improve her English and at the same time get some international perspectives on law from the UK so would like to do a semester of study at a UK university taking 30 ECTS worth of courses	
2 Juan is studying architecture in the UK and has finished the first year of his studies. He now wants to go to a Russian university and study a semester's worth of architecture courses, some from Year 1 and some from Year 2. The teaching is in English. He also wants to do a course in beginner's Russian and get credits for this. He wants the credits from Russia to count towards the Year 2 studies of his UK programme.	
3 Françoise finished her first three years of study at a UK university. She is not sure if she will continue to study the next year at the university or not. She gets a job in the summer in a French business, but after two moths misses university life and decides to continue to study in her UK university. She decides to turn up for registration for the Masters that follows her undergraduate programme.	
4 Andreas has finished the first two years of study at a UK university. He has been working part time for a small business and is offered full-time work for them for the next year. He decides he will take up the offer and work for a year, then travel the world the following year before coming back to the UK and the university to complete his degree.	

Commentary: All of these students are going to have problems because they have not understood the usual nature of the delivery of UK university educational programmes! They have not understood that the lock-step UK system (lack of individual flexibility to progress at different rates) is different to the one they may be used to in their own country.

Marie (1) does not realise that the university will only let her study in Year 3 if the subjects she has studied in her own university in the first two years closely match those taught in the UK university in the first two years of their degree programme in the same subject area. She will need to send her 'transcripts of study' and course descriptions to the university, for them to see if they match. It is unlikely there will be an exact match. In fact, the only practical way to be accepted into Year 3 is if there is a bilateral agreement between her university and a UK university where courses and teaching context have already been matched and agreed as equivalent.

Juan (2) will have the same problem and the university will probably not accept the credits he obtains in Russia for part of his Year 3 studies on his UK programme.

Françoise (3) has not fully understood the difference between UK UG and PG study: i.e. that they are not a continuous programme, as they may be in her country (especially in pre-Bologna programmes). She should have applied for the Masters when in her Year 3 and she should have made sure she was offered a place on the programme – which is not guaranteed. She is in for a nasty shock when she is refused a place at registration because she has not done this. It appears she has assumed that upon being accepted onto the UG programme she would automatically be entitled to continue onto the MA without reapplying.

Andreas (4) will be considered to have dropped out of the programme if he does this and will not be able to restart two years later in the final year. He too is in danger of having a nasty shock unless he discussed this with the programme director and the Registry Office first to arrange a possible deferred entry for Year 3. The university may well not offer this.

Programme design in the UK

A UK university is awarded a charter from the Privy Council (an ancient advisory body to the monarch) to be able to offer various levels of educational programmes. The university departments then design programmes and the university sets up validation boards and procedures to sanction new programmes that the departments have proposed. This means each university designs different kinds of programmes. No two business studies degrees, offered by two different universities, for example, will be exactly the same. In other countries in the world, the control of university programmes is much more centralised and carried out by the Ministry of Education. Various programmes are designed by experts for the Ministry and then universities apply for licences to be able to run these programmes. In this way the same programme is taught across the country in different universities. An example of such an approach is found in France.

The idea of transferable credits

In order for students to have the possibility of moving easily between universities in the EHEA, a system of recognition of studies called the European Credit Transfer System (ECTS) has been put in place. The idea is that a student undertaking a first-cycle degree (Bachelors) in a country that is a signatory to the Bologna agreement can follow this by doing a second-cycle degree (Masters) in another. Indeed, ideally, a student should be able to transfer between years while doing a first-cycle degree. Universities that have developed their administrative systems (ECTS, diploma supplement) and can prove they operate this system well are awarded a European Quality Label by the European Commission.

The diploma supplement

As well as clearly identifying the modules (courses) undertaken and the level of the studies and the grades obtained (the transcript), this document also explains clearly what the qualification is, how it is structured and assesssed and what the levels mean. The following is an example of a transcript from a diploma supplement issued by the Open University for an MBA qualification.

Year	Module	Title	Level	Credit	ECTS	Result
2006	B713	Fundamentals of senior management	7	60	30	Pass with merit
2007	B820	Strategy	7	30	15	Pass
2008	T883	Business operations: delivering value	7	30	15	Pass
2009	B825	Marketing in a complex world	7	30	15	Pass
2009	B830	Making a difference	7	30	15	Pass

Total credits counted towards this qualification: 180

Questions:

1 Looking at the transcript, how many UK credits are equal to one ECTS credit?
2 What qualifications framework level for England, Northern Ireland and Wales is used as an equivalent to the EHEA second cycle?

Answers: Each ECTS is worth two UK credits, and a UK second-cycle Masters level qualification in the UK (but not Scotland) is classified as Level 7 (it is level 11 in Scotland).

Europass

Europass is also a new EU-wide initiative which aims to help people make their skills and qualifications clearly and easily understood across Europe, thus facilitating the mobility of both learners and workers. The Europass documents can be downloaded at the website provided below and completed to form a standardised portfolio. The documents have been designed to help people record their skills and competences in a standardised way. The Europass portfolio consists of up to five documents:

Two documents which individuals can complete independently:

- Europass Curriculum Vitae (CV)
- Europass Language Passport

Three documents which are completed by the relevant organisations on behalf of the individual:

- Europass Mobility
- Europass Certificate Supplement (for vocational education)
- Europass Diploma Supplement (for university academic education)

Useful website: http://europass.cedefop.europa.eu

Tip: You may find it useful to use these documents to devise your own portfolio for when you look for work, either while a student or upon leaving university. You may wish to find out if the university you are at can help you by completing, stamping and signing the Europass Mobility and Diploma Supplement certificates. Many universities have European Offices or Erasmus Offices that you can contact to see if they can advise and help you with this.

Credits, hours of study and number of words to be written on a programme

There are no fixed rules about this, but generally for each credit awarded you are expected to do 10 hours' work (this may alternatively be called 10 hours' student commitment).

1 UK university credit = 10 hours of work

This means you should expect to put in 1,200 hours per year at UG level and 1,800 hours at PG level. The usual number of weeks in an academic year is about 32–36 weeks, so this means expecting to study a minimum of some 35 hours per week in total on a UG programme.

Even though you may be doing oral presentations, producing something or performing, for some of your credits, word counts or 'equivalent word counts' are often used to give an idea of the importance or length of a piece of work that needs to be done for credits. At UG level an assignment that brings in 20 credits is usually expected to be about 3,000 words long (seven to eight sides of A4). At Level 3 most UG programmes expect students to complete some form of dissertation (a written piece of work presenting a student's research findings on an agreed topic). This is usually worth 40 credits and is expected to be about 6,000 words in length.

On a taught Master's programme the word length of assignments may be a little higher to give practice for writing more extended texts for the final research dissertation; which is often expected to be about 8,000–10,000 words in length. This means that you may be expected to have written about 30,000 or more words in total for assessment on a Master's programme.

WARNING!

An MBA may require more than this!

Information: word length and credits

1 UK university UG credit = roughly 150 words (or equivalent of work)

WARNING!

Sticking to the word count

When you write a piece of work for assessment you will be given a word limit. This word limit will be for the main text only and does not include the bibliography or appendices, or, where it is permitted to use them, footnotes. It does however include the words used in quotes and tables.

Make sure you check the regulations at your university on what is included in word counts and then stick to the count! Usually you will be allowed 5 per cent or even 10 per cent over or under the word count without penalty. However, excess words will usually mean you have marks taken off your work, and the words beyond the limit may not be marked.

Cultural note: Many international students think their problem will be finding enough words for their assignments, however, in practice, most students find it is harder to stick to staying within the word count!

Exercise

Sticking to the word count. How do you think you can best manage your work to stick to the word count? Look at some of the suggestions below:

- Plan your assignment before you begin writing
- Divide the assignment up in to sections and assign portions of the word count to each section
- Assign the number of words to each section according to the importance of the section (or the marks each section will be given)
- Do not use up more words in each section than you have given yourself to use
- Use diagrams where possible to convey ideas as they do not use up words
- Use tables and bullets to present lists and ideas where appropriate as they use fewer words
- Regularly use the computer word count to keep track of the amount of words you are using in each section

Passing your year

You will need to achieve the necessary pass percentage for the year to be able to go on to the next year. If you fail an assignment or more than one there are rules about resubmissions.

Resubmission

If you can resubmit you need to know how many modules you are allowed to resubmit. Normally a resubmission will only attract a minimum pass grade no matter how good it is!

If you fail in your exams, you will be allowed a chance to take them again – 'to resit'. The problem with this is that usually the resits take place several months after the exams. For example, if you take exams in June you may have to return to the university in early September for the resits! This can be very awkward and stressful.

Each year's work and your degree classification

Universities may also vary a lot in how they count the final grade you achieve each year towards your final degree classification. For example a university may have the following system:

Year 1 = 0%   Year 2 = 40%   Year 3 = 60%

Or it may have the following system:

Year 1 = 0%   Year 2 = 0%   Year 3 = 100% and only in final exams (Finals)

Question: Which of the above systems would you prefer?

Comment: Most people would see the first system as more friendly and fair. Year 1 does not count – which is good as this is the year you are discovering how to study and understand what is required (finding your feet). On the other hand, the second system seems too harsh. What if you are ill during the final exams? Why doesn't any of the hard and possibly very good work done in assignments over the years count? Traditional top universities may still favour this approach, however! In all cases, the key is to make sure you know and understand how you will be evaluated.

Concern! What if you are ill or have any other misfortune?

Information: concessions panels

Students may find that for reasons beyond their control (legitimate reasons) they are not able to hand in work on time, they may not have been able to sit exams or they sat exams but were not in a condition to do themselves justice in the exams. In this case you may need to ask for a concession. One university explains this as:

> A concession is a request for permission to act outside the University regulations, degree programme regulations and/or examination conventions and is based on personal circumstances with supporting evidence and each case being considered on an individual basis.

Students who have reasons to believe that they have grounds for being awarded a concession (e.g. death in the family, physical or mental health problems) can apply for consideration for a concession. The application needs to have backing evidence (e.g. translated death certificate, medical reports from a doctor). The concessions committee looks at individual cases and makes decisions about whether a student can redo some work, if handing the work in late can be accepted without penalty, or if indeed the grading of some work needs to be reconsidered in light of the problems a student was dealing with.

Information: sit-down examination technique

Exercise

Examinations are still an important part of the university experience and can cause a lot of stress and concern. There are many guides about examination preparation and technique. Make a list of what you think are sensible approaches to take for coping with examinations.

Now look at Tables 6.12 and 6.13 and tick the ideas you had thought of. Look at the other ideas and also tick the new ideas that you feel will be useful for you to follow.

Table 6.12 Preparing for exams

Idea	✓
Design a comprehensive examination revision timetable and stick to it	
Reorganise your notes into sections so that you cover all the necessary topics of your curriculum. A mind map approach to this can be useful	
Decide which are the most important topics to revise. You cannot revise everything! You may only be able to revise 60% of the topics in any depth	
Remember it is better to have 30 minutes concentrated revision each day than two hours of unfocused revision	
Self-test each day until you have learnt the core models and formulas that you know are essential to your programme	
Choose a set time each day for revision when you know you will not be interrupted	
Collect together the necessary revision material in good time (photocopy of articles, books from libraries, copies of past exam papers)	
Make sure you know where you are supposed to be, how to get there and at what time you must arrive	
Make sure you take any necessary equipment with you (at least two working pens)	
Practice writing by hand before the exam – you may not be used to this if you use a computer all the time	
Look at previous exam papers to make sure you know how many sections there are, how many questions and how long you have in the exam	
Work out how long you can spend on each question by taking account of the relative importance of each question (see how many marks each question attracts)	
Avoid doing a lot of photocopying of articles or, at this stage, learning new material. Rather, read your materials and take your own distilled notes	

Table 6.12 continued

Idea	✓
Avoid using highlighters on texts at this stage. Again take distilled notes instead	
Work out a strategy for the order in which you will answer the questions	

Table 6.13 Doing the exam

Idea	✓
Have a bottle of water handy, make sure your watch is correctly set and visit the toilet before the start time	
Make sure you ask for a good amount of working paper so that you can jot ideas down in rough	
Even before you read any of the questions undertake a 'brain dump' – writing down the key models or formulas that you are pretty sure will be useful. This can take up to 10 minutes	
Take your time to read the questions. Stop and think. Decide which of the optional questions you will answer. Choose questions that allow you to demonstrate as much knowledge of the models you know as possible. Take 15 minutes for this	
Note down next to each question the start time and the finish time for each one and then stick to it. Add times in for the brain dump, deciding about questions and for re-reading and correcting at the end	
Do a mind map for each question using working paper. Underline the key words in the question and brainstorm ideas, indicating where any models will best fit. Number the ideas and order them and assign rough word counts to each section	
After this re-read the question and do the 'So what?' test on the ideas you have. Make sure all the points you have noted down relate to the question. If they do not, dismiss them. Answer the question asked, not the question you wanted to be asked!	
Make sure you attempt all the questions asked. Do not get stuck too long on any one question trying to make it a perfect answer. You pick up more marks in the first 10 minutes of a new question than the last 10 minutes of an answered question	
Write your answers using double spacing	
Allow yourself time to re-read your answers near the end of the exam and add in any key references or missing ideas (this is why you have written double spaced, to allow space for these inserts)	
Make sure you correctly title and put your candidate number on all of the answer sheets you hand in	

Tip: Before you enter an examination, make sure you fully understand the following words. When you understand them you can ✓ them. If you do not understand one of them, make sure you discuss the word with colleagues or your tutor.

Analyse	Illustrate
Argue	Interpret
Assess	Investigate
Comment on	Justify
Compare	List
Contrast	Outline
Criticise	Prove
Define	Reconcile
Describe	Relate
Discuss	Review
Evaluate	State
Explain	Summarise
Enumerate	Trace

Note: If, for example, you misunderstand and 'describe' when you are asked to 'critically review' you will definitely fail to answer the question properly.

Study abroad and dual awards

Built in to many university programmes are Study Abroad opportunities. These are, of course, particularly useful for language students, but are also very much worthwhile considering for all programmes of study. The experience of studying in a different culture and approaching a subject from a different perspective can be very enriching.

Study Abroad programmes are often aimed at the UK students – so that they too have the chance of some 'international exposure' – exposure that you as an international student are already experiencing by being in the UK. These Study Abroad opportunities tend to be for either part of a year (a semester) or a full year. The period of study is usually credited in to the UK programme. There are usually mechanisms for converting credits and grades from one international education system to the other, but it is always best to check how this is done before undertaking such a programme. Many Japanese and American universities have well-established Study Abroad agreements with UK universities and these agreements may often mean that students can study at the other institution for no extra cost than the fee they pay to their home university.

A number of international students studying in UK universities also themselves take advantage of such schemes. These schemes may even include dual awards of qualifications, so that students spend part of their time in one of their own country's universities and part of their time in the UK university and are awarded their home country's university degree as well as the UK university degree.

Most UK universities have Study Abroad offices, so if you are interested in the possibility of also undertaking study abroad, it is a good idea to enquire what opportunities are open for you as an international student (there may be visa issues). If possible, find out what countries and universities the UK university has such agreements with, for what programmes and at what cost.

Question: If you could also visit another country and study at a university in that country as part of your UK degree, which would it be? Why?

Perhaps you are interested in the USA because it is also English-speaking and an important country to have experience of, or you may be interested in France, because you may have studied French at school and you would like to further understand Europe while you are in the UK. Both of these opportunities would look good on a CV as it is a further demonstration of cultural adaptability and flexibility.

WARNING!

There are risks associated with studying in a new environment and culture and perhaps language and you need to consider that these may affect the grades you get for your overall UK degree classification!

Information: Erasmus exchanges

Any student formally registered at a university or higher education institute which holds an Erasmus University Charter (EUC) and who is following higher education studies which are leading to a degree or other tertiary level qualification, may apply to be on this exchange scheme. If you are a non-EU-member student and are very keen on the idea of undertaking an Erasmus year of study, check out the situation for students with your nationality with your UK university to see if you are eligible. It is only recently that the scheme has been opened to all  students including non-EU students. If eligible, you can undertake Erasmus for study placement, work placement or a combination of both, depending on the type of Charter the university holds.

The policy on funding for Erasmus exchanges changes each year so it is best to contact the Erasmus office or Study Abroad office in your UK university to check what the possibilities on offer are for you. As most Erasmus exchange programmes happen in the second year of undergraduate study, you should make investigations early in your first year and complete the necessary paperwork in good time.

Note: Grants and fee-waiving arrangements are usually available to EU students for their Erasmus exchanges.

Information: Erasmus study periods

The minimum period of study is three months and the maximum is ten months. Students are not eligible for study placements in their first year of study.

Erasmus scheme participating countries

Each UK university usually has an Erasmus office that manages the bilateral agreements between their university and universities from the current 33 countries that participate in the scheme. These countries are all the 27 EU members, and the three EEA countries of Iceland, Liechtenstein and Norway. Switzerland operates its own scheme. There are also two non-EU countries: Croatia and Turkey. The FYR Macedonia has currently a suspended membership.

Universities vary in the number of exchange agreements they have, the countries they focus on for these and the subject areas they have operating within the scheme. The Erasmus office will process all applications and will organise the payment of the Erasmus grants that EU students receive for being in the scheme.

Useful website: http://ec.europa.eu/education/lifelong-learning-programme/doc80_en.htm

Note: Intensive programmes. If you are going to study in a minority language country (e.g. Estonia and Estonian), not one of the big EU languages (Spanish, French, English, German) then you can apply to study an intensive language programme in the country you are going to before beginning your studies.

Useful website: http://ec.europa.eu/education/erasmus/doc1300_en.htm

Note: Fees. The rules of the scheme are such that students cannot be charged tuition fees by the receiving institution. It may also be the case that home students (UK and EU) have their UK university fees waived too if they are out for a full year. This is a very generous offer, so if you are a home (UK and EU) student check if this is actually the case for when you wish to go. Overseas students usually pay their full UK tuition fee if they participate.

WARNING!

If you are an EU student and if you do get such a place, make sure you do not apply for a fees loan from the SLC for the year you are away!

Website: http://www.britishcouncil.org/erasmus-about-erasmus.htm

Exercise

True or false?

Question	True	False
Overseas students cannot participate in Erasmus		
EU students cannot get a UK Erasmus grant		
International student UK university fees are automatically waived		
The receiving institution cannot charge you any fee		
EU students may not have to pay their UK university any tuition fees if they are away for a full year		
You have to pay for private classes in Hungarian if you want to study in Hungary		

Answers: F, F, F, T, T, F

Erasmus pitfalls

Exercise

Match the pitfalls to the solutions!

Pitfall	Solution
I You find that you get into difficulties obtaining the necessary credits for the time you are on exchange	A Make sure you understand the new grading system and that your programme

			director in the UK also understands how to translate the new grades
2	You find that the grading system in the other EU university is very different from the UK one, and when translated you get lower marks than you were getting in the UK	B	Do some research on the university you are going to beforehand. Check with their Erasmus office what help they can offer. Check with your UK university if they have reports from former Erasmus students
3	You don't fully understand everything because of being taught in another language and your grades are therefore not as good as in the UK	C	Make sure you meet your fellow Erasmus students – they are in the same situation as you. Many may become good friends to visit across the EU during your holidays
4	The partner university doesn't send out your transcript of grades to your UK university in time for end of year assessment for moving on to the next year	D	Attend classes in the language before leaving or go on an EILC in the summer. Check out if classes are taught in English before going. Many European universities teach programmes in English
5	You feel isolated in the new culture because all the national students have already been together for a year and share the same language	E	Take an informal note of your grades and have a transcript sheet signed off by your tutor for your UK university tutor to have a record of grades while waiting for the formal confirmation to arrive
6	You are not given much help with accommodation or with other life issues	F	Always make sure you complete your learning agreement before you go

Answer: 1, F; 2, A; 3, D; 4, E; 5, C; 6, B

Fact: Did you know that there have been over 2.2 million students who have taken part in Erasmus exchanges since 1997 and that on average an Erasmus student is likely to earn 20 per cent more in employment than non-Erasmus students?

Erasmus Mundus

This is a joint Masters and doctorate-level scheme, also operated by the European Commission. The scheme involves partnerships being formed between at least three EU and EU candidate country universities (this is known as Action 1). These universities work on designing Masters (one or two years long) and PhD programmes together, and then offer the programme to world students. International students can apply directly to the universities offering these Erasmus Mundus programmes. Programmes accepted from the consortia of universities for each masters can obtain funding from the commission for substantial 'third country' student study grants and for academics to undertake research and teaching visits. This group of universities (the consortium) can then also establish partnerships with at least one other third country (non-EU) HEI (Action 2). If this is successful then there are also grants from the Commission for EU staff and students to study at and visit the third country consortia partner HEIs.

Note: Students coming onto Erasmus Mundus programmes will need to study in more than one of the consortia partner universities. Students should check the languages of delivery of the programme in each of the partner universities.

Useful website: http://eacea.ec.europa.eu/erasmus_mundus

Chapter 7

Understanding the university administrative system, structure and support

Introduction

This chapter first describes the administrative structure of a typical university so that you can see how all the separate parts of the university work and fit together. Each part of the system is explained so that you understand how the university functions and how you can use these administrative structures to support your study experience and life at university. The chapter then looks at the key issues of accommodation and finance, and disciplinary and grievance procedures should you be unfortunate enough to be involved in these.

In any university there are two parallel structures that you are a part of: the administrative structure and the academic structure. The administrative structure is there to support you with all aspects of your university studies and life. The university has departments to manage all the following aspects of the university experience:

- Processing your application (Admissions Office)
- Processing your payments (Finance Office)
- The buildings (Estates or Facilities Department)
- Where you live (Accommodation Office)
- What you eat (Catering Department)
- Keeping a record of your studies such as recording grades and issuing transcripts and certificates (Registry)
- Organising your examinations (Examinations Office)
- Looking after you (Student Welfare Department)
- Setting up and sorting out your e-mail account (Information Services Department)

Note: International Office. Different universities have different administrative models for helping their international students. In some universities all non-British students are called 'international' (EU and non-EU) and applications and welfare are dealt with by an International Office. In other universities only non-EU students are considered international (these are called 'overseas' students) with EU students treated in the same way as home (British) students. This is largely to do with the fees that are paid by each group, with EU students paying home fees.

Which type of student are you? Look at the list in Table 7.1 and tick the categories of student that apply to you.

In some universities there is an International Office accessible to all international students, in other universities, international students do not have a special International Office dedicated to them only, but follow the same procedures and visit the same offices as all other (home) students. This requires you to be a little more confident and informed about who you need to see for different kinds of issues. The advantage is that as an international student you are fully integrated into the university and not separate from the main student body in any way. The disadvantage is that the staff you meet may not be as culturally aware and sensitive to your needs as those working in an International Office.

Whatever the design for looking after international students at the university you are in, the important thing is finding out early on where it is you go to get information on dealing with the various issues that will arise and that you need information on and support over.

A common model in many universities is to have an Integrated Services Support (ISS) Department, which acts as a central point of contact for all students: you go to this with any problem or issue and are informed as to how to deal with the issue and who to book an appointment to see. Having a one-contact-point system simplifies things for students and helps avoid the problem of being sent around the university visiting the wrong departments – something that can be very frustrating and that can make people angry because of the time and energy wasted and the stress this causes. Often the reason for this is because of bad organisational structure rather than a desire to avoid dealing with issues.

When at a UK university you have the right to expect all the different administrative and support offices to work together to provide you with an efficient and understandable service. A university that is serious about attracting and looking after international students will have worked hard on training its staff to be sensitive to cultural differences and to make sure they explain the procedures or issues you need to understand clearly.

Table 7.1 What type of student are you?

Student category	Definition	✓
International student	Any student who is not from the UK	
Home student	A student who is a national of, or is resident in and has indefinite leave to remain in the UK	
EU student	A student who is a national of, or is resident in and has the right to full citizenship of an EU country	
Overseas student	A student who is a national of and a resident in a non-EU country	

One of the most important departments is that of Student Support/Welfare (this department may often include academic study support as well as welfare support). This is a department of trained counsellors and advisers whose job it is to help students with any study, or other, problems they encounter while at university. In a well-organised and efficient university there should be good coordination between the academic departments and the support departments of the university.

WARNING!

One of the typical areas where problems can occur, however, is when the academic and the administrative parts of the university do not work together properly.

Exercise question

Which parts of the university have you heard of or have dealt with already? Complete the following chart, naming the department and thinking about what function the department is responsible for.

Name of department	Main function of the department	Service you used it for and the quality of the service
Etc.		

You can usually rate a quality of service from the following characteristics. Think of the service provided and rate it using the aspects of the service listed in Table 7.2:

Table 7.2 Rating the service you receive

Service characteristic	Explanation	Yes/No
Reliability	Did the service achieve what it is supposed to?	
Assurance	Did the person attending you make you feel confident your issue would be dealt with properly?	
Tangibles	Did the service seem properly staffed and funded? Were you attended to in a proper private space and given the time you needed?	
Empathy	Were the people dealing with you sympathetic to you as a foreign student and did they treat you with respect and understanding?	
Responsiveness	Were you able to find the right person to deal with your issue? Was your issue dealt with efficiently and quickly?	

Advice: Make sure that you always understand what is explained to you. If someone is speaking too fast for you, or has an accent you cannot understand, the best thing is to tell them that you are sorry but you do not understand too well and to ask them to speak slower. Do not pretend you understand out of embarrassment and keep quiet. If you are made to feel embarrassed or stupid then the service provider is at fault – not you!

University organisational chart

Let's now look at one UK university organisational chart. A university should have this information available on its website, and may even offer an organogram (which names the people who are in each post of the organisational chart). This is useful for you as you are then able to know who to approach, especially if the university intranet allows you, once you are registered, to access staff e-mails.

The tinted boxes indicate the administrative side and the white boxes are the academic side of the university structure. Note that each director is usually respon-

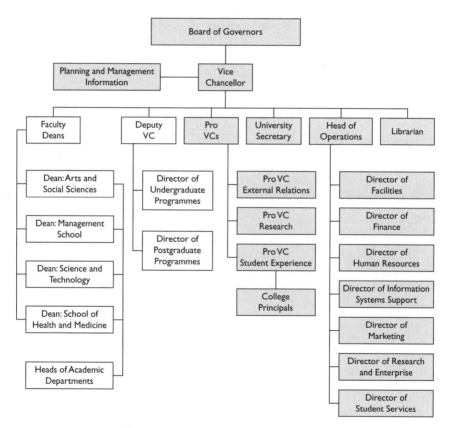

Figure 7.1 The organisational structure of a university.

sible for a range of other offices and university functions, each with their own head of department. The directors are the line managers of all of these other departmental heads and are responsible for them and the running of their departments. An organisational chart is very useful for you because if you have a problem that is not resolved at one level, you can use it to see who to approach at a higher level.

Note: The Director of Facilities in Figure 7.1, for example, will be the direct boss over a number of other offices and departments, e.g. the Accommodation Office. If you visit the Accommodation Office, or look it up on the university website, you should be able to see the organisational chart for this particular office and be able to work out who is the direct line manager of the person you deal with.

Advice: If you have a problem to do with any area of service, you must make sure that your enquiry or issue is dealt with at the correct level. If you have a problem with a service at one level, e.g. you were unhappy with your treatment by a university accommodation warden, the person to see about this is that person's direct line manager (look this up on the Accommodation Office's organisational chart). If you find that you need to go to the head of the Accommodation Office with a problem and then you are not satisfied, you can then look at the university organisational chart to see who that person's manager is at the senior level and then approach that person. This is why it is important to have a basic understanding of university and office structures – it will save you wasting time by seeing the wrong people over various issues.

Note: A little bit of homework can save you a lot of wasted time and frustration!

College system

Some universities, especially the old universities such as Oxford, Cambridge and Durham, have a full collegiate system of organisation. This means that the university is divided up into a number of separate self-administering units (Oxford has 38 colleges). To understand the college structure think of colleges as similar to federal states within a nation – which is the university itself. It is a more intimate structure for students as colleges have only hundreds of students in them. Each college has a Junior Common Room (JCR) which acts as the hub for student activities such as the organisation of parties and social events. Colleges also have their own sports clubs which play against each other on a regular basis. This provides a greater opportunity for students to participate in sport than at just the university level.

Many students like the college system because it encourages students to feel they belong to a large family with which they can identify and feel at home. In a college everyone gets to know each other quite quickly and administrative support can be personalised.

Student support and university retention

UK universities are very keen to retain their students. This is because it is not considered good practice for a university to lose students and have a high drop-out rate. One of the key statistics that universities publish in university guides is their retention rate (the percentage of students who start and finish their programmes). If a university has a high attrition rate (loss of students from one year to another), this is a cause for concern for the government and the Quality Assurance Agency. It should also be a concern for you at the application stage! Drop-out rates affect a university's reputation and position in newspaper league tables. The view will be that this university is not doing its job properly and that there must be something seriously wrong occurring with it.

This means that universities in the UK are generally keen to identify any problems students may have early on and then provide support for them to try and ensure that they do as well as possible and do not drop out. The fact that UK universities are under political and financial pressure to pay attention to attrition should be good news for you! A result of this is that universities have developed and are continuing to develop a range of academic and welfare support facilities and services. As an international student you may find that your teacher recommends that you take additional (and often free) support classes in areas such as academic writing. You may also be advised to make an appointment with an international student welfare officer if you are experiencing any unhappiness beyond your studies. It is sensible to use these free services – they are there for you!

University governance

Question: Have you ever thought about how a university is run? How the people who run the university make their decisions and who these people and the people responsible for enacting these decisions are?

You may feel that as an international student you do not need to know or worry abut this. This is probably true as long as everything to do with your studies and your time at the university goes well and you feel you are being treated properly and fairly. But this may not always be the case: therefore this chapter also explains to you the basics of how a university is governed.

Universities in the UK are 'semi-autonomous institutions governed by boards of directors that are comprised of lay members'. This means that universities are not directly controlled by the government but work in partnership with the government. The government exerts control over universities through funding and the awarding of the charters that allow them to legally offer various degree programmes.

The government also controls universities through prescribing legislation which universities must adhere to and follow (see below).

Useful website: http://www.bis.gov.uk/policies/higher-education

The administrators of universities are not appointed by the government and universities are able to set their own fees for overseas students (and increasingly so for home and EU students). They can also decide which programmes to offer and how these programmes are designed and delivered as well as setting their own entry requirements for these programmes.

Each university is governed by a board of governors. A typical board is comprised of:

- twelve independent members
- eight co-opted members (elected/chosen by the board members themselves)
- two academic nominees (voted for by the academic staff)
- one student nominee (chosen by the Student Union)
- the Vice-Chancellor (the effective chief executive of the university)

The board's main role is to:

- determine the university's educational character and mission
- oversee the university's financial viability
- make key decisions about the running of the university

The independent members of the board (which the government requires to be at least half the members of the board) are usually local people who have experience in industry, commerce, the professions or employment matters.

The Vice-Chancellor and the Senior Management Team

Terminology: In many university systems in the world the UK Vice-Chancellor (VC) is referred to as the Rector or President.

This is the person responsible for implementing the decisions of the board and for running the university through its various committees. The VC forms a directorate or senior management team which usually comprises the university's Pro VCs (active academics who take on management responsibilities), the Registrar, the University Solicitor, the Director of Finance and the Clerk to the Governing Body (Secretary). This team meets on a regular basis to oversee the day-to-day running of the university.

Note: Chancellor Another figure involved with the university structure is the Chancellor. The Chancellor is a figurehead for the university and is usually a person chosen because he or she is famous and reflects the ethos and values of the university represented. The main occasion when students will meet their university's Chancellor is at degree award ceremonies (graduation), when it is often the Chancellor who confers the degree on the students (gives them the degree). The Chancellor is not part of the university governance or executive nor a member of the board.

University committees

You may, as a student, find that you are elected to a committee to report on an issue or you may be chosen as a student representative for a departmental committee, to represent the views of students on a particular programme. You may even find yourself asked to be a member of a working group. In each of these cases it is very useful for you to have a basic understanding of how committees work. The following section introduces you to this so that you know what to expect if you are involved in committee work.

Universities are managed through a committee structure. These vary within each university, but generally there is a Senate/Academic Board that is responsible for the academic standards of the university. Various committees relating to academic issues (e.g. university partnerships, or research ethics) meet regularly and report to the Senate. Each of these committees may have further subcommittees that

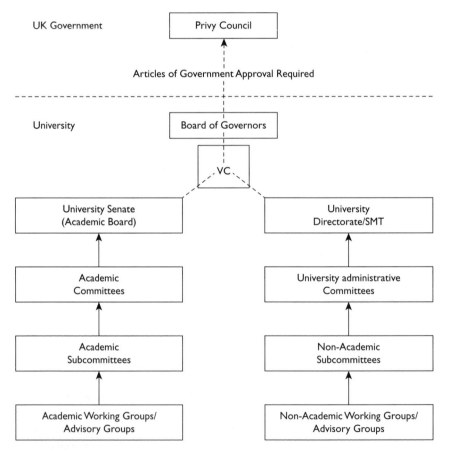

Figure 7.2 The university committee reporting structure.

report to them and there may also be more informal working/advisory groups that are formed as and when issues arise that require investigation. These then investigate issues and report to the various subcommittees: in this way information moves up to the more important decision-making areas of the university.

Membership of committees is achieved in several ways. A person may be a member of a committee because of the office he or she holds – these are called *ex officio* members (the VC is an *ex officio* member of the Governing Board, the Senate and the Directorate), other members are elected or co-opted (elected by those already on the committee).

Each committee has a membership list and the first thing a committee does, when it begins, is to set out its '*terms of reference*', a scope statement which lays out the remit, purpose and objectives of the committee, i.e. the reason for its existence. This is to ensure that it does not double up by covering what is already dealt with in any other committee in the university.

It is hoped that through such a committee structure all academic views and issues are able to be represented and the opportunity for discussion is offered. As well as an academic committee structure there is also a parallel non-academic committee structure. A Student Services' Committee usually acts as the top-level committee. The functional committees report into the Directorate – the senior management team (SMT) – as these concern the day-to-day running of the university.

All committee meetings are minuted and the minutes (record of what was said) are distributed to the members of the committee shortly after a meeting. The minutes often include 'action points' where it is indicated who has agreed to undertake what action by the next meeting. At the next meeting committee members are contacted before the meeting by the committee secretary and are asked to send in issues they wish to have discussed (items for the agenda). An agenda stating time and place for the next meeting and a list of the issues to be covered is then circulated to all members. At the meeting there is a set procedure which is managed by the chair of the committee. A typical agenda is as follows:

1   Apologies
2   Approval of the minutes of the previous meeting (these will be signed off by the Chair)
3   Matters arising (issues for discussion from the minutes including reporting back on action points)
4   Items (the new agenda items that are for presentation and discussion)*
5   Any other business (AOB)

*If you have an item and it requires some background reading and understanding by the committee members in order for an informed debate to be had, it is usually best to ask the secretary to send out any papers that need to be read to the committee members before the committee meeting. Sometimes there is not time for this and a brief document can be 'tabled' at the meeting itself for members to read there and then.

Student support offices

Accommodation Office

Most universities manage their own residential student accommodation, or they subcontract this out to specialist companies (e.g. Nido, London). Accommodation Offices are responsible for managing the accommodation for students and securing accommodation through a booking procedure (most usually an online system).

Choosing your university accommodation

Advice: Make sure you take time to select the accommodation you prefer. Look at the questions in Table 7.3.

If you are a mature student and you want to bring your family with you during the period of your study, then you may wish to consider renting a house in the private sector. Some universities also have family accommodation or 'head-lease' suitable housing from landlords, so that as a student you deal with the university and have a contract with the university for the accommodation – this is a safe option for you and one you may wish to consider.

Table 7.3 Questions to consider when choosing accommodation

Issue	Questions to ponder
Location	How far is it from the faculty you will be studying in? Which part of the city/town is it located in? Is it convenient for shopping and supermarkets? Is it on a good bus connection if far away from the faculty?
Cost and the offer	Does the weekly rate include all bills (heating, gas, electricity, Internet connection)? What is included in the rental fee? Do you have use of a kitchen? Do you have food storage space, fridge space, use of kitchen utensils? Does the room have a private bathroom and toilet or is this shared? If you have a car what is the situation with regards to parking?
Security	Is access to the accommodation controlled adequately (electronic cards, codes etc.)? Is there a security warden on the premises? Does the university rent include an insurance policy for personal possessions such as laptops? Is it clear what to do in an emergency such as a fire?
Noise	Is there a policy on noise making and do wardens ensure this is enforced? Is the accommodation in the bar area of town and is there a lot of street noise at night? Are postgraduate students provided with separate residences?
Guests staying over	If you are in UG accommodation are you able to have guests stay overnight? Do they have to be registered for insurance reasons?

Recommendation: using university accommodation for the first year

Most students choose to live in university accommodation for the first year. This way you can meet other students easily and feel secure that you are protected by university regulations and guarantees over the quality of the accommodation and the cost. In the private sector it may be more difficult to be sure of this. It also gives you time to make friends and potential housemates for the following years and to get to know the town you are in. You can discover the best areas to live in as a student as well as the costs of renting and the procedures you should follow for renting in the private sector. The university Accommodation Office and the Student Union will no doubt have information for you on this and may well run a contract-checking service for you.

Renting accommodation in the private sector

Useful website: http://www.ukcisa.org.uk/student/info_sheets/accommodation. php

Deposit payment

When you rent a property you will need to pay a month's rent in advance as well as a deposit. The rental in advance is used to secure the property for your use. The deposit is an amount usually equal to a month's rent and is used as security by the landlord/landlady (the owner renting the property) for any damage done to the property and its contents. This part of the deposit is now regulated by a Tenancy Deposit Protection (TDP) scheme.

Language note: When you rent you are referred to as the 'tenant'. The person renting the property is referred to as the landlord (male) or landlady (female).
The deposit scheme works upon the principle that a landlord/lady will protect the deposit given during their tenancy, either by a 'custodian scheme' or an 'insurance scheme'. When the tenancy (your renting period) comes to an end, the tenants should ensure they leave the property as they found it (taking into account 'fair wear and tear') and then agree with the landlord/lady how much (if anything) should be deducted from the deposit. If both sides agree, the deposit (or an agreed proportion of it) will be returned within a set number of days.

Example: You have been renting a property that had a new carpet in the living room. You organised a student party and one person dropped a cigarette on the carpet which left a burn mark. In this case, it is fair that the landlord/lady has compensation for the damage done. On the other hand, if a carpet is getting old and is becoming worn out through normal use (you walk on it each day!), then it is not fair to claim compensation for this.

If there is a disagreement over deductions to be made then the scheme has an Alternative Dispute Resolution Service which is used free of charge. When the Alternative Dispute Resolution Service is used both parties are in effect agreeing to abide by the decision of the service and it will act as an impartial and independent adjudicator to ensure that the deductions are reasonable.

Note: Landlords/ladies should use a TDP scheme and can be fined if they are legally required to do so and do not! Make sure you ask about this when you pay the deposit. Also make sure that you are given an inventory (a list) of the contents of the house that you are renting which states the condition of anything that is already damaged and make sure you check it and agree it. You do not want to be held responsible for any damage you did not cause.

Useful website: http://www.direct.gov.uk/en/HomeAndCommunity/Private renting/index.htm

WARNING!

You need to be careful about paying deposits, especially over the Internet, as there have been recent 'scams' (criminal cheating operations) that have cheated students out of their money. Before committing to a property you should:

- View the property
- Pay the deposit directly to the landlord/lady and not to third parties over the Internet
- Use the university Accommodation Office approved landlord/lady scheme – or seek their advice.

Note: Most universities actually organise house hunting events for students where landlords and landladies are invited in to the university to attend a fair.

There are several ways of finding out about the accommodation that is available in a city/town.

Useful website: http://www.studentpad.co.uk

WARNING!

Renting

In most cities in England, there is a rigid class distinction between areas of towns and cities and even streets. Areas that are middle class are associated with low crime rates, whereas other areas can become associated with crime and antisocial behaviour. Some areas may have problems of gang violence and drug taking.

Table 7.4 Finding accommodation in your university town

How to find out	Description
Letting agents (also known as estate agents)	These are high-street agencies whose business is either to sell properties or to let (rent) them. You will find agencies that specialise in student letting. Most estate and letting agents will ask students to pay certain fees when renting a house through them. The fees charged vary from agency to agency, so it is a good idea to check differences. Make sure you are always aware of all fees before dealing with them and if there are deposits involved confirm under what conditions this money will be returned. It is always sensible to get this confirmed in writing.
Local newspaper advertisements	Find out what the local newspaper is and then find the advertisement section in the back for accommodation
Student Union student noticeboards	Many students who have rented houses find they have spare rooms (a current housemate leaves, or the house has an extra room) and they advertise these rooms on student noticeboards. Visit the house to meet the others living there to see if you will get on with them before committing!
Studentpad	This is a company that works with universities to help students search for what they need. You will need a password to use the site – this is e-mailed to students in their first year around January (if the university is in the scheme). Check with the university Accommodation Office about this.

Obviously if you are an international student it is wise to make sure that you do not rent a house in such an area as you are more likely to experience problems! Most British people who are local to a city have a strong awareness of which parts of a city are best avoided for living in. It is sensible to find this out from local students or other local people before deciding to rent a property. A simple question you can ask is if there any areas of town that are 'rough' or 'undesirable' places to live. Such areas tend to be cheaper for renting, which is why they might at first seem attractive!

Tenancy agreement

You will be given a tenancy agreement for signing by the landlord. Make sure you read it carefully, understand it and agree to its terms. You should have this checked and explained to you by the university (the language of legal agreements can be difficult to understand, even for native speakers). The Student Union may run a free checking service or this may be done by the Accommodation Office.

Note the following government advice: 'Tenancy agreements can be either written or verbal, but you should use a written tenancy agreement where possible.'

Guarantors – what are they and why are they required?

UK landlords will probably ask you to provide UK-based guarantors to underwrite the rent and bills to be due on a property. A guarantor is a person who will pay the rent should students in a house not make the payments. It is a form of security for the landlord. This can be a particular challenge for international (including EU) students. Obviously an international student may not have a UK guarantor (usually a family member) they can use. It is important to discuss this issue early on with landlords and letting agencies as some may not require the guarantor and may ask for a larger deposit (usually six months of rent) or evidence of a regular income instead (if you have a part-time job, this may be helpful). Some may accept overseas guarantors – a risk for them, as UK law will not cover the situation for retrieving money owed if the guarantor fails to pay. Other ways around this are to rent from a live-in landlord or enquire with the university Accommodation Office about renting university head-leased houses – the landlord is then effectively covered because the university is the intermediary.

WARNING!

You will probably find that your university is unwilling and unable to act as your guarantor for accommodation in the private sector. You will also probably find if you are going to share a house with some British students that their parents are unwilling to act as your guarantor (to underwrite the whole household on a contract for joint and several liability). This is understandable because they cannot be sure you will not leave the UK before the contract term is over – if you do leave, they will have to pay for the missing rent and utility bills!

Note: If you do have a UK-based guarantor (a family member or friend) it is important that the guarantor is clear about whether they are guaranteeing their own son/daughter or the whole household when completing a guarantor's agreement.

Advice: The guarantor's agreement is a legal document so it can be a good idea to have it checked by an advisor if you are unsure of anything which is included within the document. Besides your university, an organisation that can help you with this is the *Citizen's Advice Bureau* (CAB). This is a charity staffed by local people – who often have a wealth of knowledge to share with you. The CAB has outposts in most towns.

Useful website: http://www.citizensadvice.org.uk

Your rights and obligations as a tenant

Tenants' rights include:

- freedom to live in the property undisturbed
- the right to live in a property in a good state of repair – your landlord should make repairs and maintain the property
- the right to access information about your tenancy at any time
- protection from unfair eviction.

You also have the right to protection from unfair rent, to challenge excessively high charges, and to have your deposit returned when your tenancy ends.

Note: If you fail to pay rent or breach other terms of your tenancy agreement you can lose your legal rights as a tenant.

The rights and obligations of a landlord

Your landlord also has the following rights:

- to repossess the property when the tenancy ends
- to take back the property if it gets damaged
- to access the property by giving 24 hours' notice
- to take legal action to evict a tenant in some instances – like non-payment of rent.

Types of tenanacy

Landlords and tenants may have other rights and responsibilities depending on which type of tenancy they have. Tenancies can run for a set period, normally of six months or longer (fixed-term tenancy), or on a month-by-month basis (periodic tenancy). The most common type of tenancy is called an Assured Shorthold Tenancy (AST).

Lodging

Another type of rental arrangement is lodging. This is when you rent a room from a live-in landlord. The landlord may be another student who owns the house. You usually have shared access to the kitchen and shared use of the bathroom facilities.

Many families in many towns also rent out rooms to students and universities may work with and have contracts with such 'homestay' families. The arrangements may include breakfast. Some families even offer half-board accommodation. Often universities use this type of accommodation when and if they run short of their own university accommodation for first-year students.

Further expenses when renting in the private sector

WARNING!

Council Tax

Council Tax is a system of local taxation, which is collected by local authorities (from the local County Council). It is a tax on domestic property that residents in the UK have to pay unless the law provides that they do not have to pay. Full-time students who live only with other full-time students or in halls of residence will not have to pay this tax. If there are any non-student residents or students who are studying on a part-time basis then the house will not qualify for this exemption. Also note that if you live in a 'house in multiple occupation' (HMO) there will be one Council Tax bill for the whole house and the owner or landlord will be liable. An HMO is where a residence has been divided up into separate bedsits.

In order to prove that you are full-time students of the university you usually need to collect a certification letter from the university student administration centre. (This is usually the responsibility of the Student Records or Registry Office.)

If you do receive an invoice for Council Tax and you do not believe you should pay it you will need to contact your local County Council offices to sort the issue out.

Useful website: http://www.direct.gov.uk/en/Dl1/Directories/Localcouncils/index.htm

Utility bills

You will probably have to pay for your bills – gas, electricity and water – in addition to your rent. It is not usual for landlords to pay the bills in leaseholds (although some landlords will still include certain bills, especially water rates, in their rent). You certainly need to have a good idea of how much the bills will normally be per month, so it is a good idea to discuss this with the landlord.

Advice: Bills will need to be shared among the members of the household so it is also important this is understood by all of the people renting the house.

In lodgings, most rents will cover the utility bills, but sometimes these will be charged extra. Telephone and Internet service are normally charged as extras.

Insurance

Whatever type of accommodation you choose, it is sensible to protect your belongings from theft, fire, loss or accidental damage while you are staying in the UK.

Companies such as Endsleigh Insurance specialise in insurance for students and can provide policies to cover clothes, books, computers, TV, hi-fi equipment and valuables.

Useful website: http://www.endsleigh.co.uk/Student/Pages/student-insurance. aspx

Note: Many university halls of residence will automatically include the cost of insurance in their charges – check this is the case, and to what value laptops etc. are covered by their policy before arranging your own policy!

University Finance Office and payment of fees

The university Finance Office is responsible for collecting your fee payments to the university – for tuition and for any accommodation you may be renting from the university. Each university has different procedures with regards to the way it collects these fees. With regards to overseas students, some universities may require the full tuition fee for tuition before you are offered an unconditional place on a programme (i.e. before a Confirmation of Acceptance for Studies [CAS] is issued to you). Others may require a smaller deposit payment only and offer an instalment payment scheme. This will involve setting up an arrangement to pay, often by opening a UK bank account and having a standing order instruction set up.

Note: Standing orders and direct debits (DD). This is a common way of making regular payments in the UK. Households use direct debits for paying utility bills. Standing orders allow the payee to withdraw an agreed sum on set dates. Direct debits are similar but the payee can vary the amount that is withdrawn from the payee. These methods of payment are safe and cost-free and by using them you do not run the risk of defaulting (forgetting to pay) – so long as you have the necessary amount of money in your account on the due days!

The same is usually true of accommodation payments. Again universities employ different payment schedules for their accommodation. This is usually set out in the accommodation contract that you will be sent and need to sign.

EU students who take out government tuition fees loans will not be invoiced by the university as the payment of their tuition fee will be managed by the Student Loan Company who pays it directly to the university.

Some universities offer a discount on their fees for full fee payment up front, i.e. all the money to be paid before you begin your programme of study. You can check if this is the case with the university you are intending to study at. You may then decide that the currency exchange rate is good enough for you to do this, or you may decide that the currency exchange rate may be better for you in the future and wait to make the remaining payments. Of course the reverse could be true and you may wait and find that the exchange rates become worse for you, in which case you will pay more by waiting!

Note: Most universities recognise that on occasion an international student may be unfortunate enough to experience disaster at home (think of the tsunamis, earthquakes, political instability and war). This may mean that suddenly a student is cut off from financial support from home. In these cases universities have funds called hardship funds that you can apply for.

Information: disciplinary action – policies and procedures

One area of which you may need to have a good understanding of how a university works is if you ever find that you have a problem with a disciplinary action being taken against you. Hopefully this won't happen – but it is a good idea to understand what to do if it does.

One important time for understanding university structure may be useful for you is if you feel an injustice has been committed against you. This could be for a variety of reasons:

- an unfair accusation
- a feeling that you have been treated without due respect and dignity
- a process at the university simply does not deliver what you feel it should
- a promise you thought had been made has been broken.

Then it is useful to understand university policies and structures and how to make a complaint in a way that is likely to be useful and successful.

Disciplinary issues and procedures

Exercise

What things do you think may be considered behaviour or actions that could bring disciplinary actions against a student by a university? Make a list called 'Things I should not do as a student'. In the exercise in Table 7.4 first match the unacceptable behaviour to an example then indicate, by ticking, if you had thought of it on your list or not

Table 7.4 Unacceptable behaviour on the university campus

Unacceptable behaviour	Example	Thought of	Not thought of
I Disruptive behaviour that affects university staff and students	A Providing false information about your previous work experience and qualifications		

2 Violent, indecent, disorderly, threatening or offensive behaviour or language	B Stating in class that all people from country X are stupid or making sexual comments about another student or staff member		
3 Fraud or dishonesty	C Using texting and Internet facilities with your mobile phone under the desk during an exam		
4 Sexual, racial or other form of harassment of anyone at the university	D Downloading hardcore pornography onto the university computer system or using a university e-mail account to send hate mail		
5 Misuse of university computing facilities	E Swearing at a fellow student in class and telling him to shut up or you will punch him		
6 The use of unfair means in exams, cheating, plagiarism or collusion	F Being drunk and laughing out loud as a fellow student presents in a seminar		
7 Damage to property of the university or of staff	G Selling illegal drugs to other students on campus		
8 Criminal offences	H Slashing a lecturer's car tyres because she or he gave you a bad grade		

Answers: 1, F; 2, E; 3, A; 4, B; 5, D; 6, C; 7, H; 8, G

Do not be surprised that if you do all of these you will probably be asked to leave the university (at best!).

Cultural note: Some of these offences may seem obvious to you. Others may be a bit more complex for you to understand. This may depend on your cultural background. In the UK you need to be particularly careful and aware of the following:

Pitfalls!

You may well have problems if you are not careful about the following. People's sensitivity to:

- reference to their own and others' sexual orientation and the issue of equality whatever a person's sexual orientation

- examples of gender and sex which may imply one group is superior or more important than the other
- any language and behaviour that may be seen to disempower, dismiss or make fun of anyone with a disability
- racial stereotypes
- negatively commenting on any one's religious affiliation or identity.

Information

Because in the UK these issues are very sensitive and important, most universities have in place 'Equality and Diversity Officers' and your university will have accessible policies on racial and sexual discrimination. You can access these if you feel your own rights to respectful and equal treatment by all university members, staff and students have been violated in order to take a complaint forward.

Areas that legislation covers are:

- Race equality
- Lesbian, gay, bisexual and transgender
- Religion and belief
- Work–life balance*
- Gender
- Disability

*This is important if you are a student with a young child. Issues of breastfeeding and provision of childcare facilities are examples of where universities should have policies in place.

Universities employ an Equality and Diversity (E&D) Officer or Officers. These people are responsible for developing the university's policies in relation to government legislation and policies in the key areas indicated above. The policies should be available to all students from the university website or in booklets available from the E&D officers themselves.

Advice: If you feel you are being discriminated against because of who you are and in one of the areas above, it is a good idea to make an appointment to see the E&D officer. It is also a good idea to have checked out the relevant government legislation for protecting people in public institutions from discrimination.

Useful website: http://www.acas.org.uk

Stop and think: Why do you think that it is seen as so important for universities to be strict about these issues?

Remember: Disciplinary procedures and equality and diversity policies are in universities to help protect all students and staff and to create an enjoyable and open leaning environment for all.

WARNING!

Cultural pitfall

It may be that in your country it is not seen as wrong or problematic to refer to people's ethnicity or even to have and voice particular views openly about other people from different groups. It may be that it is acceptable to hold firm views about the place and roles of women and men or the legitimacy and the rights of homosexuals in a society. If this is the case you need to be very careful about not transferring these concepts or ways of speaking into your UK classroom interaction. It may be that you do hold these views – this of course is a personal choice. If so, hopefully the UK university experience will make you question these assumptions. It may be, however, that deep-seated cultural views are difficult to change. In any case, the important point is that you do not contribute to creating a learning environment that demonstrates prejudice against or excludes anyone else. It is important to 'Mind your language!' If you do not you may find you have complaints made against you from other class members or even staff. It is not a defence to claim that 'In my country it is OK to speak in this way!'

Example: Mind your language! Look at the two examples of language in Box 7.1:

Box 7.1	
Male student says:	*Possible class reaction is:*
'It is not right that women can join the armed services.'	Other students who do not agree with this may see this as an act of male chauvinism, resent the student for saying this and confront the student in an emotional way over this statement.
'Some people believe that it is not right that women can join the armed services.'	Other students who do not agree with this statement will be encouraged to put forward arguments against this point of view. The topic has been presented as open for sensible, reasoned discussion, not as the expression of one particular individual student's prejudice or sexism.

Learning point: University is a place where ideas are to be debated in ways that ensure no one feels attacked for who they are or the identity they have. Respect means using language that will allow all people to participate in discussion in an open and unthreatening way. All students and staff should aim to contribute to maintaining this idea about the public learning space they share.

Example: After completing the above reading it is useful to now look at a typical university policy statement. Hopefully it should be easy to understand and agree with:

University X believes in the principles of social justice, acknowledges that discrimination affects people in complex ways and is committed to challenging all forms of inequality. To this end, University X will aim to ensure that:

- individuals are treated fairly, with dignity and respect regardless of their age, marital status, disability, race, faith, gender, language, social/economical background or being lesbian or gay and any other inappropriate distinction;
- it affords all individuals, students and employees the opportunity to fulfil their potential;
- it promotes an inclusive and supportive environment for staff, students and visitors;
- it recognises the varied contributions to the achievement of the University's, mission made by individuals from diverse backgrounds and with a wide range of experiences.

Information: the disciplinary/complaints procedure

It is important to understand that a disciplinary or complaint procedure involves many steps. At each point the issue may well be resolved and then the process finishes. If it is not resolved at one stage then it goes to the next level – this is called 'escalation'. A typical process may be as shown in Figure 7.3.

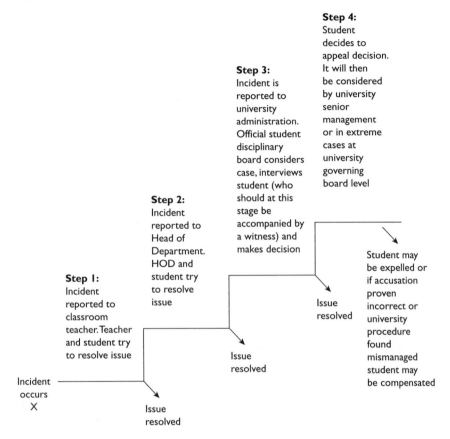

Figure 7.3 The disciplinary procedure staircase.

Information: complaints procedures

In the same way as there is a steps approach to resolving disciplinary issues, trying to resolve the issue at each stage before it becomes more official and serious, so the same is usually true with complaints procedures. In fact, it is quite revealing to look at a university's complaints procedures as a way of judging how developed a university is with regards to its management and its attitude towards its students.

As with disciplinary procedures, universities should have published easily accessible complaints' procedure information for their students. Universities often claim they welcome complaints as a form of feedback which is used to improve their service and functioning.

Advice: It is important to understand that if something is wrong you should not suffer in silence or feel that complaining will be held against you by the university. It is best to bring problems out into the open. A good university will respect you

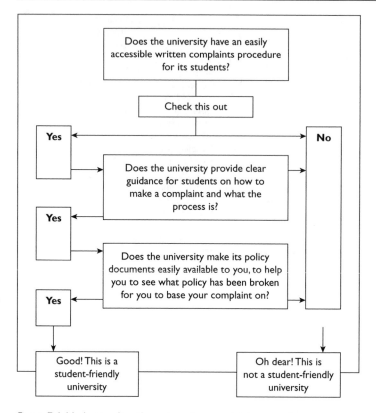

Figure 7.4 Understanding the university complaints procedure.

for this. Complaining is best undertaken in an orderly, calm manner, with rational argument put forward and backed by evidence. It is not a good idea to complain in an emotional manner and to make accusations that you do not have any evidence for.

Thought piece: If you are not being treated well and there is something wrong with the university, the university needs to know about this and improve its functioning, not only for you, but for other students who will be in your situation in the future.

Look at the following advice from one university:

> *From the University of Warwick website:*
> Don't be afraid to give feedback or make a complaint. We are committed to ensuring we deliver the best service possible and your comments help us to do that.

And the following from another university:

You should be assured that no complainant will be disadvantaged by having raised a complaint. Privacy and confidentiality will be maintained in the handling of complaints except where disclosure is necessary to progress the complaint.

Advice: You should not be afraid of making a legitimate complaint.

Students pursuing a compliant should use the complaints procedure within the university first and should take it to the final level if necessary. If after that the issue is not resolved then there is the possibility of taking the complaint to an external body: the Office of the Independent Adjudicator.

Useful website: http://www.oiahe.org.uk

Alternatively there are legal channels available, but these can be expensive.

Chapter 8

Life beyond study

Understanding and navigating British student culture

The Student Union (also known as the Guild of Students or Student Association)

Each university has a Students' Union. These are branches of the National Union of Students (NUS) and there are 600 such branches in the UK. Student Unions are for the benefit of all students, and students who are not members of the union can use the facilities of a Union building.

Useful website: http://www.nus.org.uk

The Students' Union (SU) is a national organisation with its own national president. It represents students nationally at a political level. On each campus there is usually a SU branch. Universities tend to fund their SUs through a grant which pays for the building, its upkeep and for various paid administrative posts.

Many of the administrative posts (such as the President and the Vice Presidents, e.g. 'Vice President Welfare') are full-time, paid positions and undertaken by students who have graduated and been voted for – the people holding these posts are called 'Sabbatical Officers'. Other non-sabbatical posts are unpaid and held by current students. The SU offices are usually located in a building referred to as the Student Union and this is often a building with recreational facilities for students such as a bar, an Internet café, games and TV rooms, a space for events and discos. The SU raises funds by charging admission for such events as well as by undertaking sponsored events for various causes.

One of the main administrative functions of the SU is to run university clubs and societies and to give students advice and help. Many SUs also have a social commitment and organise volunteering work by students for local charities (free help). Many international students find that volunteering is a very useful way to get to use English, understand UK society better and integrate with local people. It is also very good to have as experience on a CV and is a rewarding thing to do in itself.

If you want to know what clubs or volunteering opportunities are open to you to join as a student, you should visit the SU to get the relevant information.

Note: There is normally a small fee (called a 'nominal fee') to join specific clubs.

One of the main events of the year which is organised by the SU is the Freshers' Fair. This is organised during Freshers' Week ('Freshers' is a US term now used in the UK to refer to new first-year students). During Freshers' Week the SU promotes its clubs to new students and you can enrol at the various clubs' stands.

It is important to understand that the SU is an organisation run by its members for its members. International students are members as well and you can and should benefit from being active in using and joining in with helping the Union. Many international students get involved in running the SU by joining committees or in setting up international societies. If you want a new club to exist it is up to you to start the club and doing this will provide valuable experience in understanding how organisations are run. You often need to have a minimum number of members to begin a club and you each need to pay a small subscription. The university and the SU will then support the club by making facilities available to the members of the new club. The SU may have minibuses, equipment or room space that can be booked for use.

The NUS website (see the link above) is full of useful advice for students such as finding and renting property from landlords in the private housing sector to travel insurance. It also has an international student officer who is contactable on a Facebook wall.

Campus social life

As well as explaining the kind of activities you will do when you study and the expectations about your role in these activities, this guide also looks at the social part of your life as an international student attending a UK university. It introduces you to aspects of student life and culture that you may find useful. It is, of course, important to understand that in order to be happy as a student and to study well, you need to have a social life that is interesting and fun. Because British university life is influenced by British youth, this guide also introduces you to British youth culture.

You are encouraged to understand and assess your own social and emotional reactions and response to this culture. It is hoped that knowing about, understanding and being prepared for this culture should lessen the effects of any alienation or confusion that may otherwise arise!

Note: The UK is a multi-ethnic and multicultural country and obviously this means there are people living in the UK with the variety of religious and personal moral views that exist across the world.

Pitfall!

Because there is a community of people from most cultures living in the UK, it may be tempting for you to seek out the comfort of being with people from your 'own' cultural, social and linguistic background. Doing this does not make much sense if the motivation for studying abroad is to experience a different culture and to further develop your English!

Advice: When you have arrived at your UK university, the first few weeks are crucial for setting the pattern of who you will socialise with. It is tempting to seek refuge with people from your own background. It is also less tiring as you can speak your mother tongue. Be careful that this does not mean you end up as a member of a subgroup of students who do not mix with students from other backgrounds. If you are always with similar background students when on campus, other students may not see you as approachable, especially if you are speaking your own language when together. Make the effort early on in your studies to sit in class and work with students from other backgrounds, and to join student clubs (sports, hobbies) that allow you to meet and mix with different people.

WARNING!

Many international students complain that they have found it difficult to meet British students and to mix with them. They sometimes draw the conclusion that this must be because British students are not interested in mixing with foreign students. This may be a false conclusion.

Thought piece: Think about how easy you are making it for other students to have the opportunity to meet and talk with you: if you are with other students from your background speaking your own language, students from other backgrounds, including the British, may find it hard to meet you or may think you do not want to mix with others. Meeting people from other backgrounds involves taking some risks and leaving your own 'comfort zone'.

Information: meeting the British students

Do not expect other background students, especially the UK students, to necessarily take the first steps to meet you. The British students are also away from home for the first time and are trying to create friendship circles and establish their own social life too. For them this is easier and less risky to do with other British students, who they know will probably like the same things – just as it is easier for you to be with students from your own background. Another problem is that British people are traditionally seen as 'distant' or 'shy' (before drinking alcohol perhaps!). In fact this is actually a part of their culture, which teaches them not to be 'bothersome', 'nosey' or 'pushy' with others and to let others have their own space to get on with their own life (so long as it doesn't impose on them too much either!). This habit of giving others their own space and distance to do their own thing can appear as, and is often mistakenly interpreted as having, a sense of superiority and not wanting to meet other people. Of course there are arrogant people everywhere and in all cultures, but it would be a mistake to come to this general conclusion about the home students. It is important to remember that every culture is made up of individuals who have many different outlooks!

Information: the culture shock cycle

When you leave your own culture, especially for the first time, and live in another culture, you are going to go through the psychological process of 'culture shock'. It is important that you understand this process and avoid falling into some of its negative traps.

Culture shock is the difficulty people may have in adjusting and adapting to life in a different culture. Of course every person reacts in different ways to such a challenge, but there are some common patterns and stages that most people tend to go through that it is important to know about.

Figure 8.1 illustrates the typical process that you as an international student may experience.

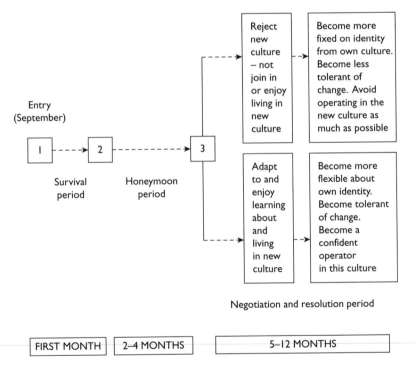

Figure 8.1 Typical stages of culture shock.

Exercise

Look at Table 8.1 and then match the stages to their explanations

Table 8.1 Stages of cultural adaptation

Stage		Explanation
1 Survival	A	You have been in the new environment for over a term. You have to deal with the new culture because you are living in it. You begin to find that you are increasingly affected by the new culture and some things annoy you. You have to find a way of living in and making sense of this new culture. Some people find this too much of a challenge, reject the new culture and decide to cling to the safety of their own culture
2 Honeymoon	B	When you arrive at the new university you simply try to survive and have little time for analysis and reaction. You just try to be at the right place at the right time and to sort out basics such as eating and getting a place to sleep
3 Negotiation and resolution	C	Everything is new and different and this is exciting and fun. You enjoy being away from the routine of you own culture. You do not yet have to really engage with the new culture in a serious way. It is like being on holiday as a tourist

Answers: 1, B; 2, C; 3, A

WARNING!

SAD, or 'Goodbye Sunshine!'

Traditionally, the culture shock cycle coincides with certain seasons of the academic year. In September it is still fairly warm, but soon autumn sets in. This can be depressing as trees lose their leaves and it gets colder. Also, because the UK is quite far north, the days get shorter. In January it is the middle of winter: it is cold. The days are very short and the nights are long. In winter a number of people start to suffer a form of depression from lack of exposure to sunlight known as Seasonal Affective Disorder (SAD). This may be especially true if you are from a warm and sunny climate. As this usually coincidences with the post-honeymoon period of culture shock, this can be a tough period for international students. However, as spring arrives, the days get longer and the flowers and blossom on the trees come out. There is new life everywhere and there is a new sense of optimism as the summer approaches. This is something many people experience living in the UK!

Box 8.1	
Symptom	*Degree of suffering:* *0 = not at all;* *5 = all the time*
Excessive concern over cleanliness and health (mild OCD – obsessive-compulsive disorder)	
Feelings of helplessness ('I am not good enough! It's all too much for me!')	
Irritability ('Why don't they just leave me alone?')	
Glazed stare (unfocused looking with your mind not really registering what you are looking at because you are worrying)	
Desire for home and old friends ('I wish I was there and not here!')	
Physiological stress reactions (e.g. biting nails, twisting your hair, losing your temper easily)	
Homesickness (missing your home and your own culture)	
Boredom (there's nothing to do of interest, the food has lost its taste)	
Withdrawal (you prefer to stay in and not go out and meet new people)	
Getting 'stuck' on one thing (running the same idea through your mind time and again)	
Excessive sleep (sleeping at unusual times and not getting up in the morning)	
Compulsive eating/drinking and weight gain (comfort eating and drinking to escape reality and forget)	
Stereotyping host nationals ('They are all mean, nasty and unfriendly!')	
Hostility towards host nationals ('They are not as nice or as honest as my own people!')	

Self-diagnosis: You need to be aware that the following symptoms may occur if you suffer from a negative reaction at stage three of the culture shock cycle (i.e. withdrawal from new culture). These symptoms may be made worse by SAD. Have a look at the list of typical symptoms in Box 8.1 and assess to what extent you may be suffering from them.

Advice: It is normal to find entering a new culture stressful – after all, you have to adjust from something you know to something you are not sure of – which means learning new rules and making mistakes. This can be embarrassing and stressful. However, there is a normal healthy level of stress we all have, but this does not mean you lose you enjoyment of things. If you find you are suffering badly from a number of the above symptoms it is a good idea to get help by arranging to meet with a trained international student support officer in the university or mentioning the symptoms to your GP (doctor). Depression is something that you can work against if you recognise its symptoms.

Stop and think: If you believe you are in danger of entering into depression, even if only a mild depression, you may be missing your own culture or your family and friends and even maybe your native climate. However, there are some things you can do to help avoid becoming depressed.

Question: What do you think these practical actions are?

Exercise

Look at the advice in the list below. Did you think of these measures?
  You can help avoid depression with some simple lifestyle measures:

- exercise every day
- follow a routine
- avoid the urge to isolate yourself from others
- make sure you join in social events where you will meet people
- challenge negative or angry thoughts
- eat healthy food instead of any junk/fast food (which you may crave as a comfort)
- avoid excessive drinking and having hangovers
- ensure you regularly set aside time from study for rest and relaxation.

Understanding the new culture: interpreting behaviour

Another important aspect of adapting and being able to live happily in a new culture is to make efforts to understand the new culture you are in. If you do not do this you may make the mistake of thinking something that is not the case and negatively judging the culture.

Cultural interpretation

Every action and behaviour by people in a culture has special meaning in that culture. The same action in another culture may have a different meaning and different values associated with it. To illustrate this, look at the following example about smiling:

Anecdote: A Mauritanian student explained that he felt uneasy with all the smiling faces he met when out shopping in the small UK town he was in: he received smiles from total strangers. The Mauritanian student was disturbed by this smiling behaviour, it didn't seem 'genuine', he joked that maybe underneath it was a form of aggression caused by fear: after all, animals bear their teeth before they attack!

Explanation: For the British a smile is a sign of social harmony, it means 'I wish you no harm.' So, apart from smiles occurring between strangers, it is also used a lot in commercial situations as a sign of willing customer service: indeed British people expect a smile when they are being attended to by anyone offering a service, and so a smile is not a sign of genuine warmth between people so much as an important sign of acceptance to do business. When the British are abroad in countries where smiling is not a necessary part of such interactions, they feel that the people (strangers) do not like them or are angry with them!

Anecdote: Another example of smiling that conveys a different meaning was with a Japanese student who, as he was a very good guitarist, offered to be a guitar teacher for some UK students. Every time a student made a mistake (often) he smiled. This began to annoy them. However, it would have been wrong to interpret the smile as one of amusement or scorn. The smile was a way to show embarrassment for himself as a bad teacher and to encourage the student!

Advice: It is a great benefit if you have an inside 'cultural informer' to help you! You will find that making a friend from the new British culture is very useful for discussing and finding out what these actions really mean.

Exercise

Look out for actions and behaviours that you find strange or difficult to fully understand. You will probably find that these have different meanings in the new British culture than in your own culture. Use the chart in Box 8.2 to help you work these out. An example is provided and worked through for you.

Box 8.2

Action that is strange or different	How this action may be interpreted in your culture	What you think it means in the new British culture	What a British informer tells you it means
Example: young people don't seem to greet each other or be introduced to each other properly (no kisses or hand shaking)	That the people don't care about each other. It can be seen as rude	British people are too shy or perhaps they are not very warm and don't really like meeting new people	Handshaking is seen as too formal and more what older people do and kissing is seen as a bit pretentious. It's more relaxed not to have routines
Add your examples . . .			

Explanation: Rules of conduct. Generally speaking, all cultures have rules of conduct and behaviour that you are supposed to follow and understand – even if not consciously. As a foreigner you are an outsider and will not fully understand these rules. Open-minded people from the host culture realise this and will not expect you to show the same behaviour and understanding – so it is usually OK to make mistakes and this can often be a source of amusement – especially among friends. There will be values and behaviours in the new culture that you find positive, but also there will be those you feel negative about too. The problem is we often see things as negative because we don't fully understand them. If you are living in the new culture for a long time and are integrating into the new culture (this may be through sharing accommodation with some British students or getting part-time work in a British business), it is worth looking at things that seem negative to try to work out what it is you do not like and whether you can see this from a different angle. Perhaps you can find some positive features in them after all!

Advice: This is a process that involves being honest about your own feelings, being open to self-analysis and trying to see things in a different way by making positives out of potential negatives. It is obvious that the more you can feel positive about being in the new culture the happier you will be and the more you will be able to integrate with local people.

WARNING!

If you believe that the culture you come from is the only right way to be – that all other cultures are mistaken and have false or incorrect values – then you are unlikely to adapt well into any new cultural environment and may not be very successful in the new culture. A person with such an inflexible attitude is often called a bigot. To work out what things in the new culture are bothering you, use the following culture allergy test in Figure 8.2:

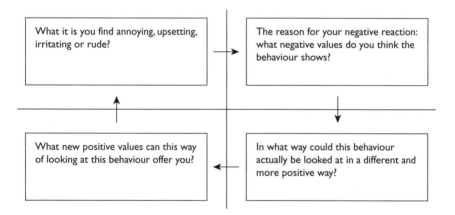

Figure 8.2 The cultural allergy-detector and antidote-finder exercise.

Example: One of the comments I often hear is that while many overseas student at first like British politeness (people saying 'please', 'thank you' and 'sorry' all the time) they then start to worry that this is not genuine or indeed strange. One Swedish student mentioned the following: 'I stepped on an English lady's foot in the supermarket the other day, and the woman said "Sorry" to me – but it was my fault – I was the one who should be sorry! What's wrong with these people!?' If we put this through the allergy detector and antidote finder, it may result in the following:

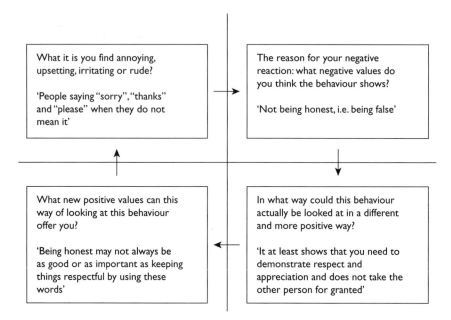

Figure 8.3 A worked example of the cultural allergy detector and antidote finder.

Comment: In fact many students when they re-enter their own cultures tend to find the lack of 'please', 'thank you' and 'sorry' annoying! If this happens to you, it shows you have undergone some cultural assimilation and will need to adapt back to the home culture!

Explanation: Identity. Of course each individual will have different values and a different identity. Not all things in the new culture will be things that you can make into something positive. There may be things that fundamentally go against your sense of what is important and right to do and believe. Identity, however, is complex and is not something that remains unchanged. Life's experiences will mean you develop your identity in different ways.

Question: What is your identity? What is important to you for your identity?

Exercise

Analyse yourself in terms of your identity by undertaking the culture flower exercise below. This exercise looks at the many different aspects of what makes up a person's identity. To do this, draw a culture flower with each petal of the flower representing different aspects of your identity. The different petals of the flower can be made up of all the things that make up your identity (who you are). Look at the example in Figure 8.4.

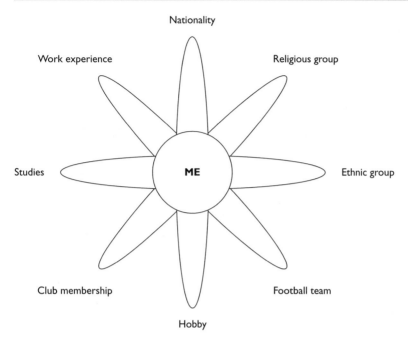

Nationality

Work experience

Religious group

Studies

ME

Ethnic group

Club membership

Football team

Hobby

Figure 8.4 The culture flower.

This is worth doing because you may find that you have many different aspects that make up your sense of identity and which are important for you. If you know what is important for you in terms of making up who you are and the values and outlook you have, then these different aspects of your identity can provide you with ways of meeting people in a new culture.

For example, as a student, you may be Nigerian, Ibo, a Baptist, a Manchester United supporter, a salsa dancer, a member of the Professional Association of Diving Instructors, studying Business Studies and with past work experience working for a charity that supports children and their families with Down's syndrome. All of these aspects of your experience may be important for you in terms of your identity and who you are. In the new culture that you come into in the UK you may be in a part of the UK where you do not find it easy to meet other Ibo Nigerians, but as the flower shows, being Ibo Nigerian is not the only aspect of your identity that is important to you or that makes you feel comfortable. You can meet new people through the other different aspects of your identity: you can join the local Baptist church and meet people this way; you may decide to go to some football matches to see your team; you may join the local salsa dancing club or attend local business-related conferences or decide to do some volunteer working for a local children's charity.

Note: One of the important things to realise about UK society is that there are, even in the smallest towns, a mass of different interest groups and clubs that welcome new members. These can often be found on the Internet or are advertised in the local libraries.

Campus culture

The more you understand the new culture, the better you can adapt to it. The rest of this section introduces you to British university youth and student culture. It explains the origins and history of this culture and certain behaviours you are likely to come across.

Note: Although individuals vary greatly in their own personal moral codes of conduct and ways of behaving, it is also fair to say that the main student culture on UK university campuses is shaped by the main group of British students there.

As a rule, this group is not particularly religious in outlook and is generally liberal and tolerant of differences in others. British culture promotes an individualistic outlook and British students tend to see life's choices as decisions that are to be made by themselves rather than made for them by their family. You will probably find that many British students have usually made the choice of the subject they study and the university they go to themselves. This is also possible because in the UK the state helps young people to be independent by offering student loans for university study, which means young people do not have to depend on their family for funding to go to university.

Making your own way in life, not expecting too much influence from the family (or indeed help!), and aspiring to become independent both financially and emotionally are seen as desirable and worthy goals (even though in reality these may be hard to achieve!). This is the same for young women and men alike.

Although this predominant British student culture exists on campuses, there are also subcultures on UK campuses. These may be religious, political or ethnic groupings. Traditionally, British families of ethic origin from outside the UK, such as families of recent Indian or Pakistani origin, may expect their children to follow parental wishes in many of life's choices. This, of course, can cause tension between the generations as their young become influenced by and assimilate to the predominantly individualistic youth culture of the UK.

WARNING!

One problem an international student may experience on a UK campus could come from other international students, or British students who identify with certain cultures and values, and who think that you should also share certain values, attitude and outlook with them because of your origin. This can be quite a difficult pressure for some students who do not wish to be stereotyped and do not believe in such an outlook. In many ways it is best, if this is the case, to make it clear early on that you are not interested in such an outlook to avoid being pestered by such groups. These groups often persist with people who seem unsure of themselves and their values!

Youth culture in the UK: sex'n'drugs 'n' rock'n'roll – a short history lesson

British youth culture is very much influenced and shaped by the youth culture revolution of the 1960s. The breaking with tradition that occurred in this period is the basis for much of British youth behaviour today. This section therefore analyses key features of this youth culture for you to better understand it.

Exercise

Look at the statements in Table 8.2 to test and understand your own cultural outlook. Identify your cultural beliefs first and then read the following sections. Then come back and complete the 'General UK cultural view' section. You will be able to reflect upon the areas that you may be surprised by, or are not in agreement with, and therefore be better prepared to understand your own reactions to the new culture.

Table 8.2 Cultural values check

Statement	My view		General UK cultural view	
	Agree	Disagree	Agree	Disagree
A woman's virginity is very important for marriage				
Sex outside of marriage is wrong				
Alcohol is a dangerous drug and getting drunk is shameful				
It is normal for young people to experiment with alcohol and other drugs				
Pop/rock music is very important for my identity				

History lesson

Since the 1960s, British youth (and especially college and university students), has characterised itself as 'liberated' from the more traditional values of older people (parents, teachers etc.) and has promoted experimenting with lifestyles and approaches to living that are in contrast to those of previous and older generations.

This is particularly true for women who have seen their role and life opportunities change greatly since the 1960s.

In the 1960s, because of the development of a youth culture in the UK, people talked, and may still talk, about a 'generation gap': the difference and lack of understanding between parents and their teenage children. This may be disappearing now as many of the 1960s and post-1960s generations are now themselves parents.

Reflective exercise: You may find if you are from a more traditional culture that there is a big gap between your parent's way of life and outlook and yours, and especially the outlook promoted by British youth culture. How far are your parents likely to understand the behaviour and outlook of the young generation in your country, or, from what you know, the young generation in the UK? What things may they not be aware of or understand?

The sexual revolution

The invention and promotion of the oral contraceptive pill, which became widely available to British women in 1961, allowed for the possibility of sexual relations free from the fear of pregnancy before marriage. This was the basis of the 'sexual revolution'. The concept of 'casual' or 'recreational' sex (sex for pleasure rather than procreation) developed among the younger generation, freed from the fear of unwanted pregnancy. This sexual revolution has continued to develop since the 1960s with the result that an increasingly tolerant and liberal attitude towards sex has developed in the general public. This also applies to general public attitudes towards the lesbian and gay movements. Gays and lesbians have increasingly moved from a position of hiding their orientation to being bolder about proclaiming it and to openly fighting prejudice against them. For this reason gays and lesbians have increasingly been encouraged to 'come out of the closet' and not be afraid of being different from heterosexuals. If you come from a country where for religious or cultural reasons homosexuality is illegal and where homosexuals are persecuted you will certainly notice this aspect of sexual permissiveness.

The drugs revolution

At the same time in the 1960s, the psychotropic drug, LSD, appeared on the youth scene. It was promoted as a 'counter-culture' drug by writers such as Aldous Huxley and Ken Kesey and by the American psychologist, Timothy Leary, who invented the phrase 'Turn on, tune in and drop out.' Psychedelic experiences greatly influenced painters and rock musicians of the period and student campuses were often at the forefront of developing a new youth culture. In 1967 the Beatles released their famous psychedelic rock album *Sergeant Pepper's Lonely Hearts Club Band*. Since the 1960s, drug taking and different drug types (alcohol, LSD, cannabis, acid, ecstasy, speed, amphetamines, cocaine etc.) have become associated with different youth movements, lifestyles and fashions. Youth groups made themselves distinctive by adopting different styles of dress and music. Well-known youth movements (which are depicted in many British films) have been: mods, rockers, hippies, punks, new romantics, heavy metal and death metal fans, grungers, goths . . . with new movements seeming to be created with each generation of teenagers. Many of these movements have started in the UK, no doubt because of the development of the London-based pop and rock industry. These movements and fashions have become globalised and have tended to influence youth culture across the world.

The music revolution

Because youth movements provide a strong psychological sense of identity for the young, the music associated with each movement is important to youths as a way of identifying with a particular group and its values. Each group has very different musical tastes and because of this they have often developed a strong dislike of each other.

Because the UK is a multicultural society there are also youth movements associated with specific ethnic groups. These too have their rituals, fashion, preferred drugs, music and ideological outlooks.

Music for many youths in the UK is therefore often linked to an individual's and group's identity and outlook on life. You may find that conversely classical music and folk music that reflects a national heritage is not listened to by young people in the UK as much as in your own country. This may be because such music represents the older generations or a higher-level social class or a nationalism that young British people prefer not to be identified with. The issue of class is important and will be looked at in more detail later in the guide.

Student politics

Although the original youth movements of the 1960s were seen as anti-establishment and politically rebellious (this culminated in the youth revolt of Paris 1968), over the following decades youth movements have become less political and more about fashion and commerce than politics. Youth culture is big business. As a result UK students have, over the past few decades, been seen to be rather apolitical compared to the 1960s generation. You may therefore be surprised (perhaps even disappointed) if you come from a culture where youth like to engage in political debate and action, as this is not currently a major preoccupation and issue of discussion among many British students. This, of course, may change in the future! There has, for example, been recent student unrest and protest in the UK over the rise in tuition fees for students to study at universities.

Being plugged-in

Another crucial aspect of youth culture today is being 'plugged in'. The Internet and the mobile phone have opened up a world of rapidly changing communication. As well as giving unlimited cheap and instant access to friends (e.g. Skype), the Internet links people across the world into social networks such as Facebook and Twitter. For a young person today the mobile phone and access to the Internet is fundamental. Not being plugged in as a young person can result in isolation and a sense of being out of touch.

Question: The above information is designed to give you a context for understanding British youth today. How much of this brief history did you already know and understand?

Reflective exercise: In what ways is the above history of the youth movement in modern Britain similar to your experience of the youth movement in your country? In what ways is it different?

Sex and culture

Comment: Whilst there are movements and campaigns on campuses to promote chastity among students (often from religious groups), most British students would see it as perfectly normal to have sexual relations with other students, even if this is not necessarily part of a stable relationship.

Pitfalls!

There can, however, be several negative consequences to this liberal approach to physical intimacy among British youth. Important consequences it is best to be aware of and plan against are:

- Unwanted pregnancy
- Sexually transmitted diseases (STDs)/sexually transmitted infections (STIs)
- Emotional confusion and upset.

Background

British secondary schools and family doctors as well as many parents have accepted the reality of sexual activity among young people. Schools take steps to prepare young people for this and, through education, try to protect them from the attendant dangers of pregnancy and STDs. Despite this the UK has a problem in these two areas. There are higher levels of teenage pregnancy in the UK compared to the rest of Western Europe and doctors warn they are seeing a worrying rise in STDs among the young (genital warts, chlamydia, genital herpes, trichomoniasis, gonorrhea).

Information

The following is adapted from some advice taken from a student designed website aimed at UK students:

It's great being at University isn't it? We are away from home for the first time with no one around to tell us what we can and can't do! This new freedom can make us all go a little wild! We will no doubt be very busy getting to know new people and forming new relationships. Having a good time – often with alcohol involved – can mean we lower our inhibitions and take more risks.

But remember that STIs and unplanned pregnancies are at an all time high and still increasing in number, it's better to be safe rather than sorry. Remember that it only takes one mistake to lead to a lot of misery and important negative consequences.

The safest way to have sex is to use condoms. For most people this can be off-putting, but it is essential to use them to reduce the risks of STIs and pregnancy at the same time. One tactic is to try to make a joke out of using one, as making it fun reduces tension. Anyway remember that condoms are there to protect both of you.

No other contraception covers both of these aspects for both of you. Think about the fact that if someone refuses to have sex with a condom you should wonder why. The truth is that no one can ever be sure of their own or their partner's sexual and STI history and while some STIs may not show symptoms in some people these people may still be infectious.

Reflective exercise: What do you think of this advice? Is it helpful for you? Had you thought of this before or is there new information for you to think about in here?

It is strange that with this state education policy and the ready availability of various forms of contraception in the UK (from hormonal implants to the wide availability of male and female condoms – the 'femidom') British youth seems to suffer from these problems at higher rates than other European youth. Possible reasons are:

- Educational policy focusing on the functional rather than the emotional aspects of sex, which makes it seem detached and unreal to students.

- Young women feeling pressurised to be sexually active before they are emotionally ready because they may think this is expected of them to be accepted by boys.
- Easy access to, and high levels of, alcohol consumption by the young may lower defences and reduce the likelihood of using effective protection during sex.
- Abortion is free and provided by the National Health Service to women who wish to have it.
- The British welfare state offers some financial and housing help to young single mothers.

Another reason may be cultural: the attitude towards sexual permissiveness among young people in other countries may be different and more conservative.

Reflective exercise: Think about your country and the attitude among young people. Is it different? What is the attitude towards a young single girl if she gets pregnant? What kind of help or support can she expect from the state or society?

Note: In the UK, abortion (termination of pregnancy) is legal and provided by the NHS. This has been the case for a long time and in the UK this does not currently raise the same level of controversy as it does in other parts of the world such as the USA.

Question: What is your attitude to abortion? Why do you think the UK is not generally a country for which this is an important political issue?

Stop and think: How does this background information compare to your own sex education and the approach to sex among the young people in your country? In what ways do you see your own approach and attitude as different from what is described here? If it is different why do you think this is?

Sex and culture: Emotional relationships, falling in love and considering experimenting with sex is inevitable for university students away from home and free to make their own decisions in this regard, perhaps for the first time. This is complex enough in one's own culture where you are more likely to know the rules and read the signs to do with flirtation. You may have a better idea in your own culture of what is expected and permitted in certain circumstances and what is not. When you enter another culture, or mix with young people from other cultures, this can become a lot more complex and confusing and mistakes can be made.

Exercise

Look at the following two stories, and then consider the issues arising from the following questions:

Story 1: 'Jasmine' was from an East Asian country and from a middle-class, conservative family. She had come to a UK university to do a Masters and she ended up sharing a house in town with two other female Masters students – one British and one Swedish. One night they decided to have a 'house party' and invited their fellow classmates along. Jasmine did this by personally inviting members of her class. 'Jacobo' was one of the students invited to the party by Jasmine and went along as he assumed that she was interested in him because of the personal nature of the invite. To him this was significant. He had heard that Latin men are attractive to Asian women. He felt flattered and was curious to sleep with an Asian woman. Jasmine was not used to drinking alcohol but drank as everyone else was doing so – she didn't want to be a killjoy. She enjoyed dancing with a fellow international student – 'Jacobo' from Central America. The next day Jasmine recalled that towards the end of the evening she had been guided to her bedroom by Jacobo where he had expected her to have sex with him. She had managed to fend him off and he had left angrily. In the morning the previous night's events seemed unreal. The alcohol had clouded her thinking and she realised that Jacobo had been pressurising her to act in a way she didn't want to. She felt angry and humiliated that he had assumed he could act in this way with her. She didn't feel there was anyone she could talk to about this and having to work with him in class after this became so upsetting and stressful that she was unable to continue to concentrate on studying properly and decided to give up her Masters and return home.

Story 2: Hamid was 18 when he came to the UK to study English for a year – he had obtained a scholarship for this from the Ministry of Education in his North African country. In class he was often paired with Sachiko, a slightly older Japanese woman. She was studying English for a term in the same class as him as part of a visiting Japanese university group. Hamid's spoken English was better than Sachiko's and she admired his ability. One evening the class decided to go out together for an evening meal. Sachiko sat next to Hamid. They walked back to their university accommodation block together and Sachiko went into Hamid's room to listen to some music. Sachiko was sexually experienced and Hamid wasn't, so Hamid had sex for the first time. Over the next few days Hamid found himself becoming obsessed with Sachiko – he couldn't think of anything else but her and wanted to be with her all the time. Other classmates noticed this and disapproving of this reported it to the accompanying Japanese professor. The Japanese professor had a meeting with Sachiko and told her that others in the group had seen her going into a young foreign man's room at night. He told her that this was shameful behaviour and he would have to tell her parents about it if it didn't stop immediately. The next day Sachiko told Hamid she didn't want to see him any more and he was not to sit with her in class. She felt angry at her classmates and the professor because she liked Hamid, but she also didn't want her father to find out. Hamid was bewildered and very upset and lost all interest in his studies. He did not know what he had done wrong or why Sachiko had suddenly cut him off. She felt she couldn't explain why.

Reflective exercise: In both stories cultural differences and attitudes have negative consequences for the young international students involved. Because of sexual relations going wrong the students in these two examples gave up their studies. What lessons can you take from these two examples? How might the problems have been avoided?

There are several possible areas for problems to occur in such situations. One is the problem of assuming that people from other cultures will interpret your behaviour, behave in the same way and have the same understandings and reactions as young people from your own culture. Another problem is that of sexually stereotyping people from other cultures, e.g. 'young women from country X are free and easy' or 'men from county X are only interested in sex and not emotional engagement'. Taking greater risks when away from the reservations and behavioural controls that you may experience in your home culture can cause difficulties.

Reflective exercise: Do you think any of these factors could have influenced the actions in the stories above and could have led to the problems experienced?

Advice: As with all intercultural communication, assuming you know what the other person is thinking or that people from different cultures have the same outlook as yourself is dangerous. Checking and discussing attitudes and understanding is important. Sexual relations, while a complicated area to talk openly about, is no exception and as shown in the above examples, the consequences of not having the same understanding as each other can be damaging for those concerned.

Sex is a vital part of human life and is an especially important part of students' thoughts and lives. It is not, of course, something that only leads to negative outcomes as the examples above show, but can be a positive and fun intercultural learning experience. The rest of this section looks at the more fun part of sexual behaviour from an intercultural perspective. This is designed to help you think about sexual flirtation and culture and to help you make some sort of sense of the rules that may be in operation as regards sexual flirtation in the UK.

Flirtation: reading the messages

Flirtation is what we humans do when we are interested sexually in another person. There are many ways that we signal this interest to each other and many of these would seem to be universal, but some may be culturally specific – and these may be confusing.

Reflective exercise: If you are interested in another person, what are the flirtation signs that you use and recognise in your culture? Try the following exercise. Think of as many signs as possible and their meaning:

Male flirtation sign

Sign	Meaning

Female flirtation sign

Sign	Meaning

In the animal world flirtation is often a display by the male to attract the female (male peacocks open their big tail fans, stag deer fight each other with their antlers) and it is ritualistic. Although we humans also have a set of signs that we use to signal interest, these may be different from person to person and from culture to culture. There is no 100 per cent certain way of knowing if someone is flirting with you and wants to be more than just an acquaintance or a friend! To complicate this some people like to play the flirtation game as a way of seeking attention and making themselves feel important. Problems can arise particularly when mistaking friendliness, or games played for sexual interest. Whatever games may be played there is one vitally important rule that must be followed:

The unbreakable rule: 'No' means 'No'.

Having understood this, there are, however, signs you can look for and become aware of.

Exercise

Read the following story of two imaginary British students flirting with each other. Underline each point where you think there is a flirtation sign occurring and explain what it means.

Scene 1:

Two students meet at the library issuing desk. Over the past few weeks they have been noticing each other by catching each other's eye. The young woman finds she has again caught the young man's eye. She smiles but looks away quite quickly. The man moves closer to the woman:

♂: Hi XX – How's the course going?

♀: [Looks up and seems surprised] Oh Hi XX, Fine. You?

♂: Nearing the end now, thank God! I can't wait to read something I want to for a change!

♀: [Smiles] Yes, I know what you mean! [Flicks her hair]

♂: Hey let's get a coffee. I need my caffeine fix. Come and join me.

♀: [Looks hesitant and looks at her watch] Oh OK. It'll have to be quick, I've only got 10 minutes to kill.

Scene 2:

The man buys two cups of coffee after checking what the woman wants. He takes them to seats located away from the main open area of the coffee bar. The woman follows the man and sits opposite him. They chat about the course until the woman looks at her watch again.

♂: OK, I guess you have to be on your way now. Hey! I'm going out with some friends tonight to celebrate handing in my last assignment. We're going to this really great pub – the Cat and Fiddle. Do you know it?

♀: [Shakes her head]

♂: Look. Come along. You'll love it.

♀: I don't know. I have to prepare for a 10:00 a.m. seminar tomorrow and . . .

♂: Oh that's OK – a little break will be good for you then. We won't be there all night anyway – I've got an important squash match tomorrow too. What's the seminar on?

♀: Oh boring . . . Customer behaviour in banks – you know their attitude to waiting and queuing. Stuff like that . . . We had to observe customers and analyse their behaviour.

♂: No kidding! No bank robberies at the time I hope!

♀: [Laughs] Nothing so exciting I can assure you.

♂: OK. I'll meet you at the library at 7:30.

Scene 3:

In the pub towards the end of the evening.

[The man sits next to the woman. The man's thigh presses against the woman's thigh. The woman does not move away. The man shows the woman a trick to do with flicking beer mats, she cannot do it so he places his hand on hers to teach her. She does not withdraw her hand and seems to enjoy learning the trick.]

♀: Well I guess I'd better get back.

♂: I'll walk you back to your place.

♀: No, no. That's OK. I don't want to be a bother.

♂: No bother. I've got to pass by your place anyway.

♀: [Gathers coat – male helps her put it on]

Scene 4:

In front of the woman's accommodation.

♂: Thanks, that was nice. Shame about the seminar tomorrow. Hey you've got something in your hair [Looking closely at the woman's hair the man then brushes her hair with his hand to clear it away]. [After a pause, with both of them lingering] Tell you what – you can practice the presentation on me – so long as you make me a cup of coffee. Is it a deal?

Comment: Box 8.3 lists behaviours that are often associated with flirtation. How many of these did you notice being used in the dialogue above?

Box 8.3	
Behaviour	*Comment*
Raised eyebrows	Shows interest
Eye contact	Held for a bit longer than is normal. Regular brief instances across a room
Sideways glance	A strong signal of interest
Hair flicking	Female
Playing with accessories	Female: earrings, twirling hair, fiddling with necklace Male: playing with necktie, jingling change in pocket
Leaning in towards the other person	Getting closer than normal
Open body language	Not turning away, crossing arms or legs or pulling back
Looking at lips or other body parts	'Checking each other out'
Laughter	Laughing at the other person's jokes
Finding excuses for and ways to touch	Light touching, pressing thighs together
Complimenting the other person, especially on their appearance	This becomes flirting if it is more than what is usually expected

Cultural difference: Although much flirting behaviour may be universal – e.g. dilated pupils may be a biological sign of attraction – there are also cultural variables with the use of the above set of signs. Concepts of personal space, touching and eye contact may particularly be different. The routines that two people may engage in as they move from one level of flirting to another will also be cultural. In some cultures there are very clear rules and sequences of actions that are followed: not following them in some cultures could even be dangerous for the people concerned. This may mean that if you come from a culture where flirting is ritualised, you may find the uncertainty in the UK difficult. We will now look at some of the cultural differences that may exist:

Personal space: Different people from different cultures are brought up (socialised) into expecting a certain physical closeness or distance between people as normal. This distance changes between different cultures. In some cultures people are more comfortable closer to each other than in other cultures where people are more comfortable further apart. This is about how much personal space people feel they need. One sign of flirting is getting nearer to the other person, i.e. going beyond the normal distance that another person considers their 'personal space'. Flirting is often about reducing the personal space zone.

Reflective exercise: Look again at the dialogue above. How is space used to send messages?

Note: Inviting someone into your bedroom is of course a very definite invitation into your personal space and towards intimacy.

Touch: In some cultures touching is part of ordinary friendship and means nothing more, e.g. kissing or holding hands (this can occur between friends of the same sex). In other cultures kissing or hand-holding is not understood in this way, but is rather a sign of intimacy. In some cultures people touch each during normal interaction more than in other cultures without it having a flirtatious meaning. This can also cause confusion.

Eye contact: In some cultures it may be normal to look at the person you are speaking to directly, i.e. eye to eye. In other cultures, for example the UK, it is not usual to look someone in the eye for very long – although it can be longer than in some other cultures. Looking at someone longer than normal is a way of showing some sort of interest.

Other uses of eye contact are catching someone's eye repeatedly, winking (a male activity that can be used to show a secret liking when directed at a female) or deliberately averting your gaze if you are not interested. When people from different cultures have very different eye contact norms this can lead to misunderstanding and confusion (someone used to short periods or very little eye contact may seem uninterested when this is not the case, or someone with much more sustained eye contact norms may appear to be too interested and 'in your face' to those not used to this). The messages can easily be misread because of cultural differences.

Routines: In the above example the routine is a traditional one in which it is the male who is the one who is the chaser/driver and the female the decider/controller. This is a traditional male–female flirtation pattern in many cultures, but as women are becoming more emancipated in the UK and may be more forward themselves this pattern may be changing. You may find that if you are from a culture where women do not behave as the chaser/driver you find it difficult to know how to respond when you come across this behaviour!

Note: In the example dialogue above it is the man who does the 'chatting up', who 'invites the female out', who pays for the coffee and who makes the suggestions on actions. The male also adopts the traditional role of protector – paying for the coffee, helping the female to put her coat on, walking the female home. The female adopts the role of decision maker and possible line-drawer – allowing the flirting to develop as far as she wants it to or stopping it when she wants to. In the above dialogue the female could have beaten the male off at many points offered by the male, e.g. when invited for coffee she could have said she didn't have time. The female also adopts the traditional role of 'playing hard to get', i.e. of not wanting to seem an easy win for the male (averting her gaze, saying it would be difficult to go out as she had to get home early).

Note: Sexual politics and gender roles. *Scenario 1*: a male holds a door open for a female coming after him. The female is angry and tells him she can open a door for herself. The male is confused and feels angry.

Analysis: What is going on in this scene do you think? Who is right and who is wrong?

Scenario 2: Veronica, an international female student, was used in her culture to dressing up in what she felt was a very feminine way. This involved fishnet stockings, long high-heeled boots, a short, tight mini-skirt, a tight leather jacket and quite obvious lipstick and eye shadow, as well as long, dyed blonde hair. She liked dressing this way, but noticed that in the UK dressing in this way provoked 'wolf whistles', winks and comments from passing men and also hostile looks and sometimes rude comments from British females.

Analysis: What is going on in this situation do you think? Who is right and who is wrong?

WARNING!

Date/acquaintance rape

One problem that appears to be on the increase, and is perhaps also under-reported, is what is called 'date' or 'acquaintance' rape. It is about people not understanding or respecting the borderlines of friendship relationships. In many cases there seems to be confusion about the willingness to have sex. This may be about misreading or confusing signals, and of course with two people from different cultures the confusion can be greater. The danger is that males may mistake friendliness for sexual interest; they may expect females to play hard to get. They may mistake true lack of sexual interest for coyness and think the female is really simply expecting the male to be persistent and forceful.

One frequently commented upon aspect of female 'message sending' by international students in the UK is that of the way some young British women choose to dress when they go out for the evening to party. International students from more conservative cultures may be intrigued, confused and sometimes shocked to see women in UK high streets exposing skin, even in the depths of winter.

Note: It is important to realise that much of this way of dressing is due to fashion. Some UK youth fashions deliberately set out to shock and draw attention to the users of the fashion by challenging more established ways of dressing. Another aspect of 'going out' in the UK among youths is for groups of the same sex to dress up together and go around together, and each person may be dressing to compete with the other members of the group. Dressing in this way is often part of 'letting off steam' (also known as 'letting your hair down') i.e. having fun, after having worked a conventional week in a more conventional role.

Drugs and culture

Drugs are mental stimulants and are used in all cultures. In the Andes the indigenous people chew cocaine leaves to give themselves energy at high altitude; in Asia opium and heroin are used, often in ceremonies; in Jamaica 'ganja' (cannabis) use was made famous by certain Rastafarians (e.g. Bob Marley), with its use being linked to spiritual experience; in East Africa khat is chewed as a stimulant. These and many other drugs have been used for hundreds of years in these cultures. Now, in the modern world, drugs are commercialised illegally and sold, mostly to young people who use them for recreational purposes. Drugs are big business and can be found, for those who want them, on many university campuses.

Addictive drugs

Some drugs are well known to be addictive – this means that as you use them your body and mind become dependant on them to function and once you are 'hooked' you find that without them you feel mentally and physically unwell. The need to take the drugs on a regular basis can lead to economic and social problems. There are an estimated 280,000 problem drug users in the UK, most taking heroin and crack cocaine, and the use of these drugs is estimated to lead to around 2,500 deaths a year. People addicted to these drugs are often referred to in the popular press by the negative word 'junkies'. Areas where such addicts gather to inject their drugs (to shoot up) are often identifiable by used needles on the ground. These can be dangerous objects as they may transmit diseases such as HIV or hepatitis C if they puncture your skin. Another problem of such addiction is that heroin addicts may resort to crime to find the money to 'fuel their habit'. Some researchers suggest that as much as 20 per cent of 'acquisitive crime' (stealing and robbing) may be a result of drug addition. For this reason some countries have legalised drug use to try to control the needles and take away the need for crime to obtain the drugs. The drugs are instead supplied by the medical profession to registered drugs users.

> **Reflective exercise**: What are considered to be drugs in your culture? Who uses them and what is the attitude towards drug taking among young people in your culture? What is the legal situation regarding possession of these drugs?

The legal situation in the UK

Note: In certain countries in the world certain drug use and possession is punishable by death. In other countries of the world certain drug use is legal – this is the case in Portugal, which in 2001 became the first European country to officially abolish all criminal penalties for personal possession of drugs, including marijuana, cocaine, heroin and methamphetamine. In other countries drugs laws are not imposed and drug use is tolerated – famously the case in Amsterdam in the Netherlands which has cannabis cafés. This understandably leads to confusion in the minds of international students about drugs and the law in the UK.

The Misuse of Drugs Act of 1971 made the possession and supply of drugs illegal in the UK. Drugs were classified into three categories:

Table 8.3 Categories of illegal drugs in the UK

Class A	These include cocaine and crack (a form of cocaine), ecstasy, heroin, LSD, methadone, methamphetamine (crystal meth), magic mushrooms containing ester of psilocin and any Class B drug which is injected
Class B	These include amphetamine (not methamphetamine), barbiturates, codeine and cannabis
Class C	These include anabolic steroids and minor tranquillisers

Note on cannabis: The most common drug that you may encounter socially, besides alcohol, is cannabis. Although cannabis use is illegal in the UK, punishment is usually minor, resulting in a confiscation and a 'cannabis warning' for small amounts. It is worth noting however that this warning will appear under your name on government databases and in Criminal Records Bureau (CRB) security checks. There is evidence that cannabis, especially the more potent varieties, can bring on mental problems: if you have mental health problems, taking a drug – any drug – excessively, is going to make your problems worse and this may be even truer when you are navigating living in a foreign culture. Another potential problem is that of mental addiction to the drug. With regular use, a cannabis user can become unmotivated. This may lead to the user being more likely to be late for or absent from class or struggling to keep up with studies and it can lead to a downwards cycle towards failure on a study programme.

WARNING!

International students must be aware that drug using and supplying is a serious offence under UK law. Although often the full prison sentences are not applied, it is important to know that the penalty for a Class A drugs offence is a maximum sentence, for possession, of seven years imprisonment with an unlimited fine, and for supply, life imprisonment and an unlimited fine. For class B the maximum for possession is five years or a fine or both, and for supply, 14 years imprisonment or a fine or both.

Music festivals

The UK is increasingly famous for having music festivals, and these cover a very wide range of different types of music. Famous festivals, for example, are at Glastonbury and Reading.

Useful website: http://www.thefestivalcalendar.co.uk

Attending a summer music festival is a ritual among UK youth, with the full experience involving camping out, partying, sleeping off hangovers and even having mud baths! It is best to prepare properly before going. Many festivals are also part fairs now with stands offering all sorts of food and products and different groups running workshops to accompany the event.

Pub culture

One of the most frequent places that people in the UK go out to and socialise in is the pub, and students are no exception. British pubs (public houses) are famous the world over. A pub, and visiting a pub, has a certain set of 'rules' (pub etiquette) that it is useful to know about and follow for a smooth visit.

Exercise

Look at the pub visit routine in Box 8.4 and put the events in the right order.

	Box 8.4
1	Pay for the round
2	Wait for one of your friends to offer to get the next round (one of your drinking companions should do this when most of you are ready for a refill)
3	Ask your friends what they want and offer to get the first round
4	Order the drinks, answering any further questions from the barperson
5	Enter the pub and go to the bar
6	Take the drinks over to your friends and settle down at a table and drink and chat
7	Help take the empty glasses (empties) back to the bar and say goodbye and thanks to the barperson
8	Greet the landlord/landlady/barista
Answers: 5, 8, 3, 4, 1, 6, 2, 7	

Note on payment: Unlike in some other countries, you need to pay for the drinks upon point of order. There is a cultural tradition in the UK that people, in turn, buy 'rounds' of drinks, rather than each person individually buying their own drink (unless this has been agreed otherwise by the group).

Note on pub food: Most pubs nowadays also serve food ('pub grub') and can be cheaper places to eat than restaurants. Most UK pubs do not offer tapas or small dishes of food to accompany drinks. People usually buy packets of crisps or peanuts instead.

Note on pub beer: The British take great pride in their beer. It is often brown in colour and served at room temperature and is pumped into the glass. Another word for this beer is 'bitter' or 'ale'. The lighter-coloured blonde beer found in most of the rest of Europe and the world is called lager!

Chapter 9

Life beyond the university

Understanding and navigating British life and culture

Introduction

This chapter looks at UK culture beyond the university. It particularly focuses on aspects of UK culture that you may notice as different or strange but that you may need to understand and engage with. The aim of this chapter is to help you to be better placed to understand and participate in the life and culture of the UK as an international student. After a general introduction to modern Britain, the information is provided under separate sections. It will give you a basic understanding of UK society and also provide you with some exercises to develop your awareness of this culture and your own response to it. The final part of this chapter, 'Streetwise', is designed to help you avoid certain pitfalls and possible dangers and to stay safe during your stay in the UK. It is not designed to frighten you: the UK is generally a safe environment to be an international student in, but the overriding concern here is that it is 'better safe than sorry' and being safe is often about knowing things beforehand.

General introduction: who are the British?

Question: What do you know about the British? Where are they from? What is the ethnic composition of modern British society?

WARNING!

It is wrong to assume that the 'real' British these days are exclusively white people. There are other races and ethnic British communities that are just as much British in all regards as the white population. Black communities in Bristol, Liverpool and Manchester are not simply recent results of immigration but have a long history going back centuries. You should not assume that anyone who is not white is from a foreign country or will have much of a sense of being anything other than British.

Advice: Being 'colour blind' when interacting with the British is a good way to avoid making such a mistake. It is best to let a person decide if they want to discuss their ethnic origins. It is usually something that one finds out at a later stage of friendship than on first encounters. In many ways Britain and certainly London is now 'super-diverse'.

The British ethnic mix

The historical ethnic origin of the British is an amalgam of:

* Pre-Celts and Celts arriving some 15,000–7,500 years ago
* The Roman invasion and occupation from AD43 to 410 – which brought people from all over the Roman Empire to the British Isles
* The Anglo-Saxon invasion and occupation (fifth and sixth centuries)
* The invasion and occupation by the Norse people (Vikings) who especially settled in the north and east of the British Isles (ninth–eleventh centuries)
* The invasion and conquest by the Norman French in 1066.

As well as this mix of ethnicities from conquest and invasion, Britain has a long and more recent history of immigration. Liverpool has the oldest black population dating from 1730 and the oldest Chinese community in Europe dating from the nineteenth century. Huguenots (French Calvinist Protestants) came to Britain in the late seventeenth century and many Irish and Jewish people arrived in the nineteenth century. After the Second World War there was substantial migration from Africa, the Caribbean and South Asia – a legacy of the British Empire. There was also substantial immigration from Poland. Recently, with the entry of former East European countries as New Accession States into the EU there has been substantial immigration of young people to Britain from the former Eastern Europe.

The census in 2001 showed that 92 per cent of the 62 million UK population was 'white'. The nearest other ethnic population in size was British Indian at around 2 per cent of the population. From the 2011 census a large, new, growing category of people is 'mixed race' and the non-white population now stands at 16.5 per cent.

Note: Most of the 'non-white' ethnic groups tend to concentrate in the bigger cities and especially London.

Note: Immigration is a hot political issue in the UK at present and one consequence of this is the tightening of regulations for entry of overseas students. It was felt that previously the student visa route was being used illegally by people not interested in studying but in entering the country to work.

Religion

Christianity

The official religion of England is Anglican Christianity, as practised by the Church of England. The Church in Wales is also Anglican. In Scotland the official Church is the Presbyterian Church of Scotland. Other Christians in each country also include the Roman Catholics and the Methodists. The Queen (the British monarch) is Supreme Governor of the Church of England. It is a Protestant church and its leader is the Archbishop of Canterbury.

Note: This has not always been the situation in Britain. Historically Britain has been a Catholic country for much longer than a Protestant one (the religion of the state became the protestant form of Christianity in the mid-sixteenth century): Roman Christianity took root in Britain in the sixth century. Much of the religious inheritance, the beautiful cathedrals and churches, were built in Catholic Britain.

It is worth noting from the 2001 census that 53 per cent of the population described themselves as Christian (many of these Church of England). However, in reality, religion is an increasingly unimportant aspect of life for many – even those who may claim to be Christian. When people describe themselves as Christian, it may be they see themselves as culturally Christian rather than meaning they have a firm Christian religious outlook on life. Also about 30 per cent of the population declares themselves non-religious. This makes for a society that does not appear to be very religious. Seven per cent of the population is also comprised of people from other religions: Muslims make up about 3 per cent and Hindus about 1 per cent of the population. The other religions that make up the remainder are the Jewish, Buddhist and Sikh religions.

Religious tolerance

An important message is that Britain is a multi-faith society in which everyone has the right to religious freedom. Although Britain is historically a Christian society, people are usually tolerant towards the faiths of others as well as those who have no religious beliefs. As an international student it should be easy for you to practice your faith freely in the UK. Many universities offer mosque or multi-faith prayer facilities for their students.

UK social structure and class

Key to understanding British society is understanding British social class structure. Although it is argued that class distinctions and divisions are not as rigid as they used to be, that there is more class mobility between the generations now than before, certain important facts about class remain evident. An example from the university education sector makes this clear: Oxford University currently takes 55 per cent of its undergraduate British students from state schools and 45 per cent from private (also confusingly called 'public') schools. However, only 7 per cent of the British school population go to private (public) schools.

Brief history of class in the UK

The historical origins of British class-based society are unclear: some suggest that it is a consequence of the Norman invasion of 1066 and the subsequent structuring of society based on a French-speaking, landowning elite ruling over a conquered Saxon peasantry.

Certainly, after the French invasion, education, delivered in Latin and French, was for those who would progress to well-paid administrative jobs working for the Court. The other form of learning was copying the work of parents or learning on the job through becoming an apprentice to a tradesman and craftsman. The Industrial Revolution further served to divide people into a working class (factory workers) and a managerial class.

The first Industrial Revolution in the world occurred in Britain in the nineteenth century. There was no system of social welfare to protect workers from exploitation, and this led to great urban poverty and hardship as workers came in from the land to live in overcrowded and unsanitary conditions in the cities.

Note: This movement is now paralleled in the developing world today.

During the Industrial Revolution women and children worked unregulated hours and in dangerous conditions – there was no Health and Safety legislation to protect them from the machines they operated or from exposure to dangerous chemicals. Children as young as four were at times employed.

Note: Child labour is now considered by wealthy countries to be a human rights violation, and is outlawed. However, in poorer countries in the world child labour still exists.

One consequence of this was that the family, as a unit, was undermined because while parents worked in the factories, younger children, who did not go to school, were often left to look after themselves in the streets. It can be argued that the origin of street gangs and rebellious youth in the UK stems from this nineteenth-century period.

The government made efforts to deal with the problem on many fronts. One was education, with state primary education becoming obligatory in 1870. Before then formal education was only available for young children in church schools (both Anglican and Non-conformist).

While enforced state education has undoubtedly changed many lives for the better, schools were also perceived by certain street youths as a way of trying to control and change them – to take them away from the freedom of the street and to try to instil middle-class values in them to make them less rebellious and easier to control. This view of education as not necessarily something benevolent and in the interests of certain working-class children is an attitude that is still surprisingly prevalent in parts of the UK today, with teachers often seen by youths as enemies or repressive instruments of the state.

Reflective question: What is the view of education in your country?

- Is it seen as an instrument of good and advancement offering opportunity to families and their children?
- Is there a view that it is also a negative factor that is there to try and control and pacify certain youths?

Note: In many developing countries in the world education is often not resourced sufficiently by the state and a good education is often a luxury beyond the financial reaches of many. In such countries education is generally understood to be vital as a way to escape poverty and move up the social ladder. Sadly a decent education remains a dream for many. As an international student it may surprise you, if you value education in this way, to notice an apparent disregard for free education and the lack of a study ethic among British youth.

Reflective question: Are you surprised by this view of education held by certain youths? Is it the same in your country? Can you understand it? How does this attitude seem to vary from yours?

In the UK people's class status tends to determine their life opportunities, their way of life (lifestyle) and often their tastes and attitudes. Different social classes have different outlooks on life and can be thought of as having different cultures.

Exercise

If you want to further understand the UK culture generally you may be interested to ask UK students their views on class in the UK and to which class, if any, they feel they belong and why. You can ask British friends about how class may be reflected in the items listed in Table 9.1:

Table 9.1 British culture and class influence

Factor	Class influence and examples of these
People's names	
Supermarkets used	

Food	
Where you live	
Hobbies and pastimes	
Sport	
Education	
Clothes and fashion	
Musical tastes	
Way of speaking (accent)	
Other	

Class divisions

The answers will probably be very complex, but generally people will label themselves as either working class, middle class or upper class. Some may divide the categories into lower middle class and upper middle class or may feel that they are in transition from one class to another (e.g. working class to middle class).

The north–south divide

Of key importance is where you are from – North or South – with the North being considered traditionally more industrial and working class than the South and Southerners being viewed stereotypically by Northerners as more 'posh' and snobbish and less 'down to earth' than Northerners. Southerners may conversely stereotypically view Northerners as 'gruff' and 'unsophisticated'. This North–South view of the UK divides the country along a line drawn from Ipswich to Oxford to Bristol.

Housing

Another important factor is where you live and the type of housing you are from. British cities and towns and even villages tend to structure themselves along class lines with streets being typically working class or middle class. For this reason the government can use postcodes as a way of determining the value of property in each street for Council Tax purposes. The upper class tend to live in detached country houses known as mansions or country estates (many of these are beautiful buildings with private collections of art and are open to visitors on certain days). After the Second World War there was a housing shortage and the Socialist government of the time constructed state-owned housing for the masses with controlled rents: areas of towns had 'council estates' built in them. In the 1980s the Conservative government offered many of these council houses for sale to their tenants and so in council estate areas today there is a mix of state-owned and privately owned housing – which has caused a further class division.

Reflective question: Do you have a class system in your country? Does it work in the same way as in the UK? If so what class do you consider yourself to be in your country?

Introduction to British politics

The British do not, as a rule, spend much time discussing politics. It is not a preferred topic of conversation, as it may be in many other countries of the world. Political interest in and awareness of what is happening in other parts of the world may strike you as rather low. British news does cover the basics of what is happening in the world, especially if there is a disaster or catastrophe, and newspapers do carry international sections, but generally the news is focused on UK events and happenings. The joke that a paper could carry an article on the front page about the Queen of England breaking her toe and the news in a small column on the second page that half the world has ceased to exist after being hit by a meteorite may strike you as not so improbable!

The UK is a constitutional democracy, which means that there is a very complex and subtle arrangement of power in the country between the monarchy and the elected government. The important point is that the UK is not a republic and neither is it a full-blooded monarchy either. People elect their parliament from the political party choices available through regular elections (every four years). The government, which is led by a Prime Minister, then runs the country, passing laws and implementing its ideology through laws that have to be passed first by votes in the House of Commons and then in the House of Lords.

As well as giving permission (be it largely symbolically) for the formation of governments, the current Queen is, in fact, also the head of the armed services and the Church of England. It is perhaps little surprise therefore that the British people take such a keen interest in the Royal family and in who is likely to be their next monarch!

The main political parties to choose from are:

- the Conservative party (right wing and an advocate of private ownership)
- the Labour Party (socialist in origin, still broadly left of centre and an advocate of state control)
- the Liberal Democrats (promote an ideology that mixes strands of thought from both the Conservative and the Labour parties)

Note: The Green party in the UK only has one parliamentary seat, but this may not reflect the true support that a small party has in the population. This is because in the UK there is not a proportional representation voting system but a 'first past the post' system.

British hobbies and pastimes

The British are a nation of special interest groups. They are very keen on amateur-level sport or drama, and take keeping fit seriously. They also have a love of their countryside. You will find evidence of this in the local city library – where a list of local clubs is available, many of them advertising for new members. Towns and cities also put on a wide range of exercise and keep fit sessions at local sports centres. All towns have local football, rugby, hockey and other sports clubs.

Advice: If you want to meet the British, joining local clubs and societies is an ideal way to do so.

The great outdoors

Walking in the countryside is a British pastime. You will find that the whole country is crossed with thousands of public footpaths that take you through beautiful countryside, many of the pathways starting in town and city centres. These pathways are all indicated on detailed Ordinance Survey maps available in local bookshops at very reasonable cost (the Explorer 1:25,000 scale maps are ideal to use). Using these pathways is a very fun way of discovering the local area and it keeps you fit!

Streetwise

In this section we will look at social aspects of Britain that you will encounter. The aim of the section is to inform you about and explain about certain aspects of life in British streets. While in general the UK is a safe country for people in the street, as with everywhere it is also best to be aware of potential dangers or problems that can occur.

Driving on the left

While you may know that the British drive on the left, it is easy to forget this when you are walking in the streets or crossing roads. Tourists and international students who come from countries where cars drive on the right need to remember that in the UK this is the opposite. Always make sure that you do not step out into a street without looking first. Make sure you look both ways and for traffic approaching from your right!

Alcohol

The most common drug in the UK, and one which is deeply part of the culture, is alcohol, and this has traditionally been beer or whisky.

One of the most noticeable and most commented on aspects of British life by international students is the British approach to drinking alcohol. British youths can drink alcohol from the age of 18 years. This is much earlier than in the USA, where many states restrict alcohol to youths and where the legal drinking age is 21 years.

Alcohol is very widely available in the UK. The UK has a drink driving limit of 80 milligrams of alcohol per 100 millilitres of blood, so it is not unusual to be with British people who will drink some alcohol and then drive. This may seem shocking for people from countries where there is a zero tolerance of alcohol in the blood of a driver.

> **Reflective question**: What is your experience of drinking alcohol? What is your attitude? How are you going to approach drinking alcohol during your time as a student?

Alcohol and health

The UK government tries to promote sensible drinking and offers the following guidelines:

> Men should drink no more than 21 units of alcohol per week (and no more than four units in any one day). Women should drink no more than 14 units of alcohol per week (and no more than three units in any one day). Pregnant women should not drink or smoke at all.

One unit of alcohol is 10 ml (1cl) by volume, or 8 g by weight, of pure alcohol. Table 9.2 shows what one unit of alcohol is about equal to:.

Table 9.2 Units of alcohol in popular drinks

Drink type	Strength (% alcohol by volume)	Units	Units
Wine		**Small glass (125 ml)**	**Large glass (175 ml)**
	12 %	1.5	2.1
	14 %	1.75	2.45
Beer		**Half pint**	**Full pint**
	3 %	1.0	2.0
	4 %	1.1	2.2
	5 %	1.4	2.8
Spirits		**Single shot (25 ml)**	**Double shot (50ml)**
	20 %	0.5	1.0
	40 %	1.0	2.0

Suggestion: You can use the above information to monitor yourself to see if you are staying within the guidelines or if you are increasing your consumption and therefore risking damaging your health.

Anyone who watches the British drinking (and this certainly includes students), will realise that the guidelines are seldom followed and a consequence of this is that British people are damaging their health. Liver damage and obesity are consequences of drinking too much alcohol, and the government is worried about the cost of this to the nation.

Drunkenness

Perhaps the most noticeable aspect of alcohol drinking is the drunkenness in the streets on Friday and Saturday nights. People from countries and cultures where alcohol is not drunk or where it is drunk but in a different way, may be shocked at the way alcohol is consumed in the UK. In Latin countries such as Italy or Spain alcohol is traditionally served in bars with food and is drunk for the purpose of enjoying the taste and flavour. Using alcohol with the sole purpose of getting drunk is still uncommon in these cultures. The British, because they use alcohol as an escape mechanism from normal working life, have many expressions for getting drunk that you may hear being used. These include: 'to get hammered', 'to get pissed', 'to get sloshed', 'to get bladdered', 'to get plastered'. Young people often put the word 'well' before these to emphasise them, e.g. 'to be well-bladdered'.

One of the noticeable aspects of British drinking, especially youth drinking, is therefore that of 'binge drinking'. This is drinking a lot of alcohol over a short period of time with the intention of getting drunk. Pubs tend to encourage this kind of behaviour by offering happy hours (two drinks are available for the price of one). It is this kind of drinking that leads to the somewhat chaotic scenes on many British high streets on Friday and Saturday nights, with young people worse for wear perhaps collapsed on the floor and police trying to calm down those who have become aggressive.

Binge drinking is often undertaken by groups of young men or women who are out to party and as part of the fun they may dress up according to a theme. Do not be surprised, therefore, to meet groups of drunken youths dressed as Roman centurions (or in flimsy togas), or young women dressed as fairies. You may even meet individuals dressed as comic strip heroes such as Batman or Tarzan. One good excuse for such an evening out among friends is to celebrate a friend's forthcoming marriage. For men this is called a 'stag party' and for women a 'hen night'. On these occasions it is also not unusual to see men dressed as women (badly).

Drinking culture infiltrates all aspects of British social life. The university sports teams may spend an hour-and-a-half playing hockey, football or rugby to follow it by hours of drinking in the sports pavilion or local pub. It is not expected among team mates that a person will just play a team sport for the sport itself!

WARNING!

There is therefore a lot of social pressure in the UK to drink alcohol.

Advice: If you are a Muslim or non-drinker you should make this clear from the beginning so as not to be constantly declining offers of drinks or, if you are a Muslim and see establishments whose primary objective is the sale of alcohol as 'haram' (forbidden), having to make excuses for not meeting friends in the pub.

Note: It is important to also realise that you do not have to drink alcohol to have a social life and a good time in the UK. Most establishments now sell non-alcoholic beer as well as other non-alcoholic drinks.

Violence

This section is designed to make you aware of the possibility of violence against you when you are in the UK. The vast majority of students do not experience any violence against them, but unfortunately there are some who do and this section is designed to ensure that you at least are aware of the danger so that you do not become a victim of violence yourself.

Perhaps one important aspect of being an international student in the UK is that for a number of international students this is also the first time that they have lived away from the protection of their own family. It may be that you have been sheltered from life in the street in your own country. Now in the UK you will not have this protection, so becoming 'streetwise' is important.

People in Britain are very concerned about crime. This is probably because crime statistics suggest that British citizens are more likely to be the victims of crime than most other European people in their countries. A lot of the crime is burglary and robbery as well as what is called antisocial behaviour (this can involve targeting and harassing individual people who are different). As far as murder is concerned, the murder rate in the UK is still low compared to many other countries, but violent crime is increasing as there is an increase in the use of weapons such as handguns and knives, even though these are not openly on sale.

Antisocial behaviour

One difficult problem affecting the quality of life for some people, particularly those living on some council estates (state-owned social housing), can be that of antisocial behaviour. In this circumstance a gang or a family may terrorise a neighbourhood, picking on anyone who resists them and making life very hard and unpleasant for people, sometimes attacking them physically. When any youth is successfully prosecuted for antisocial behaviour, he or she may be issued an Antisocial Behaviour Order (ASBO) which means he or she is not allowed to be in certain locations.

WARNING!

One problem for international students is that they too may be targeted by such people because they stand out as being different and often from a more privileged background. This can be quite frightening and difficult to deal with. The key to not being in this situation is mostly to do with making sure that you do not end up living in an area of town where such problems exist.

Gangs

One of the reasons for the increase in crime is the growth of youth street gangs. These are not to be confused with criminal gangs who fight each other for control of districts to be able, for example, to control the drugs trade.

Street gangs are not only male but female too. They tend, in their majority, to be located in the bigger cities (London, Manchester, Birmingham, Liverpool, Glasgow, Nottingham and Sheffield). Many gang members are teenagers who have been excluded from school for bad behaviour and who are mostly unemployed, bored and see no future for themselves. Gang attacks are particularly dangerous and violent because they are collective acts, often by many people against an individual who has no chance of escape or defence.

Carrying weapons

Youths who live in areas where there is fear of gangs may feel they have to carry a weapon in case they are attacked. This can mean that if they are stopped by the police they are then prosecuted and get a criminal record. The maximum sentence for carrying a knife in a public place is now four years in prison.

Stop and think: Do you have similar troubles in your country from youth gangs? How do you avoid trouble? What signs do you look for to see if trouble is present?

Avoiding trouble: If you see it or hear it, avoid it!

One of the key ways to avoid trouble is to learn to spot the signs of trouble ahead before you are caught up in it. If you see a group of young men or women who look drunk or high on drugs and who are blocking a pathway or display threatening body language, it is sensible to cross the street or turn round and keep out of their reach. The following observation is interesting to think about:

> People walk into a 'rowdy party' group rather than avoid the situation for various reasons: young male adults, who do recognise the danger, often keep going and deny the reality, or feel capable of handling it because to give in to feelings of anxiety is to feel weak and not in control. But are these feelings worse than getting beaten up? Macho feelings interfere with good sense! Young women are set upon by girl gangs because they often just don't believe

that other girls can be dangerous. It is also true that people may believe that if they mind their own business, they will not be the victims of an attack. Unfortunately gang attacks in the UK are very random and for victims it is simply about being in the wrong place at the wrong time.

Exercise

Make a list of tactics that you think will help you avoid being the victim of an attack, either a gang attack or a mugging. Now compare it to the list in Box 9.1. How many of these had you not thought of?

Box 9.1

Trouble avoidance tactics	Thought of it ✓
Learn to spot the trouble signs, notice them and then avoid people who are showing these signs	
Learn about your town and the areas that British people consider to be the bad areas. Avoid going to and especially living in these areas	
Avoid being by yourself late at night or in deserted streets. Try to be with people or in streets where there are other people too	
Do not be afraid or embarrassed to cross a street or turn around to avoid what looks like possible trouble	
If near a group of troublesome teenagers, do not make eye contact with them, do not answer them back, keep moving and do not allow yourself to be stopped. Avoid being surrounded. Run before this happens	
If running, run towards other people and be prepared to shout for help	
At night get a taxi from a recommended taxi company (one recommended by the university). Book the taxi return before going out (time and place). Do not stop an unknown taxi in the street	

Do not sit in railway carriages by yourself or anywhere away from light and other people	
It is best to prepare how you will get home before you go out (make a note of the last train or bus time). Alternatively, if there are no buses or it is late plan to stay over with friends so that you don't have to travel back alone	
Avoid showing off expensive mobile phones, carrying expensive laptops or wearing jewellery in public	
If attacked do everything to avoid falling to the floor (easier said than done – but serious injury mainly occurs when you are kicked when on the ground)	

Avoiding trouble: Planning ahead

It is also very important to think about avoiding walking or being in places by yourself where you can be trapped: it is not sensible to walk in narrow passage-ways or be on the top deck of double-decker bus at night. Trouble also seems to be more likely to occur at certain times of day and in certain places: e.g. at pub closing time, at empty railway stations in the evening or at or around nightclubs.

As well as gang attacks, another motive for violence may be theft. Violent attack for robbery is called 'mugging'.

Racial discrimination

Both EU and overseas international students may unfortunately, at times, experience racial discrimination. There are two forms of this. One is overt racism. This is when somebody shouts at you (maybe from a passing car) and makes racist comments, or refuses to serve you in a shop. This kind of racism is not often experienced as it is generally seen as unacceptable behaviour by most people.

There are people in the UK, however, who may not be in favour of a multi-cultural society and who do not like the fact that the UK is becoming more mixed. They worry it is changing and being taken over by people who do not hold what they consider to be traditional British values or who do not speak English or understand and adapt to British culture. There is a political party called the British National Party (BNP) that represents mostly white people who tend to hold this view. The BNP is against immigration in general, be this economic migrants or asylum seekers (people escaping danger in their countries). There is a feeling in the BNP that such people come to the UK to take advantage of the benefits of the welfare state, help that they feel is to the cost of the British people.

Another organisation to be aware of as a foreigner in the UK is the English Defence League (EDF). It is a street organisation that claims to defend Englishness and to oppose the spread of 'extremist Islam' in the UK. The movement particularly highlights the fact that British troops are fighting in Islamic countries and being killed doing this and that some Islamic people from resident Islamic communities in the UK do not support these troops.

WARNING!

If you are an Islamic student and wear clothing and attire that demonstrates this, any comments made by the public or hostility directed at you is probably from people sympathetic to the views of the two above-mentioned organisations. Unfortunately the subtleties of different views and outlooks within Islam is often not understood. The fact that there have been some examples of terrorist acts committed by international (or former international) students in the UK does not help the general suspicion that can exist.

Another form of racism that is much more difficult to understand and deal with is that of 'institutional racism'. This is the systematic negative treatment of certain individuals because of their ethnic origin by an organisation. A difficulty combating institutionalised racism is that there is not one easily identifiable perpetrator. When racism is built into the institution, it appears as a collective action. The police were accused of this through their response to the murder of a black teenager, Stephen Lawrence, in 1993. Universities are public organisations and as such may be prone to institutional racism, although universities that take internationalisation and the recruitment of international students seriously should have made efforts to eliminate any such tendency. Examples of it may exist, however, for example in the different treatment by nationality of certain students by certain administrative departments in a university, or indeed similarly differential treatment of students by an academic. Institutional racism is linked to stereotyping: an example may be that a university helps or is tolerant of a certain student from country X who gets into debt but is not tolerant of another one from country Y to the same degree, as there might be a dominant view that people from country Y 'cannot be trusted'.

Advice: If you are in a situation where you believe you are experiencing institutional racism, i.e. you have been treated differently because of your race, gender, nationality or sexual identity, you should not keep quiet about it. It is a serious issue and needs confronting. You must insist on the right to equal treatment. Every university should have an Equality and Diversity Officer you can meet with about any such concerns. Universities must enforce the Equality Act 2010 and this Act is applicable to nine areas of potential discrimination.

> **Reflective question**: In what way do you think people may be discriminated against and what might they need legal protection for? There are now nine separate 'protected characteristics' or 'equality strands'. Try to think of what these nine areas might be.

Answer: There are the 'big six': sex, race, disability, sexual orientation, religion or belief and age, plus three new ones – marriage and civil partnership, gender reassignment and pregnancy and maternity.

Comment: Had you thought of all of these? In what way do you think a pregnant student or a student who is a young mother may be discriminated against, or how might a person who has changed their sex be discriminated against?

WARNING!

For international students, overt and covert racism may well exacerbate feelings of culture shock and homesickness which may not only adversely affect academic performance and perception of the university, but also general well-being. Dealing with racial discrimination is not an easy task, partly because complaints made by students may not appear to have much substance. It is easier to handle overt forms of discrimination when verbal or physical abuse is present, but the more subtle aspects, e.g. insinuations about intelligence, moral standards, attitudes, the targeted use of humour etc., are difficult to assess. It is therefore very important to take any such concerns seriously yourself. The university should take such complaints very seriously indeed.

Note: International students may experience racial discrimination from both UK and other international students as well. Whether this is intentional or not it can cause tension and stress both in the classroom and socially.

Crime

Question: What are the typical crimes that you think you need to be aware of and be careful about avoiding as an international student in the UK? Is crime something that worries you?

Useful website: A website that lists and explains common types of crime in the UK is: http://www.direct.gov.uk/en/YoungPeople/CrimeAndJustice/TypesOf Crime/index.htm

Different parts of the UK have different rates of crime and different parts of the same city vary as well. The following website is useful for noting the amount and types of crime in different areas of the country. It searches areas by postcodes.

Useful website: http://www.police.uk

Obviously being a victim of any crime is distressing, particularly when you have to deal with this in a foreign culture and speak to police in a foreign language. Crimes that you need to be aware of as a foreign student include hate crime, burglary, street crime and rape or sexual assault.

Hate crime

This is when you are attacked for who you are – because of your skin colour or race (by racists), or attacked for being gay or lesbian (by homophobes), or attacked for being disabled either physically or mentally.

Useful website: http://www.nus.org.uk/hatecrime

Burglary and theft

One of the reasons why students are victims of property theft is because they are easy victims. When students rent houses they may not realise that they need to pay attention to house security, i.e. use window locks and have security locks on doors.

Advice:

- **Keep doors and windows locked**. One of the key things to look out for when choosing a student property is whether the accommodation has decent window locks (ideally key lockable) and deadlocks fitted on all outside doors. Even on campus you need to pay attention. Be aware that thieves commonly take advantage of the relative anonymity of a large student population to sneak in and out undetected, particularly at the start of the university year when most people don't know one another. It is best not to let people into your building that you don't recognise. Always lock your bedroom door, even if you are just nipping down the corridor!
- **Insure and mark your belongings**. It is sensible to insure your belongings against theft. There are many insurance companies that provide insurance for students in the UK and many campuses have a student insurance office. You can shop around online to get quotes too.
- **Make a back-up of your hard drive**. As well as insuring your laptop, it is also sensible to make a back-up copy of your hard disk and keep this somewhere hard to find. That way if someone steals your laptop you can get it replaced. But how would you replace three months of work on your final dissertation or a lifetime's worth of your favourite music?
- **Keep lists of the make, model and serial numbers of any electronic items**. Also mark them with your postcode using an ultraviolet pen, as this may help the police track them down if they are stolen.

Street robbery (mugging)

Because criminals are on the lookout for an easy target, it is a good idea to avoid attracting their attention and avoid being in the wrong place at the wrong time.

Rape and sexual assault

In the UK as with any other place in the world, taking sensible precautions to avoid exposing yourself to possible danger is important. This means not walking alone at night in dark unpopulated streets, it means not catching unlicensed taxis in the street if alone and it means making sure that friends know where you are and that you can contact each other by mobile phone. It is worth noting that male, as well as female, rape is a danger. Another danger that is worth being aware of is the reported growing use of date-rape drugs among students on campuses: it is wise to be aware of their existence.

Question: What exactly are date-rape drugs? Technically speaking, any substance that renders you incapable of saying no or asserting yourself can be used to commit rape. This can include alcohol, marijuana or other designer or club drugs like ecstasy. However, the term 'date-rape drug' usually applies to the drugs rohypnol, gamma hydroxy butyrate (GHB) and ketamine hydrochloride.

WARNING!

These drugs can be easily slipped into drinks and food and are very fast-acting. They render the victim unconscious but responsive with little or no memory of what happens while the drug is active in their system. The drugs are virtually undetectable, being tasteless, odourless and colourless. All traces of the drugs leave the body within 72 hours of ingestion and are not found in any routine toxicology screen or blood test – doctors and police have to be looking specifically for them and they have to look quickly! Without any memory of events the victim is often unaware that they have even been raped, and if they are aware or have suspicions they make very poor witnesses.

Advice:
- Be wary about accepting drinks from anyone you don't know well or long enough to trust.
- If you are accepting a drink, make sure it's from an unopened container and that you open it yourself.
- Do not serve yourself drinks from open punch bowls at parties.
- Don't put your drink down and leave it unattended, even to go to the toilet. If you do this discard the drink when you return.
- Notify other females you know about the effects of this dangerous drug and have a 'buddy' system of looking after each other at parties. In fact if you go

to lots of parties a safe practice is to take it in turns to be the sober one who checks on the others.

Useful website: http://wn.com/date_rape_drug

Terrorism

While there is no way to know when or where a terrorist attack may occur, the government does inform the public of the threat level. This is most noticeable in airports, when there may be extra security checks taking place. For this reason it is always best to arrive for flights in plenty of time at UK airports.

The main terrorist attacks tend to be in the major cities and especially in London, as this creates the biggest amount of chaos and prestige and news for the terrorist group concerned. The last major terrorist attack was on 7 July 2005 when Al-Qaeda-inspired British suicide bombers attacked the London metro and bus system. Previous to this the main terrorist threat was from the IRA (Irish Republican Army) and more recently the 'Real IRA' – terrorist groups who believe that violence can achieve a united Ireland (uniting north and south) free of any UK control.

As the main targets tend to be transport networks, avoiding public transport as much as possible or large crowds (e.g. famous big nightclubs) and public gatherings when there is a terrorist threat are precautions that can be sensibly taken.

Chapter 10

After you finish your studies

When you finish your studies you will no doubt have several possible courses of action and be planning one of these:

1   Stay in the UK and work
2   Move on to another country and work
3   Return back to your home country.

This chapter will look at issues to do with each of these options.

Staying in the UK to work

This option makes sense from an experiential and financial point of view. However, for overseas visa national students, this is not easy.

It is sensible to start investigating and planning what you need to do if you wish to work in the UK after finishing your studies early on in your study period. Do this by keeping up to date with this information from the UK Council for International Student Affairs (UKCISA) and the United Kingdom Border Agency (UKBA).

Useful websites: http://www.ukcisa.org.uk/student/info_sheets/working_after_studies.php
   http://www.ukba.homeoffice.gov.uk/workingintheuk
   Also make an appointment to see the university International Student Adviser or Careers Adviser to get as much help and information as possible.
   See if you can find out the right information for the issues listed in Box 10.1:

Box 10.1	
Question	*Answer*
What visa do I need to get?	
Do I need a sponsoring employer?	
How do I find a sponsoring employer? What is the Sponsor Register and how do I access it?	
Is there a need for the Labour Market Test?	
What salary must I be offered to be considered for graduate-level employment?	
Is there a cap on the number of Tier 2 visas issued to graduating international students?	
Can I transfer to a Tier 2 visa within the UK?	
When should I begin my job hunting?	

Note: You must make your application before your current permission to be in the UK as a student expires.

Curriculum vitae

Advice: It is essential to design a good curriculum vitae (CV). Use the Careers Office to help you with this process. Make sure that the CV is checked thoroughly by a UK expert in CV design. It only takes saying the wrong thing in a CV or application letter to be dismissed from a shortlist for interview.

Moving to another country

Again, if this is your plan, you should start your enquiries early. Make sure you check the following:

- The kind of visa required and how to apply
- The requirements you need to meet to be accepted for entry
- Whether you need to legalise and translate your qualifications
- Whether the qualifications gained in the UK are recognised in the country you wish to go to, and if not how to get them recognised.

Returning to your home country

While this may seem the easiest option, you need to be aware of a widely experienced phenomenon called 'reverse culture shock'. This is what you may well experience when you have been living out of your home culture for a length of time.

Typical symptoms of reverse culture shock are listed in Table 10.1.

Note: It is important to realise that this is quite a natural set of experiences that many people feel upon re-entry into their old home culture. The effect will die down for most people as you learn to readjust and understand the people around you again and not resent them.

Of course not everyone experiences this syndrome to the same extent. But those who do can have quite a bad time, especially as they were not expecting this reaction. Being aware of this before it happens should be helpful to you.

Table 10.1 Reverse culture shock

Symptom	Experience ✓	Rationale
Nobody cares about or asks much about your travels and overseas experience		The people you left behind have developed their own lives and when you left you stopped being of immediate interest to them. Understand people live for what is around them on a day-to-day basis
You may feel trapped		You might find life back home boring. You may have a sense that you have gone backwards. People seem narrow-minded. Making this obvious to your old friends will not make you popular
Normality seems hard to cope with		When you are overseas even mundane tasks such as a visit to the supermarket can be interesting. This is no longer so when you are back home. People back home also seem to be obsessed with trivial things
People just don't understand you		You will have developed some new opinions while overseas. The people back home probably have not. You will have made international friends and you may be seen to prefer them to your old friends
My former friends seem to be jealous of my experience		Be aware that if you start talking a lot about your amazing experiences people may not like this. It is best to wait until you are asked about your experiences before telling them!

Staying in touch

Graduation

Most universities organise quite spectacular graduation ceremonies and if you are interested in attending these you need to reserve places for yourself and any friends and family as well as book the necessary ceremonial gowns. You also need to think about visa issues, if the graduation is within the expiry period of the visa and what to do if it is not.

Alumni groups

One way of keeping in touch with your university is to join it as an alumnus. Most universities have national alumni groups that you may wish to join and also have alumni magazines and social media sites that will keep you up to date and in touch with the university.

Glossary

Chapter 1

Active reading   Reading with a purpose – to achieve something

Engage in something   To encourage you to be interested in something

Pitfall   A common danger and trap

Reflective learning   Learning that requires you to stop and think about something and to become aware of your own perspective

Self-development exercises   Exercises that you do by yourself to increase your understanding of yourself

Chapter 2

Anecdote   A short story taken from life that acts as an example

Career   Professional work pathway you take in life, for example a career in law (i.e. to be a lawyer)

Check out something   Investigate and make sure about something

Chore   A daily task that has to be done, e.g. cooking or shopping

Download   Saving a file to your computer from the Internet

Foundation year/programme   A year of preparation before you begin your UG programme

NHS   The National Health System, i.e. the system of doctors and hospitals for treating ill people

Option   An option on a study programme is a course (module) you can choose to do

Out-of-town stores   The big supermarkets and stores found on the edge of towns and cities

Overseas students   Students from outside the EU/EEA

PG qualifications   Postgraduate (also called Masters) level study

Prestigious university   A university that has a good name and reputation and is difficult to get in to

Recognise a qualification   A qualification is only valid if the authorities in a country accept it as legitimate

Repatriation The cost of sending you home if you are badly injured or dead

Requirements The grades and certificates necessary to enter a programme in a university

Scenario An imagined future

Study abroad Any studying that is undertaken by a student in a different country from their own

Opt for something To choose something, for example a programme of study

UG qualification Undergraduate (also called Bachelor) level study

Chapter 3

Accreditation Acceptance of and the awarding of credits for a subject studied

Aptitude test A test to determine if you have the necessary qualities to study for a particular profession

BA/BSc Bachelor of Arts/Bachelor of Science

Bursary An award of money that does not need to be paid back

CAS Certificate of Acceptance of Studies

Conversion degrees These are programmes, usually at Masters level, which prepare you in a new subject area to the one you have studied at undergraduate level

Crime-ridden An area with a high level of crime

Default The automatic amount/position if there is no evidence to indicate anything different

Defer Postpone/delay

Disabilities Physical or mental problems that affect a person's ability to do something

Electives These can also be called 'options' and are modules that you choose to take. They are not core (i.e. obligatory) to the programme

Eligible Meeting the conditions for entry

Ethos Values and ways of thinking

Exemption Not having to do or achieve something – usually some study on a programme because an area of study has already been undertaken

Fee status Category of fee payer

Graduate Someone who has graduated from university and holds a first/ bachelor's degree

Honours degree A degree for which the full credits have been awarded (in England this is 360 credits)

Incentive An encouragement – usually a reward

Integrated programme Part of the whole

Keep an eye on To regularly check something

League table position University ranking

MA/MSc Master of Arts/Master of Science

Maintenance grant Money that is given to a student by the government to help cover living costs

Means-tested   The amount you receive depends on your family income: means-testing assesses this figure

Ordinary degree   In Scotland this is a three-year degree (four-year degrees are called Honours degrees). In the rest of the UK an ordinary degree is a degree that is not completed to the standard of an honours degree

Ordinarily resident   Living in the UK as a legal UK resident and not for the purposes of education

Pathway   Your educational journey or route

Personal statement   A positive description of a person's qualities and abilities

Scholarship   An award of money to study

Threshold   The minimum amount required

To practice   To work professionally, e.g. as a dentist

Top-up degrees   Degrees that are awarded for completing only the final year of study of a programme

PGT/PGR   Postgraduate Taught/Postgraduate Research

Recognition   Acceptance as legitimate

Sandwich degree programme   A Bachelor's in which a year of work experience is built into the programme

Subject to something   To depend on something

Subsidised   Partly paid for

Terms (of repayment)   The conditions for repaying monies

Chapter 4

Bank Holiday   A national holiday

Call round   To visit someone

Clutter up (space)   To occupy and block

Communal space   The shared parts of a house or accommodation block, e.g. living room, corridors

Considerate   Thoughtful and understanding

Drop off (your luggage)   To leave (your luggage)

Drop out   To leave university before completing a programme of study

Early on   at an early stage

Have a word with someone   To talk to someone about something

Homestay   Accommodation offered by a university in which you have your own room but live with a British family

Housemate   Person you share accommodation with

ID card   Identity card

Local   From the immediate area

Long-haul flight   A flight between continents of over eight hours

Pick-up service   A bus or taxi service that meets you and takes you to your destination (usually for free)

Pre-departure event   A meeting with a university representative in your country about travelling to and settling in to your university in the UK

Prescription (from the doctor) A form that indicates the medicine you need to pick up from the chemist/pharmacy

Put up with something To tolerate

Settle in To adjust and become comfortable

Tend to (do something) To be in the habit of doing particular thing

Take something further To take further action (usually to make a formal complaint)

Tips Useful ideas

Utensils The things you use to cook, e.g. pots and pans

Warden The person who is employed to look after an accommodation block

Chapter 5

Arising from Produced by

Attend to To be concerned for

Audit Systematic check

Back (up) an argument (up) To support

Bank on something To count on or be pretty sure of something

Break something down into To divide something into its constituent parts

Bribery Paying money or giving favours for someone to advantageously do something for you

Blank canvas A mind that has no previous knowledge

Catch you out To trick you or cause you to make a mistake

Charter An understood set of rules

Cluster A groups of similar things

Cohort The particular group of students you are part of as a class

Come along To develop

Come on! Be positive! – or, hurry up!

Come up with (an idea) To deduce and suggest

Comfort zone The area of experience and thinking you are familiar and 'at home' with

Counter productive Against the best way of doing things

Deliver (a programme) To arrange the teaching

Drop in (on someone) To visit unannounced or without an invitation

End up with To conclude

Field of knowledge Area of expertise

Fit To match, to go with

Follow up on something To revisit and further investigate

Get in the way To block

Get on with someone To understand and work well with someone

Grade inflation The increase in giving high grades (which makes the high grades less meaningful)

Ground rule Agreed basic rule

Hand in To give/deliver

Harsh Hard and unforgiving
Hold back with an opinion To refrain from mentioning
Hold you back To stop you progressing
Interaction Discussion and agreement
Loan period Length of time for borrowing
Log book A record with regular entries
Mainstream Commonly accepted
Misconduct Incorrect and illegal behaviour
Modular degree A degree made up of many different courses from different disciplines
Pace Timing/speed
Peers Your fellow students (people of the same age)
Plagiarism Copying
Pose a problem To become or to suggest a problem
Practicum Learning experience based on experimenting in a laboratory
Prompt To encourage
Put in time/effort To spend time on/to use up effort
Random Unorganised and unsystematic
Rote learning Memorising or learning by heart
Self-esteem Your own belief in your own worth and abilities
Settle down To become focused and attentive
Show promise To have a good basis for future development
Slip by To pass by
Source Origin
Strict Unforgiving
Set targets To design goals and aims
Shared Used or undertaken by more than one person
Snooze To half sleep (nap)
Tag Label
Take a back seat To be passive
Take on To understand and use
Talk something through To discuss and analyse
Trap Danger
Turn of phrase Elegant and correct way of expressing yourself
Valiant Brave
Viva voce Oral examination
Waive a fine (or fee) To decide not to implement
Well-being Your physical, mental and emotional state
Work something out (for yourself) To determine

Chapter 6

Academics People who teach and do research at universities
Appendices Examples and pieces of evidence attached to the end of pieces of work

Assignments Pieces of work that you hand in for marking (assessment)

Bind (a thesis) To present it formally with a cover

Blank (mind) To not be able to think of anything you have learnt

Cram To try to study everything in one go before an exam

Cope with To manage successfully

Core (modules) Essential and obligatory

Criteria Descriptors

Critical Analytical and able to agree or disagree with ideas based on arguments you have made

Cryptic Complex to try and understand

Eligible Legally entitled

Ethics Moral standards

Faculty A collection of university departments that are in similar areas of knowledge, e.g. Arts and Humanities

Formative marking Marking that indicates how much you have learned and what you need to learn for the future

Framework Structure

Have grounds for something To have a legitimate reason

In line with Similar to

Intercultural competence (ICC) The ability to understand and communicate well with people from other cultural backgrounds

Jot down ideas To write quickly and roughly

Keep on top of something To have studied and learnt what you need to know and not fallen behind

Keep track (of something) To remain aware of

Lack of Something that is missing

Learning outcomes The points you should have learnt and the skills you should have developed after studying a programme

Light of (in light of) Taking into consideration

Merit To be worthy of

Mix up something To confuse

Monitor To watch and control

Objective Based on evidence beyond your own opinion

Overlook something To ignore

Oversee To watch and control

Penalty Sanction

Personality clash Two people who do not get on together

Prejudice Bias or unfair preference

Quotes Pieces of writing you copy and reference from published sources

Rigour Thoroughness

Sanctions Punishments

Scheme Plan of action

Self-directed Organised and able to be responsible for one's own learning

Set out (an argument) To explain your position

Skimpy Insufficient
Spare time Free time
Subjective Your own opinion without evidence
Summative (marking) Giving a final grade or score to show your achievement
On time At the due date
In time Before the due date
Transcript Printed document listing credits and grades obtained for programmes studied
Turn up (for) Arrive unannounced or without an appointment
Umbrella The higher level or overarching structure
Up to you Your responsibility

Chapter 7

Bills Invoices from utility (service) companies
Breach To break an agreement or rule
Chauvinism Believing men are superior to women
Collusion Cheating with an accomplice
Compensation Money paid for damages done
Comprise To be made of
Confer To give
Confidentiality To keep secret
Deal with (something) To manage
Direct debit (DD) An instruction made by you to your bank that a payee can take out varying sums of money for services offered on a regular basis to you
Discrimination Unfair treatment
Due Money owing or work to be handed in
Eviction Removal
Fault (at fault) Wrong
Grievance procedures The action you take if you have a serious complaint to make
Half-board Accommodation that includes a meal per day
Hardship Experience of extreme difficulty
Hold something against someone To hold a grudge against someone and take negative future action against the person
House hunting Looking for a house to rent
Hub Central meeting point
Instalment payments A part payment
Intermediary Person or organisation in between
Lay member A member recruited locally and not appointed by the government
Line manager The direct manager of an employee
Mind (your language) Be careful what you say
Parties People or organisations named in a contract
Retain To keep

Risk Possible danger
Run out/ run short of Not to have any more left
Scam A clever way of cheating you
Sexism Believing one sex is superior to the other
Spare Free or left over
Standing order An instruction you make to your bank to make fixed amount
    payments to a certain account payee bank account on a regular basis
Terms The conditions of a contract
Up front payment Payment before you begin
Utility bills The money you have to pay for electricity, gas and water
Vary To differ
Way around something A method of avoiding something

Chapter 8

Bigot Someone who thinks their way of doing things and their people are always
    right, without any evidence that this is the case
Catch someone's eye To notice someone
To chat up To try to attract
Confiscation Taking away
Coyness Ritual demonstration of shyness
Crucial Very important
Deal An agreement
Enrol To join
Flirtation Giving signals that you are attracted to someone
Hangover Headache and feeling unwell from too much alcohol
In your face Too direct
Off-putting Makes you not want it
Outlook The attitude you have and way of seeing the world
Pretentious False and showing off
Withrawal Not to participate and to be alone

Chapter 9

Binge drinking Drinking too much alcohol too fast and getting very drunk
Harassment Being picked on and given negative treatment
Mugging Robbery
Stand out To be obvious and an easy target

Chapter 10

Narrow-minded Uninterested in ideas beyond your immediate experience
Only take doing something To make the mistake of

Index